T0302314

ROUTLEDGE LIBRARY EDITIONS:
WORK & SOCIETY

Volume 21

YOUTH, UNEMPLOYMENT AND TRAINING

YOUTH, UNEMPLOYMENT AND TRAINING

A Collection of National Perspectives

Edited by
ROB FIDDY

Routledge
Taylor & Francis Group

LONDON AND NEW YORK

First published in 1985 by The Falmer Press.

This edition first published in 2024
by Routledge
4 Park Square, Milton Park, Abingdon, Oxon OX14 4RN

and by Routledge
605 Third Avenue, New York, NY 10158

Routledge is an imprint of the Taylor & Francis Group, an informa business

British Library Cataloguing in Publication Data
A catalogue record for this book is available from the British Library

ISBN: 978-1-032-80236-7 (Set)
ISBN: 978-1-032-82025-5 (Volume 21) (hbk)
ISBN: 978-1-032-82030-9 (Volume 21) (pbk)
ISBN: 978-1-003-50259-3 (Volume 21) (ebk)

DOI: 10.4324/9781003502593

Publisher's Note
The publisher has gone to great lengths to ensure the quality of this reprint but
points out that some imperfections in the original copies may be apparent.

Disclaimer
The publisher has made every effort to trace copyright holders and would
welcome correspondence from those they have been unable to trace.

Youth, Unemployment and Training

A Collection of National Perspectives

Edited by
ROB FIDDY

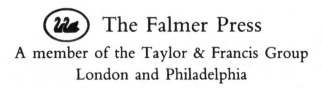 The Falmer Press

A member of the Taylor & Francis Group
London and Philadelphia

UK   The Falmer Press, Falmer House, Barcombe, Lewes, East Sussex,
            BN8 5DL

USA   The Falmer Press, Taylor & Francis Inc., 242 Cherry Street,
            Philadelphia, PA 19106-1906

First published 1985

Library of Congress Cataloging in Publication Data

ISBN 0 905273 86 9
ISBN 0 905273 85 0 (pbk.)

Typeset in 10/11 Bembo
by Imago Publishing Ltd, Thame, Oxon.

Contents

Contents

Acknowledgement

I gratefully acknowledge the consistent help and support from members of the Centre for Applied Research In Education (CARE) at the University of East Anglia, Norwich, in the production of this book. In particular Barry MacDonald and Nick May — and Gundi Daymond for her skill in translating from French and German.

I am also grateful to the Economic and Social Research Council for their support of my doctoral studies in post-school courses for unemployed youngsters which led directly to this collection of papers.

Introduction: Youth, Unemployment and Training

Rob Fiddy

I saw some graffiti today: 'Work For All Soon ... Third World War Imminent.'

Now, it is, of course, uncertain that a third world war would produce a boom in the service industries, let alone the armed forces, as the first and second world wars did. It is even uncertain that a third world war is imminent. But it is interesting to speculate on how many walls, in how many countries and in how many languages this message could have been written still to make the same amount of sense.

Training and unemployment — is the relationship between these two elements of life for youngsters to result in a post-school sentence of frustrated ambition or a welcome release from years of toil? The answer depends upon what one is led to believe life after school to be about, what one would like life after school to be about and how these expectations and aspirations may be accommodated. Homo Laborious, the work ethic and the dole queue are, after all, creations of society.

Not too many years ago, the late Professor Lawrence Stenhouse said that a piece I had written criticizing British policy towards unemployed youngsters had only highlighted the more transparent aspects of that policy. He said that attempts to put the work ethic on ice and at the same time to 'blame the victim', in order to assuage some of the possible repercussions of structural unemployment, must surely be well understood by all to be, at best, stop-gap measures. Indeed, he must have been right. Work experience programmes in this country have done little to offset increasing levels of youth unemployment and even in the early years of schooling pupils are predicting for themselves a life on the dole. Nevertheless, billions of pounds are regularly allocated in Great Britain for the continuation of variations on the work experience theme. See-through or not, it seems that there are few alternatives emanating from central policy planners which can provide a meaningful environment for youngsters which is not impinged upon by a status derived from work, the lack of it, or its surrogate the work experience placement.

In the 1960s the 'white heat' of the technological revolution was looked forward to as heralding a life of increased leisure. But it appears that, whereas the increase of non-work time has come about willy-nilly for a high percentage of the population and with particular significance for the young, education and training policy makers have chosen to emphasize that which is least readilly available — employment.

But is there a realistic choice available to policy makers who may be haunted by the thought of gangs of youth on the streets? To declare that education is not for work begs the question 'then what is it for?' An effective and plausible answer not only requires alternative strategies but also a fundamental shift in the national perception. It is not entirely appropriate to assume that policy makers have the necessary power to change attitudes. Attitudes change in spite of policies and notoriously in spite of education. But such a shift is already visible amongst youngsters, even if the viable alternatives are not forthcoming, and could be supported by policy. It is here where the legitimate perception of alternatives is fudged by the increasing emphasis on vocational training both during and after school. The notion is promoted that the relationship between education and the economy is direct and set. Maybe one of the first questions to be asked for the future is 'should it be?'

The examination of to what extent this also holds true for other countries is the purpose of this collection of papers.

GREAT BRITAIN

This first section is a re-investigation of the situation in Great Britain. Re-investigation because, in one sense, this book follows on from *In Place Of Work: Policy and Provision For The Young Unemployed*[1], a previous compilation of papers which dealt primarily with the British experience. In the introduction to *In Place Of Work*, I said that:

> High levels of youth unemployment are to be found all over the Western world, and many governments have explored problem-solving strategies which pose alternative courses of action ... To be able to provide a complete range of alternatives would require an additional volume however.

This is the additional volume. It includes contributions on nine different countries.

I also said, then, that:

> Any overview of activity in the area of provision for the young unemployed could not fail to notice a breadth of practice and a state of rapidly changing policy.

The first section deals, in part, with the rhetoric of the most recent shift in British policy for school-leavers — 'The Emergence of the Youth Training Scheme'. But whatever else transition is about it concerns people. The first paper in this section features Saville Kushner's case-study of the conflation of personal and political pressures which form the context for current curriculum development in the area of the transition from school to (un)employment.

Note

FIDDY, R. (Ed.) (1983) *In Place of Work: Policy and Provision for the Young Unemployed*, Lewes, Falmer Press.

Vocatonal 'Chic': An Historical and Curriculum Context to the Field of Transition in England

Saville Kushner

Preamble

It was the summer of 1981 — shortly after the street disturbances which involved so many urban youth in Britain. Many educational researchers must have donned their fieldwork costumes and sped into the field to take the temperature of the urgency. This one was no exception. Amongst other students, I spoke to Maureen, a seventeen-year-old living in Kirkby. She was short, quite heavily built. Her hair was cropped in the modern style and she wore a black leather jacket with zips — permitted because she was about to leave school (for art college). Her face was rounded, but came to a point at the chin — accentuated by a small mouth with tightly drawn lips. She looked down at the floor, avoiding my gaze then suddenly straight into me with her own deeply set dark blue eyes. She didn't smile a great deal — but nor did she look sad or detached. The young boys who were 'rioting'? She condemned them for vandalizing and 'shaming' their home ground and for fighting battles with the police which they knew they would never win. She supported the mothers who removed the barricades from the streets when the disturbances threatened to spill into Kirkby. Even so, she had a residual sense of empathy with the rioters. Why?

> 'Because it concerns us. Because there's been a label put on the people that's causing the riots — and we fit into that label.'

> 'What's the label?'

> 'Youth. I mean, that's us all over isn't it? I mean you can't help it, like. You were born in 1963 and you're in 1981 and you're seventeen years old. You're part of it.'

> 'Do you mind being put in the same category?'

> 'I don't know. I mind in the sense that there's a small minority causing the disturbances. But I don't mind in the sense that they're causing the disturbances for a good cause.'

It must be confusing to be an adolescent in today's world. It certainly sounds so, notwithstanding the one-dimensional and often laundered accounts of adolescent interviews so frequently published these days. But it is no less confusing for adults who work on adolescent problems. Kathryn was a fieldworker on an action research project in Maureen's school — offering consultation to the staff on the development of careers education and school-leaver preparation. On one of her visits she ran a training session with the senior staff. She gave them an exercise which allowed her a few moments to relax, to look out of the window across the flat playing fields at the old new-town estate. She felt pressurized, as she frequently did — especially on these long-distance fieldwork trips 150 miles from her home in the heart of the home counties. Kathryn sat back in her chair but with tight shoulders betraying the stress. She smiled a lot — revealing a natural buoyancy — but the smile also had a tightness suggesting a wanting to be out of it and back home. She wrote a fieldnote — as usual, intent on recording even the most intimate moments:

> 'Out of the window there's a blank landscape and a kindly people. I have an uneasy awareness of the political and ideological implications of some of the things I have been saying this afternoon. Helping a school to come to terms with the fact that we are not *all* entering a world in which we are to be without work ...'

There are many ways of approaching the study of 'transition' from school. However you choose to do it you eventually face the need to handle contradictory and paradoxical data. Data which articulate people's life-chances, aspirations, attacks and defences on self-esteem — models of self and of man and woman. Maureen finds it hard to reconcile apparently contradictory aspects of her adolescence — Kathryn finds it equally hard to observe and interact with adolescent issues. If the actors experience complexity then the observers must. And yet we live in a world where educational policy and, increasingly, practice are strident in their assertion that the solutions are easy to define and to implement. This chapter tries to portray something of the complexity by approaching transition from within — to offer the reader a feel for it. By looking at the experience of the project Kathryn worked on in some intimate detail, it may be possible to reach for general understandings of the problems adults have in discovering and meeting the needs of adolescents. What is missing is the adolescent perspective itself. That is extensively developed in the evaluation report from which this chapter is culled[1] — but the intention, here, is to explore difficulties adults face. Since the research project features prominently in the following account it is appropriate to commence with a little background.

The Project

In 1976 the European Commission set up its first educational programme of research and development. Reflecting the primary concern of the decade the main theme of the programme was 'The Transition from Education to Working Life'. In Britain six projects were funded. In Sheffield and London, projects worked in schools; in Wales they operated in training workshops; in Scotland on work experience courses; and in Bradford a project worked in further education. One of the smaller projects in the programme was based at the National Institute for Careers Education and Counselling (NICEC) and was entitled the Careers Guidance Integration Project (CGIP — usually pronounced phonetically as 'See-Jip'). CGIP was jointly funded by the Department of Education and Science and the European Commission. It ran from 1978 to 1982 and it received a total of about £75,000 in funds. The Project's proposed aims were to explore the potential for the on-site training of teachers as careers educators and to do this through their induction into new forms of organizing and presenting the careers curriculum. Their major theme was to be 'Integration', implying the dispersal of responsibility for careers education across internal (usually departmental) boundaries in schools and colleges as well as across external boundaries. This was thought of in terms of developing wider 'communities' of advisers and counsellors, breaking down the traditional role of careers specialists. The Project's working style was based on consultancy techniques. Typically, they would generate data, either in interview or in discussion groups, and they would feed that data back to teachers in order to stimulate reflection and critique. Plans for action and change were anticipated as a consequence. One major source for the proposal lay in an earlier study by Bill Law and Tony Watts reported in a book entitled *Schools, Careers and Community*[2] in which they explored 'integration' within an action research framework. CGIP was to be staffed by Bill Law (Director, part-time), John Miller (part-time) — both of whom were on the tenured staff of NICEC — and a Research Fellow (full-time but on a short-term contract). Kathryn Evans — who came with a background in teaching and in management consultancy — was appointed to the Fellowship. Later in the Project she became its Director. The DES sponsored an independent evaluation of CGIP — this chapter represents a part of that evaluation.

Throughout its four years of existence, CGIP had to struggle to maintain its themes. In the early part of its life careers guidance and 'integration' were marginal to the interests of schools; by the end of its life schools were under pressure to respond to the changing social and economic context and sought CGIP's assistance but for their own, often limited, purposes. In all CGIP worked in about twenty schools and colleges. Whilst they were able to assist some of these to engage in curriculum reflection and even innovation, they made little headway in encouraging schools to open up their gates to the wider community. The Project's final report gives an extensive self-analysis of the conditions surrounding their successes and failures. What I do in this chapter is to place CGIP in the wider political and social contexts in which education and training combine to produce a field of study we call 'transition'.

It has been observed[3] that technological innovations might run for twenty years before they can be expected to have wide impact, and that social innovations take something closer to fifty years. In 1984, in the first year of the operation of the 'New' Training Initiative, the innovation proposed by the Unemployment Act of 1934 comes of age. Under that Act was established a scheme for the vocational training of unemployed adolescents parallelling in crucial details the Youth Training Scheme. As Rees and Rees[4] point out, the scheme of 'authorized courses of instruction' did not have the coverage of the contemporary Youth Training Scheme. Nonetheless, the source of the Act was a non-educational Ministry (Labour) which sought to prosecute the scheme through a specially created executive agency (the Unemployment Insurance Statutory Committee) which parallels the current Manpower Services Commission (MSC). As Rees and Rees point out, referring to the previous and the current major recessionary periods, 'there are straightforward similarities in the responses of the state to the problems of unemployment'. However, these two particular initiatives are features of a longer historical process which has, throughout the modern history of education, sought to establish a relationship between vocational training and schooling, and which has simultaneously sought a resolution to the problems of regulating the supply of juvenile labour. During times of economic recession measures to cope with unemployed youth become the focus for that process and vocational training values assume a fashionable status. In intervening periods of relative prosperity these values tend to be subdued, though the discourse of vocational education continues and the values are maintained and rehearsed. There is always an industry/education interface.

The Careers Guidance Integration Project was funded in the same year, 1978, that Becher and Maclure published their review of the 'golden years' of curriculum reform[5]. Their prognostications for curriculum change still focussed on the major agencies for educational innovation — the Department of Education and Science (DES) and the Schools Council. The Manpower Services Commission was briefly mentioned:

> The main impact of an energetic, centrally directed and financial policy for skill training will be in the Colleges of Further Education. But there will also be backwash in the schools. True, the DES has made efforts to defend the status quo of local educational administration and local curricular autonomy. When the MSC/TSA (Training Services Agency — now fully merged with the MSC.) discussion document on 'Vocational Preparation for Young People' (1975) criticized the educational preparation of school leavers and remarked on a need to provide remedial courses for young workers in basic literacy and numeracy this was perceived as another threat to invade the 'secret garden of the curriculum'. But this was only to be expected, if the schools are recognized to be temporary custodians of the curriculum, not owner-occupiers.

Through the brief life of a curriculum project the DES virtually lost the battle for the defence of educational territory; the Schools Council suffered an inevitable demise; the MSC came to directly fund new curricula in schools and became the largest single curriculum development agency this country has yet seen; and the schools' custodianship of the curriculum is under serious question. The persistent industry/education interface is shifting, searching for a new equilibrium.

The National Institute of Careers Education and Counselling (NICEC) is an independent institution which operates at the interface — funded by both industry and education. Its discourse softens the sometimes strident demands of industry into the massaging tones of educational ideals; and simultaneously seeks to sharpen up the vocabulary of education with the language and concepts of Grubb and Tavistock developed for (amongst others) the reflective management trainer. When NICEC secured funding for CGIP they guaranteed a continued foothold in schools — a substantial one for them, though CGIP was one of the smaller of the European pilot projects.

But interfaces are problematic areas. Typically, they are places of uncertainty where definitions are hard to fix. When the dynamics we are describing come into play, those who work there notice the tensions generated. About halfway through the life of CGIP, Kathryn (by then the Project Director) sought an independence from NICEC whose survival strategy she felt conflicted with the needs of the Project. In an internal note she wrote:

> As an institute, we are in a position to take a stand on good practice. But we have the same problem as government policy-makers. We can take a horse to water but we can't make it drink. 'We' have some reputation in the field built upon a developmental approach to Careers Guidance. From the outside I'd say we looked liberal, more engaged with the personal than the political. As I understand it, a degree of ambiguity in NICEC's role is deliberate, perhaps leaving leeway for internal differences of approach and scope for picking up outside work over a broad area. We are selling our services and making a living ourselves. We can draw the line at doing certain things but, in general, we are trying to provide a service.
>
> There's tension between this and taking risks. This is why I raised the question within CGIP of keeping some distance between that Project and the training and development work of NICEC, *while it's still an experimental project.*[6]

By the end of the Project, without having fully secured that independence from the host institution, Kathryn stood back and took an overview which embraced the role of NICEC:

> As we move towards a national Youth Training Scheme, and parallel developments such as an integrated 17+ pre-vocational qualification in schools and colleges, so the need to consider the relationship between education and vocational and pre-vocational training will increase.[7]

The history of vocational training in Britain is a supermarket for comparisons. The workhouse schools date back to 1723 and, through MSC-familiar eyes, look for all the world like institutionalized work experience. The prestigious Mechanics Institutes with their mission to bring science to the working classes, to enculturate young workers into the new industrial society — a national programme by the mid-1800s — bear a more than passing resemblance to present-day Information Technology Centres. The ill-fated Day Continuation School proposals of the 1918 Education Act and their ephemeral successors in the County Colleges proposed by the 1944 Act suddenly appear alive and well in those marginal outhouses on the Further Education College campus which embody MSC training provision.

Each had its place in the development of modern day schooling — a development which Hamilton[8] sees running parallel to the development of industrial production systems. He defined the class as the basic analogue embodying common features of education and industry — group work, standardized treatments and tasks, instruction and control. And he shows that production and pedagogy shared, in one case, a prestigious mentor — Adam Smith. The institutions which were the vehicles for such developments were the ephemera of a society struggling to reconcile the potential for creating wealth with the creative potential of wealth. The struggle persists. The society, heralded fifteen years ago with the establishment of a Chair of Leisure Studies, has seemingly appeared too early and instead of leisure we still think in terms of enforced idleness. And so, our institutions, as expressions of that same struggle, reappear in not too unfamiliar a form.

The question, of course, is whether our contemporary institutions are as ephemeral as their antecedents. The MSC, for example, is designed, structured and prosecutes its duties as a temporary system. It is deployed essentially as a pragmatic instrument whose operations are geared by year-by-year flows of cash. (There is little historical evidence to suggest that central agencies of government — educational ministries or otherwise — have been committed to long-term development in vocational training provision beyond schools.) At the same time it is clear that in-school provision of vocational curricula has always been problematic — not least through the resistance of schools and the reluctance of central education authorities to impose a public curriculum. Contemporary pre-vocational innovations in the secondary school (the TVEI (Technical and Vocational Education Initiative) programme) — emanating from the Prime Minister's office and under MSC auspices — are designed to bypass the nodes of resistance (the DES itself was bypassed in the planning). They do not, for example, start from the assumption which fuelled the curriculum reform movement in the 1960s — that the secondary curriculum is obsolete and in need of renewal. Both the TVEI programme and the DES-funded 14–16 curriculum programme for 'low-achievers' are intended to create alternative curricula by attracting expertise in schools and LEAs. Part of their appeal is money and resources; part of it, also, is that it offers direct participation in what we characterized earlier as fashionable vocational values.

The persistence of ad hocery — the failure to resolve educational and economic aims in schooling — has entailed failure to set up a permanent system to mobilize, train, or socialize youth of post-compulsory school age. This in turn has frustrated the emergence of a robust policy to deal with the problems of youth in transition. The pendulum has frequently swung from in-school to out-of-school policies as successive raisings of the school-leaving age have been delayed by alternative measures such as Day Continuation Schools and the County Colleges, both proposed to offer full- or part-time training to students of post-school age. The current tensions arising from increasingly overlapping roles of the Departments of Industry/Employment and the Department of Education are a contemporary manifestation of longstanding competition. The 1934 scheme for a national training system post-school came from the Ministry of Labour and offered money to a non-educational authority for what was — albeit in unconventional form — educational provision. Territorial incursion has worked in the other direction, of course, as education authorities, since 1910, operated their own youth employment service in opposition to the Board of Trade, Ministry of Labour and Department of Employment in succession. The resolution of the ensuing role competition was, as Heginbotham noted, that:

The Education Committee's officers gave vocational advice and the Board of Trade officers found the actual jobs. When the supply of jobs did not match demand there was, as might have been expected, friction.[9]

Such territorialism is not uncommon in systems of provision for adolescents — whether between educational and non-educational authorities or between competing educational institutions. One of the more prominent examples is the frequently sharp competition between Sixth Forms and FE colleges, both hungry for the clients who bring in what little money is currently available for expansion. CGIP worked in both types of institutions seeking to encourage the development of guidance provision for adolescents in each. In one school they were working with a committed Head of Sixth, but against a tradition which had been quickly established in a school which had only been open for less than ten years.

Fordham School is not unusual in having to work with a growing number of students who do not fit into the traditions of the sixth form. There, traditions centre around 'A' levels, independent study and small group teaching. For some staff sixth-form teaching has been the most rewarding part of school work, and the school sixth form has been important to the whole school as a source of prestige. To belong to the sixth has been considered a privilege ...

The policy of an 'open' sixth challenges these traditions. We have encountered teachers who remain implacably opposed to the policy, believing that the sort of young people encountered in their interviews have no place in school. Even those who support it are faced with two sets of problems. The first concerns their own skills and experience in offering coherent courses to these students ... The second, related set of problems concerns resources. The further education sector has always been more responsive to a changing market for its services than schools, and it is geared to respond quickly. The major current response is to demands from Manpower Services Commission, backed by funding for temporary posts.

For schools, the response is slower. The last major change was ROSLA; and, in a way, current changes could be seen as a further raising of the school-leaving age. Then, however, the change was backed with money for curriculum development, accommodation, materials and staff. The dilemma for the Head of Sixth at Fordham School is that he has to cope within existing levels of staffing, accommodation and teaching materials.[10]

Shortly after that report was written, the government announced the TVEI programme which may, in the long run, give schools a resource to improve their own response time in line with further education (FE) colleges. (It encourages schools to take on BTEC and City and Guilds courses, for example, which offer a comfortable basis for the 'new' curriculum.) But the conservatism of schools has been one of their protective mantles and making them more 'demand conscious' may produce changes of a structural nature.

The underlying issue can be framed as a crucial question — what is the appropriate institutional base for the education of the adolescent?

The ramifications to this question are complex. In exploring them my focus will be on schools — as was CGIP's, though they also worked in FE colleges. The question of the appropriate institutional base for transition preparation is principally a question of how far we might expect schools to go in framing a response to the pressures to prepare adolescents for economic life — how appropriate are our curriculum traditions, and how sacrosanct?

The extemporized classroom settings which typically house MSC and other transition training courses are as forlornly familiar as were the classroom 'mobiles' which once substituted for capital spending programmes and which frequently allowed schools to 'banish' to the far reaches of the playground marginal curricula such as careers education. Prefabricated huts in the corners of FE college campuses, rented rooms over coffee-shops in the town centre, a single classroom ensconced in an industrial complex — the variety alone is a challenge to the familiar 'sameness' of school. This may, of course, be merely an accidental feature — the consequence of MSC's need to acquire instant space outstripping its capacity to institutionalize it. Together, however, with innovatory strategies to develop, teach and assess curriculum, the MSC in particular is suggesting, if not creating, a real alternative to more conventional secondary school curriculum. 'Social and Life Skills', 'Preparation for Living', the universally familiar educational elements of the 'new' vocational curricula, differ in ways that deter easy generalizations — though they tend to share familial features. There is a tendency for them to be objectives-based — linking planned content to assessment. They tend to be premised upon instructional styles of pedagogy. Their knowledge content is unrelated to the 'disciplines' and 'fields' of knowledge which underpin the mainstream school curriculum. They have no curriculum antecedents in institutions of higher learning.

They do, however, have a history. Bloxham attributes 'Life and Social Skills' (LSS) courses to the rise of the MSC and characterises them as deriving from a deficit model of the student. The questions she addresses explore:

> The arguments by which it has been decided that the consequences or causes of unemployment of young people can be linked to a lack of 'social and life skills' ...[11]

The Centre for Contemporary Cultural Studies — radical critics of contemporary events — see LSS courses as promoting 'a willingness to organize one's life according to the demands made by employers'.[12] Such arguments tend to place curriculum critique in the context of contemporary political critique. However, this family of curriculum has a more substantial history than such critique implies. Unconventional curricula appropriate to the personal and social needs of adolescents undergoing the putative transition into adulthood were advocated, for example, for the Authorised Courses of Instruction operated under the 1934 Act. A report on the scheme written in 1937 (National Advisory Council for Juvenile Unemployment) noted that;

Saville Kushner

> A technique of instruction is being developed to suit the needs of a service that differs in many respects from that of other educational institutions.

Then, as now, industrial advocates could use juvenile unemployment to exert leverage over educational discourse. Claims were made for new-style curricula to cater for the needs of students who were seen to be in deficit — not through lack of disciplinary knowledge — but through lack of the skills of 'citizenship'. The Ministry of Labour took a view we might recognize today that the longer-term clients of the Authorised Courses of Instruction 'tend to be of a type who find difficulty in securing employment owing to some defect of physique or character' and went on, in a report of 1938, to talk about responding with 'adjustments' to curriculum and pedagogy. The Ministry of Labour was active in the whole field of transition from school to work in the inter-war years and beyond and, in 1938, they were producing pamphlets for schools covering (in an interesting contrast) *Choice of Careers* and *Choice of Occupation* (the former included librarianship and veterinary science; the latter, laundry trades and engineering). The education authorities were forced to respond and, in doing so, were compelled to adopt the new vernacular which focussed on the primacy of 'skills'-based learning. In 1947 the Ministry of Education published a Central Advisory Council report entitled *School and Life: a First Enquiry into the Transition from School to Independent Life*. The report talked about breaking down the traditional boundaries around schools and creating a wider 'community' of educators and counsellors, and acknowledged pressures from industry:

> We have to ask ourselves how far the needs of industry ... prescribe the aims of education and how far ... systematic education can serve the needs of industry ... without departing from its proper purpose.

Their prognosis was, ultimately, defensive of schools whose objectives were held to differ from those of industry. 'The object of employment is the product; in education it is the process that matters.' Nonetheless, the report found it difficult to handle the issue — defending traditional schooling whilst acknowledging the public demand for vocational curriculum more related to the perceived needs of adolescents. Their ambivalence shows through at every point of the report:

> The basic skills required at school are also needed in employment ... Elementary mathematics, the use of English, recording facts, some manual training ...
>
> Certain qualities which are social as much as industrial are called for. Regular time-keeping ... precision ... persistence, speed and accuracy ... There is nothing uneducational in training for such qualities ...
>
> The danger to be avoided is that of subordinating the whole personality to a narrow conception of industry's needs ... It is not enough to prepare the young scholastically, technically, vocationally for their work in the world while neglecting to prepare them socially, personally and emotionally.

CGIP confronted much the same dilemma in their research. Their substantive interests lay less in the industrially-orientated curricula based upon 'work skills' than in careers education, the 'integration' of counselling resources ('integration' implying, amongst other things, breaking the internal and external boundaries which currently define conventional schooling). In their final report they concluded:

> The reasons why it has been difficult for us as a Project to encourage schools to look across their boundaries into the community seem to be:
> — There is little consensus inside or outside schools as to what the enterprise of schooling is for. If exam successes are to remain a key measure of school achievement, then 'integrative' activities will not be allowed to distract from that achievement.
> — Many schools see themselves as inculcating superior values to those of the surrounding community. They do not want to collaborate with what they are trying to resist.
> — School structures are set up to serve an academic, rather than a practical, curriculum. How *do* you use 35 minutes in the middle of the day to undertake a community project?
> — The curriculum and internal organization of most schools are organized on a hierarchy of 'worth'. Project and practical work is low in status.
> — Young people's own attitudes to school are fixed by tradition. Their expectations govern what they count as 'work'. They need first to unlearn what we have already taught them schools are for — before they can begin to use school in a new way.
> — Teachers tend to control activities for their own reasons. Loss of control, and the threat of anarchy, are considerable fears for teachers. There are risks attached to 'letting go' and experimenting.
> — Money and resources available give a clue to policy priorities. County upper schools were all designated 'community colleges', but their community activities are vulnerable, as education is cut back to basics.[13]

The challenge to schooling persisted — a challenge to the exclusive right of schools over preparation of youth for adult roles. In 1934 the Ministry of Labour was setting up an alternative vocational training system as well as accrediting employers to offer vocational education courses. In the immediate post-war period the challenge created division within the national system. One battleground at that time was the dichotomy between vocational education and vocational training — under the flares of reconstruction and the new drive to underpin educational development with manpower planning criteria (as recommended, for example, by the Barlow Commission). In 1949 the Ministry of Education published a report of a Special Committee on Education for Commerce. The Secondary School Examination Council had just proposed extensions of academic studies into the (then novel) unit commonly known as the sixth form. Vocational educators saw the 'gap' and moved in. The Special Committee's report noted:

> The traditional form of secondary education has been that offered in the grammar school; its content is familiar and its merit fully recognized. Nevertheless, in the opinion of many of those interested in educational problems this form of education is unduly literary, linguistic and abstract for the needs of many young people who would be better placed in schools of another type. Such young people would find greater stimulus in a form of education which uses practical work and daily experience in order to bring home and make vivid the relevance of theory.

In an appendix to that report Professors Plant and Smith, members of the Committee, added a note of reservation about placing too great a reliance on the dichotomy between vocational education and vocational training. Their note prefigured the debate that was to become prominent and acrimonious and which was to focus on the 'binary' system proposals of the middle-1960s. Plant and Smith were principally concerned about the impact of institutionalizing such distinctions and of, consequently, gearing educational provision to job-stratification. That 'gearing' principle, however, underlies much of this rather obscure report and, in a sense, suggests a resolution that was in keeping with the tenor of educational debate of the moment. The stratification implicit in the recently introduced tripartite system (grammar, technical and 'modern' schools) was only an element (clearly the major element) in a recurring advocacy of institutional stratification, though the general argument was based more directly upon arguments for alternative curricula (arguments echoed in contemporary rhetoric concerning the education of the putatively 'under-achieving' 40 per cent).

A final report worthy of mention gives a hint as to the detail in which such proposals were considered. A Ministry of Education report of 1945 entitled (prophetically) *Youth's Opportunity* pursued the ultimately fruitless line towards the County College proposed in the 1944 Act, recording its own antecedents in the Fisher Act of 1918. The Report opens with an analysis of the failure of the Day Continuation Schools noting, in particular, 'the lack of suitable teachers'. The scheme had attracted enthusiasts but had failed to find a professional expression of that enthusiasm:

> There was no properly thought out course of training for them and few of the assistant staff had adequate experience of working boys or girls or of their working environment.

Even with good staff, however, the Fisher proposals were bound to fail owing to the necessity to inhabit 'makeshift' buildings. The new curricula had no distinctive environment to counter the students impression that 'they were, in the most literal sense, being sent back to school'.

The evidence of student views reported by CGIP and by its evaluation suggest strongly that students do not easily reject school. The institution of the school is one they all recognize — and which many see, perhaps surprisingly, as benign. Schools may, for example, be incompetent in a student's view in confronting contemporary employment dilemmas — but they are not malevolent. Transition agencies, however, particularly training schemes for unemployed youth, are commonly seen as exploitative and a part of the problem itself.

There is one further ramification to the question of the appropriate institutional grounding for the education of the adolescent. We have seen some evidence of inter-ministerial competition for the resources to administer and change school curriculum. In recent years there has been at least one major casualty in the ensuing tussle — the Schools Council has been forced to give way to the MSC as the leading source for curriculum renewal. The MSC, with the massive funding it enjoys, is a formidable in-fighter which has been proved capable of leading collaborations with the DES. The new breed of administrators in the Commission are more accustomed to seeing policies implemented quickly — and with resources — than are their counterparts in the DES. As leading advocates of the new vocational curricula they cut a fine administrative dash. Their political elan lends a quality of modernism and polish to curricula they promote — they offer the new vocational 'chic'.

The CGIP Final Report noted, in respect of the relationship between 'schooling and YOP':

> It has been difficult for schools to find a coherent voice in influencing this relationship; not least because massive funding has been at the disposal of MSC, while spending on schools has been cut back. MSC, too, is not subject to the pluralistic decision-making constraints of the education service but can directly, and relatively swiftly, respond to demands.[14]

One political lesson of the 1980s has been that no assumptions or conventions need be regarded as sacrosanct. What is appropriate is what is, amongst other things, modern. And, though our system of school and LEA governance is new in terms of political history, some allege that it is already outmoded. The ultimate impact of *ad hoc* agencies in such volatile political arenas is hard to gauge.

In asking what is the appropriate institutional base for the instruction of the adolescent we are, in fact, asking the more focussed question 'Are schools still appropriate places for their education?'. The ad hoc measures we have alluded to and which have sought to develop a vocational training system tend to have been framed as a challenge to secondary schools. And yet they have persistently failed to carry the challenge through — the 'secret garden' of the curriculum, at least until the arrival of the Technical Vocational Education Initiative (TVEI), remained relatively inviolate. Even so, the pressure for new curricula persists. Are schools appropriate places to develop new curricula aimed at transition imperatives — preparation, self-awareness, social skills? If a particular kind of pedagogy is needed, are schools the best places to discover them? What, indeed, does an appropriate curriculum look like?

This last question was, in many senses, the most taxing question addressed by CGIP and its evaluation. The evaluators took a view of curriculum broader than the conventional view which focuses on content (curriculum objectives, materials, assessment techniques) — what Becher and Maclure call the 'public curriculum'. Like them they sought a more complex definition of curriculum to account for the fact that students' learning derives from experiences and stimuli from far wider sources than lesson content — such sources include the social and political relations the student observes in school, the architecture, the presentation of provision, the teaching style. You may, for example, teach a course on the history of trade unionism basing it on a single text and using a given pedagogical technique — say small group discussion. To teach that in a carpeted sixth form common-room as part of an examinable 'A' level course would be offering a wholly different learning experience to offering it as part of a non-examinable Life and Social Skills course to one-day release students in a 'mobile' classroom at the edges of a college playing field. To vary the teaching style to one of instruction ('chalk-and-talk') would be to further change the curriculum by changing the status of the learner. A critical variable in this version of curriculum we might think of as 'access'. If, in the above model, we gave every student a copy of the text and allowed the group to negotiate their own approach to the topic, we have created the possibility of such a radical shift in classroom protocol and student status as to have made the curriculum wholly distinct as a learning experience from any of the other forms we have mentioned. How does this relate to our theme? It does so through the agency of a second major question.

In their Final Report CGIP ask the question 'What curriculum is appropriate for the society we are moving into?' That question is currently being vigorously addressed by many educational and non-educational professionals. For the purpose of this chapter I will focus the question onto what is, perhaps, its most critical element, and I will focus, also, on a more immediate 'threat' to the curriculum as it evolves in practice, in classrooms.

In considering contemporary curriculum for adolescents, what are the changing factors in the relations between teachers, learners and knowledge?

Let us start by looking at two vignettes of CGIP's work in schools. I spoke earlier of the tensions resulting from the dynamic interface between educational and industrial values. If those tensions are real then they will be observable in curriculum practice. In these vignettes we will hear teachers talking of experiencing shifting relationships with their students in classroom exchanges which appear less predictable than they perhaps once were. Both pieces concern the introduction of 'Life and Social Skills' courses. Such courses — intended, usually, to induct students into adult patterns of behaviour — are a central element in the new curricula offerings. They are universal in post-school training settings and increasingly popular in schools. The type of curriculum content typical of these courses and comprising the syllabus Kathryn offered to Kitbridge School includes analysis of emotions, empathizing with others, development of self-presentation and interaction skills, etc.

CGIP staff were talking to two teachers at Kitbridge comprehensive school about the introduction to the curriculum at a 'Life Skills' course. The two teachers — Jenny, a Deputy Head; Gill, the Careers teacher — had taken a curriculum outline from Kathryn (along with some materials) and had tried to sell it to other teachers in the school. Both were experienced teachers — Jenny was a veteran of the Humanities Curriculum Project, one of the national curriculum projects of the 1960s (directed by Lawrence Stenhouse) which worked through teacher development to ways of handling controversial issues in the classroom. The Life Skills outline, when presented to staff, had evoked conflict. Feminists among the teachers had immediately objected to the use of a story which began 'Jacob Risby owned a garage ...' Kathryn asked Jenny and Gill whether objections had been made to undertaking any Life Skills teaching or simply to the nature of the material. What were the 'dissenters' worried about?

Jenny: ... they see in here (pointing to the course outline) a great deal of political manipulation which I personally don't see.

Gill: There's accusation of it being biassed towards the middle classes —

Jenny: — and that it's always a lot of, well, manipulating people so that they won't have riots. That the Wood Green riots were, in fact, a way of 'coping with life' —

Gill: — that it's a way of getting you to conform. But you see, there are others of us who disagree with that. We look at it more objectively.[15]

But Jenny sees in this Life Skills curriculum potential for self-exploration. More so than any curriculum she experienced as a student.

Jenny: I discounted the experience that my parents had had — totally wrote it off. I'm quite surprised that more of our girls are more responsive to that sort of recounted experience ... they listen very much more than I did when I was young.[16]

But that, in a context of a Life Skills curriculum, makes demands on the teacher to reveal her own experience.

Jenny: There are some girls ... who would, I fear, use any of my revelations against me ... All of us, as human beings, feel quite inadequate to deal with Life Skills. Most of us look at it and say — 'I've got a bit of that, I haven't got any of that, none of that' — and we're used to being in control of our own subject and here we're not ... Study Skills I can do quite well ... I have quite patently succeeded in overcoming my difficulties in studying, haven't I. Whereas I don't think I'd actually manage to pass an exam in these sorts of things.[17]

Jenny sits, casually musing over the Life Skills course outline during a lull in the conversation. She checks off items on the list of objectives. 'Some days I can't do any of these things', she says half under her breath.

At Dane Park School Bill Law and Kathryn were supporting a team of teachers who were developing a social education curriculum. At one point in the collaboration the teachers came up against demands made by the curriculum which, though clearly appropriate, were felt by some to raise professional dilemmas. Bill recorded the event:

Identifying consequences.   The final session of this visit proved to be concerned with the consequences of giving the students a substantial voice in class. We reminded them of the sorts of things that had come from the Project's survey of 'What the Students Said', and we asked them, in small groups, to brainstorm the options that they could see for their students on leaving school in a place like this.

The list was diverse, and referred to such options as 'prostitution', 'suicide' and 'bumming around'. It led to some heart-searching on the part of the teachers. Two issues were identified: 'Should the classroom contain references to such 'unsavoury' facts of life?'; and 'How can a teacher make the same kind of authoritative pronouncements of these matters as he or she can on topics in other subjects on the curriculum?'

Our views on such matters could hardly have been in any doubt by this time. We could hardly argue for the linking of classroom with the world beyond the school gates, and then argue that references to unsavoury facts in the world should be filtered out. We had, moreover, already argued that as 'self-disclosing adult' a teacher has no more authority on such matters than his or her own personal experience can support; he or she may well be less 'expert' on some issues than some of the youngsters.

At this point, the medium becomes the message. While we were prepared to say how *we* — as individuals — saw it, it would have been self-contradictory for us to prevent the voicing of views, that the voicing of views should be prevented; or to adopt the role of 'experts' telling teachers that they should not adopt the role of experts!

One or two teachers began to wonder in the discussion how they could deal with issues like suicide — except in terms of their own personal opinions.[18]

These two vignettes are examples of events encountered by CGIP typifying changes taking place in classroom expectations which pressurize the traditional professional roles of teachers. In their review of the curriculum reform movement, MacDonald and Walker outline a succession of fifteen major changes in schooling and its administration which, at that time, would 'most likely impinge on the world of curriculum projects'.[19] The list included ROSLA, comprehensivization, changes in assessment and examinations, economic cutbacks, etc. If we were to rewrite that list eight years later we would have to add as a prominent feature the growing sophistication of adolescents and their demands on teachers to handle difficult and controversial issues in class. This is not new but its prominence is. Jenny remembers the period of change at the time MacDonald and Walker were writing and sees the contemporary version:

Jenny: Sometimes I catch myself in the middle of something — in an English lesson — and I think — yes, that's a 'life skill'. There's a kind of germ in the air about these things, isn't there, that goes round schools from time to time — and you can just pick it up. And you don't quite always know where it comes from. Sometimes it might take a long time to germinate. It is a little like assessing the impact of the Schools Council. There was a great lack of take-up there — and yet when I think in my teaching time before the Schools Council — it was a sort of watershed. Lots of things have changed as a result of that.[20]

Jenny has a historical perspective that allows her to compare curriculum climates over two decades. But that does not guarantee that she will draw from the experience of those years. Although the Humanities Curriculum Project grappled with similar issues to those Jenny faces — handling controversial value issues in classroom — she does not return to the Project for the disciplinary support she feels she needs in teaching Life Skills. For her HCP belonged to another time. The materials were stored in the school basement — they were out of date.

Publicly there has been a devaluation of the experience of the curriculum reform movement as the Schools Council has been reduced in size, status and function. The vigour with which the Council was attacked by the DES as well as by Government Ministers was evidence of the strongly held conviction that it had failed in its task of improving and reforming curriculum and examinations. Of itself, the Council's demise is a public discouragement to revisit the experience of their 125 or more (until 1977) curriculum research and development projects and there is, at least prima facie, a case for arguing that the baby went out with the bath water. Some recognition of that, and of the continuity of issues despite the alleged failure of the Council, has come recently with the commissioning by the Further Education Unit (FEU) of two HCP-style teacher packages on youth unemployment from Professor Jean Rudduck, one of the original developers. CGIP was sure, as they recorded in their final report, of the continuity between current curriculum issues and those which were addressed by the curriculum reform movement:

Much of the underlying philosophy of careers work is at one with progressive, child-centred views of education. Much subject teaching is based upon knowledge to be acquired on the 'storehouse' principle. Careers teachers coming new to Careers work face many of the problems faced by those attempting curriculum innovation in the 1960s and 1970s in student-centred discovery-learning projects. These projects attempted to work with processes, not just facts to be stored; to centre their work upon the needs and characteristics of their students; and to share the learning process with them. These innovations raised similar questions of rationale and method and even questioned the traditional and accepted expertise-based authority of the teacher. Careers work today is encountering similar problems.[21]

These issues confront teachers who engage those elements of the new programmes which cover Life Skills, Careers Education, Social Education, etc. Such emerging curricula face a common problem — how to maintain teacher authority in classroom activities which emphasize areas where teachers are conventionally unskilled; where activities are, in CGIP's words, 'centred upon the needs and characteristics of their students'. It is in such activities that professional resources become stretched as they were amongst those teachers who had to cope with the impact of ROSLA and for whom such projects as Geography for the Young School Leaver, Project Technology, HCP and others were set up. And yet, there is a problem, evidenced by Jenny and the

Dane Park teachers, of capturing the experience of those who have faced the issues earlier.

The Schools Council will be properly judged in time and may emerge as the court of the 'golden years of curriculum reform'; or as the ineffective tool of the teacher unions that has been alleged. For the time being at least it seems that their experience will be lost to the new curriculum developers. In one sense that may inevitably lead to a reinvention of the curriculum 'wheel'. But there is another sense in which the process might be more valuable than 'reinvention' along suggests. It may well be that new generations need to revisit their problems in their own time, in their own way. What we might be seeing is a purposeful break with a tradition that is already bound up in a past history of others' adventures. Certainly many of the claims of the new programme designers are founded upon allegations of failure of their earlier counterparts. The new curriculum developers may well be entitled to their own adventures.

Meanwhile, teachers and students pursue the educational enterprise from day to day. Teachers continue to exercise their professional skills and judgments against a backdrop of growing pressures to acknowledge a diversity of wider social problems. Jenny talked of the single-issue pressure groups calling on her school to invest curriculum with 'dimensions' of 'multi-cultural' issues, equal opportunities, vocational needs, the special examination needs of black students, etc. 'If we have any more dimensions it'll be all dimension and no subject matter.' One of the problems she found in reconciling these demands with the resources available was a structural imbalance in schools. 'We have never really recovered', says Jenny, 'from the rupture of pastoral from academic staff'. That rupture came, itself, in response to external pressures for schools to handle the personal and social problems of their students. That Life Skills, careers education and other such elements of the new programmes need an integration of pastoral issues with academic milieux was one of the tenets of CGIP. Their view of the potential for achieving that mix by the time they came to write their final report was not optimistic.

> Many teachers remark that they feel too much is expected of them. They are expected to compensate for social ills, such as lack of family support and breakdown in community life. Where there are no apprenticeships or unskilled work for young school-leavers, they are expected to socialize students into work skills and attitudes they would once have learnt on starting work. They are expected to lay the groundwork of preparation for the manpower needs of society and at the same time to maintain educational standards and academic success. All this with less and less resources, both to supply the essentials of a balanced educational environment and to encourage the professional development of teachers.[22]

Four Models of Deficit

As a last section to this paper it might help to add an analytical tool to the history I have sketched. Measures to cope with the needs of adolescents tend to have been framed as remedial measures, and the remedies tend to have derived from some perception of deficit which pinpoints a shortfall in existing provision. It is an attempt to formalize these perceptions of deficit as models which will constitute our analytical tool. But first I need to say what I mean by a model of deficit.

There are three stages to the development and use of a model of deficit. First, a shortfall is noticed or identified in educational (or training) outcomes. (Say, standards of numeracy are falling and employers are concerned about the quality of recruits.) Next, culpability is established and a culprit identified. (In this example, perhaps teachers are the focus for blame in abandoning tried and tested methods of mathematics teaching in favour of experimental curricula.) Finally, a remedy is designed and legitimated with reference back to the problem. (An objectives-based, mastery-learning scheme is proposed to replace modern maths syllabi under the claim that it is 'proof' against teacher modification). The models tend to emphasize student, school and culture deficit.

Student Deficit

This is the one which is perhaps most familiar to contemporary readers. Sue Bloxham highlights the model:

> ... despite the massive growth in youth unemployment, extended across a much wider achievement range, government special measures still identify the young people and their lack of skills as the problem, rather than directing provision towards solving the problems that the young people face ... YOP continues to take a 'deficiency' view of the causes of youth unemployment, arguing that training in basic skills is needed to help young peoples' employment prospects.[23]

In its popular form applied to the problems of adolescents, the model involves a tendency to 'blame the victim' — in this case, claiming that unemployment is at least partially rooted in unemployability. Hence the measures taken are of a remedial character and we would recognize the products most easily from curriculum offerings in 'work preparation', 'work experience', 'life and social skills', 'job-hunting skills', etc. Since the deficit is usually taken to be observed or assumed (rather than researched with students), curriculum tends to be based upon behavioural aims and objectives — for example, to improve interviewing style; to improve punctuality; to learn to value the 'world of work'. One implication of the model for curriculum evaluation is that the initial assumption of deficit in the student has a tendency to protect the curriculum. Since the rationale for arriving at curriculum content is the shortfall in behaviour that might otherwise be expected of the student, the early assumptions tend to become frozen and evaluation will tend to focus back onto the student (to see how the 'treatment' works). Curriculum process becomes narrowed down to, at best, a redefinition and transmission of those assumptions rather, for example, than an exploration of student needs, a negotiation between the teacher and student on a relevant content or, indeed, style of teaching.

School Deficit

We can think of this deficit model as falling on schools in one of two guises — either through allegations of curriculum shortcomings or of teacher shortcomings. It could be argued that the curriculum reform movement which flowered throughout the 1960s was based upon the former, and the more contemporary attacks upon teachers and upon the teaching profession are representative of the latter. Furthermore, the two can be thought of as related by a common public concern to challenge the right of schools to exclusive guardianship of the secondary curriculum.

Deficit in curriculum

I will take one example to illustrate the thrust of the major curriculum reform projects from the 1960s and their common origins in a deficit view of curriculum. It is drawn from Stenhouse[24] in which he offers brief case studies of fifteen major curriculum initiatives. This particular one comes from a description of the 'History 13–16' project.

> In the late 1960s the established place of history in the curriculum was being challenged by a variety of reformist movements. In 1968 the Historical Association's journal, 'History', carried an article by Mary Price on 'History in Danger' which analyzed the problems being encountered by the subject and defined a number of curative strategies. The article summarised teachers' fears of the 'real danger of history disappearing from the timetable as a subject in its own right'. These teachers saw history 'surviving only as an ingredient of social studies or civics, or combined courses of one kind or another ...

Later in the book, Stenhouse discusses the origins and impact of the curriculum reform movement. He broadens the source of the desire for reform from localized areas of curriculum concern to a general concern with schools. From ROSLA on:

> Curriculum research and development was adopted by the state system through the agency of the Schools Council, and applied to the problems of the comprehensive school. No longer was it a matter of updating the curriculum for the academic: it was an attempt to meet the problems of extending a genuine secondary education to people who were not of that elite.

Deficit in teachers

Though Stenhouse's own Humanities Curriculum Project sought curriculum research and development through the pathways of teacher development, there was never a strong rhetoric of teacher deficit. MacDonald and Walker, writing of the comparisons between the American and the British curriculum reform movements noted the confrontational style of American developers.

> British debate about the schools, on the other hand, with few exceptions, is conciliatory if not positively self-congratulatory. To borrow a standard phrase from the pupil report-card, 'could do better' is the tone typically struck in this country by curriculum developer

and critic alike when referring to the performance of the teaching profession . . . Partly, of course, this is a matter of cultural style. But it is also partly a consequence of the fact that almost all of the participants in the discussion have at one time been schoolteachers and still remember their own inadequacies and difficulties.[25]

The flavour of debate has since changed. Teachers are sure and easy targets of attack from many quarters and particularly, perhaps, from many who never were teachers and who are free of the memory of experienced difficulties. Researchers, the CBI, the unpredictable HMI reporters, MSC, local employers and the media — all engage freely in a scrutiny of teacher competence. Measures being proposed at the time of writing include the continuing push to include parents and employers in traditional areas of teacher decision-making in schools; the introduction of teacher competency test procedures; the revamping of teacher-training to render it more accountable to central authority; and MSC participation in teacher-training.

Cultural Deficit

There is a third model — cultural deficit — that we might use to explore the sources of contemporary challenges to curriculum.

MacDonald and Walker conclude their chapter on a comparison of American and British curriculum innovation by asking the question:

What degree of 'respect' was shown for the established system, its institutions, its processes, its personnel, its achievements? In America, too little. The bombardment of the system in the early sixties was followed by the attempt to 'move in' new institutions, new processes, new personnel with new goals. Such takeover bids for social systems are likely to fail for two reasons: they will be resisted because they strike at the self-esteem of those they need to co-opt; and the resistance will be successful because power is much more widely distributed in social systems than those at the centre realize.[26]

It is still too early to say whether the school system will be able to resist contemporary takeover bids, though the argument, surely, does not look so clear-cut as it might have done in 1976. What is clear, however, is that many of the measures currently being taken to combat adolescent and institutional difficulties with post-school transition constitute attacks on basic assumptions and conventions in education. The principal attack is on the assumption that educational issues need to be confronted by educational professionals.

The education system has, hitherto, enjoyed a resilience to outside interventions. When the Engineering Industries Training Board (EITB) published proposals for school curriculum and examinations in 1979 and presented them at regional conferences of teachers they were met with massive and hostile resistance for what was taken to be their assertiveness.[27] There is a sense in which the education service has been accustomed to non-educational authorities having to negotiate access to the 'insider' curriculum discourse. As Kathryn noted in an internal project note:

> ... In schools there is a tradition of professional integrity. Schools are hostile to interventions designed to influence academic standards or to reduce autonomy ...[28]

Such predispositions underpinned the writing of Miles whom I quoted earlier on what he called 'linkage failure'. Temporary systems, set up to generate new curricula, face the problem of 'linking' back into the permanent system in order to fully establish their products. Much of that linkage in Britain was a matter of cultural alignment — investing the product with the vocabularies, meanings and symbols of classroom life. The cautious construction of the 'partnership' principle which characterized the relationship between educational administrators and practitioners was itself an acknowledgement of the cultural hegemony of the educational veteran. And, of course, the administration produced education veterans of its own — officials who, against the run of Civil Service procedures, were stable-bred in the DES; Chief Education Officers like Clegg and Newsom who were curriculum innovators.

But only four years after the debacle suffered by the EITB the Manpower Services Commission is welcomed by local authorities and schools. We could almost turn Miles' principle on its head and see the vocational/industrial culture as the most recent conqueror of the education system. In some parts of the country — those with long histories of mass unemployment — the MSC and its host of affiliates are coming to be seen as the 'providers' and the schools as the 'supplicants'. 'Linkage failure', in such circumstances, might leave schools stranded.

These models are intended to reflect the way people — including the research community — perceive the problems of transition. What research and evaluation take place in the transition field tend to be subject to interpretation according to the predispositions of the user. To produce accounts grounded in research and which challenge overly simple definitions of the problems is itself a problem that has not yet been worked through by the research community in education. Conventionally, that community has shown itself to be more useful where educational process is to be simplified and rationalized, and we can think of testing, setting curriculum objectives, establishing criteria for 'effective' teaching, producing matching models to marry given students with given careers, etc. American school systems have proved the most responsive audience to such approaches and they have exploited the opportunities to implement simplified solutions. The results have created some misgivings among critics of education. Michael Apple, a radical amongst American observers of the curriculum, talks of the common treatment of curriculum issues as technical problems and of the consequences in the demeaning of the teacher professional. In doing so he paints a bleak picture of the contemporary American classroom:

> It is nearly impossible, now, to walk into an American classroom without seeing boxes upon boxes of science, social studies, mathematics and reading materials ... lining the shelves and in use. Here, a school system purchases a total set of standardized material, usually one which includes statements of objectives, all of the curricular

content and material needed, prespecified teacher actions and appropriate student responses, and diagnostic and achievement tests co-ordinated with the system. Usually these tests have the curricular knowledge 'reduced' to 'appropriate' behaviours and skills.[29]

Such curricular and curriculum contexts have their proponents in Britain as well — and the field of transition is one of the more popular arenas in education for their aspirations.

We have already developed the necessary ingredients for such a brew and they are active in our education system. This is not to say that traditional British classrooms are not already modelled on industrial values and relationships — the Hamilton quotation earlier makes precisely that point. Where Apple's classroom differs from the classrooms seen in the case studies is the lack of freedom for teachers and learners to create their own relationships. Curriculum invoked on such a principle tends to be rigid and unadaptive and, therefore, out of step with the needs and characteristics of its users. It is, of course, central to the rhetoric of transition that curriculum emanates directly from those needs and characteristics.

But such a curriculum — based on the needs and characteristics of educational management — is relatively undemanding to conceive of and to design and suits many expectations of transition. The research base is highly developed and trades on its accessibility (lists of objectives, effectiveness criteria, discrete assessment measures) and on its relative ease of use. Curriculum that is in step with the needs and characteristics of students in transition, on the other hand, requires the marshalling of a complex and often inaccessible array of factors — of which student agendas we have spoken of as the most prominent. CGIP were not altogether optimistic about the prospects for such a curriculum and about the prospects for the lessons they learned and published. I close this chapter with a last extract from the Project's final report. Kathryn borrowed (from the evaluators of the Strathclyde EC project) a distinction between 'institutional' networks (school, FE, YTS, careers service) and 'cultural' networks (based upon the students' own contacts and associations). It was not hard to encourage teachers to use the former — they were, after all, sources of support.

The cultural network is more difficult for the teacher to use. For a start, it is owned by the student and represents his or her personal, and often private, space. What right has the school to attempt to colonize this network, and why should it seek to do so? This is a pertinent question where there is a gulf between the values represented by the school and the values of students. A number of schools we have worked with saw themselves as providing an oasis of protection against the prevailing values of the community. They were 'closed' systems, and deliberately so. Faced with riots in their locality, were they to bring discussion and debate about their causes and consequences into the school? There are influences which teachers may seek to keep out. Notions of integration between school and community have their limits as well as their potentialities.[30]

Notes

1 KUSHNER, S. and LOGAN, T. (1983) *Made in England: an Evaluation of Curriculum in Transition*, CARE Occasional Publications No. 14, Norwich, University of East Anglia.
2 WATTS, A.G. and LAW, B. (1977) *Schools, Careers and Community*, London, CIO Publishing (General Synod Board of Education).
3 MILES, M. (1964) *Innovation in Education*, Columbia, Teachers College Press.
4 REES, G. and REES, T. (1982) 'Youth unemployment and state intervention' in REES, T. and ATKINSON, P. (Eds) *Youth Unemployment and State Intervention*, London, Routledge and Kegan Paul.
5 BECHER, T. and MACLURE, S. (1978) *The Politics of Curriculum Change*, London, Hutchinson.
6 CGIP internal notes, February 1980.
7 CGIP final report, 0/3.
8 HAMILTON, D. (1980) 'Adam Smith and the moral economy of the classroom system', mimeo, DES, University of Glasgow, March.
9 HEGINBOTHAM, H. (1967) 'The development of the youth employment service' in LEICESTER, J. and FARNDALE, J. (Eds) *Trends in the Services for Youth*, Oxford, Pergamon Press.
10 CGIP final report, 10/22–3.
11 BLOXHAM, S. (1983) 'Social behaviour and the young unemployed' in FIDDY, R. (Eds) *In Place of Work: Policy and Provision for the Young Unemployed*, Lewes, Falmer Press.
12 Centre for Contemporary Cultural Studies (1981) *Unpopular Education*, London, Hutchinson.
13 CGIP final report, 9/12.
14 *Ibid*, 0/2.
15 Evaluation fieldnotes, February 1982.
16 *Ibid*.
17 *Ibid*.
18 CGIP final report, 8/14–5.
19 MACDONALD, B. and WALKER, R. (1976) *Changing the Curriculum*, London, Open Books.
20 Evaluation fieldnotes, February 1982.
21 CGIP final report, 0/5.
22 *Ibid*, 0/3.
23 BLOXHAM, S. (1983) *op. cit.*
24 STENHOUSE, L. (Ed.) (1980) *Curriculum Research and Development in Action*, London, Heinemann Education.
25 MACDONALD, B. and WALKER, R. (1976) *op. cit.*
26 *Ibid*.
27 See KUSHNER, S., LOGAN, T. et al (1983) *Decision-making in the Secondary Curriculum*, E204, Unit 10, Educational Studies, Milton Keynes, Open University Press for a fuller account.
28 CGIP internal notes, February 1980.
29 APPLE, M.W. (1982) 'Curricular form and the logic of technical control' in APPLE, M.W. (Ed.) *Cultural and Economic Reproduction in Education*, London and Boston, Routledge and Kegan Paul.
30 CGIP final report, 9/8.

The Emergence of the Youth Training Scheme

Rob Fiddy

In September 1983 the Youth Training Scheme (YTS) officially superseded the Youth Opportunities Programme (YOP) as the major provision for unemployed school-leavers in this country. The new scheme met a mixed response. For example Len Murray, the General Secretary of the Trades Union Congress (TUC), said of the scheme:

> The YTS can represent a major step towards ensuring that all young people, on leaving school, have the opportunity to acquire a preparation for working life on which to build their future careers.[1]

He did admit, however, that it would 'not be easy to achieve this objective.' Nearer to the grass roots Suzy Croft and Peter Beresford, of Battersea Community Action, proclaimed that:

> The government has placed an enormous ideological, economic and political commitment in the YTS ... It and its predecessors offer government a perhaps previously unenvisaged opportunity to regulate the lives and information received by young people on an unprecedented scale.[2]

Sir Terence Beckett, the Director-General of the Confederation of British Industry (CBI), had, earlier, expressed doubts about the viability of the new scheme: in his view the recession would make it difficult for employers to provide adequate training opportunities and the futures of the scheme's 'graduates' would be far from rosy. 'The Guardian' reported him as saying that 'nothing could be worse for young people who have received additional training if there is no prospect of a job at the end of it'.[3]

Few previous initiatives in the area of education and training have provoked such a spectrum of reaction. Certainly the economic climate, particularly as it has affected the employment chances of the young, is not one to encourage critical ambivalence amongst those who have ready access to the media. At the time of writing, over 50 per cent of under eighteen year-old school-leavers are unemployed and the Manpower Services Commission (MSC) themselves (whose aegis includes the YOP and the YTS) predict a general rise to 63 per cent by the mid-1980s, with peaks in some areas of the country to 90 per cent.

The most obvious critical response to the YTS from the young is to be found in their non-attendance. In the first month of operation the YTS offered 371,000 places (out of an eventual 460,000) of which less than 25 per cent were taken up. This apparent lack of general confidence in the benefits of the, as yet, largely untried YTS may well have its antecedents in the well-documented accusations of the YOP's failings — mainly in that it afforded employers the cheap labour of trainees on the scheme and offered little in the way of post-YOP job chances. What credibility the early YOP had slipped away as it rapidly expanded to cope with increasing levels of unemployed school-leavers, whilst at the same time the numbers of its graduates gaining employment fell.

Try as the MSC might to promote the YTS as having learned and benefited from YOP's mistakes, the message on the street seems very often, so far, to be 'more of the same'. This in itself, at least in terms of organizational rhetoric, is a misunderstanding of the new scheme. YTS training is of longer duration than YOP's. It has formal requirements for off-the-job education and clearly specified learning objectives. But most importantly for potential trainees it butt-joins school experience. Because the YTS can be entered straight from school, whereas the YOP was for school-leavers who had experienced a period of unemployment, it is in competition with other vocational options. This is one of its features which has led some representatives of the further education sector to declare that the YTS proposals were attempts 'to restructure youth and decrease the power of the trade unions (and) to undermine further education'.[4]

What is the YTS, and why has it sparked such controversy? In May 1981 the MSC produced a consultative document entitled 'A New Training Initiative' which dealt with the future for national industrial training. The government endorsed the MSC's findings with a White Paper in December 1981 which projected 'A Programme for Action', with three major objectives:

i)   to develop skill training including apprenticeship in such a way as to enable young people entering at different ages and with different educational attainments to acquire agreed standards of skill appropriate to the jobs available and to provide them with a basis for progress through further learning;

ii) to move towards a position where all young people under the age of 18 have the opportunity either of continuing in full-time education or of entering a period of planned work experience combined with work related training and education;

iii) to open widespread opportunities for adults, whether employed or returning to work, to acquire, increase or update their skills and knowledge during the course of their working lives.[5]

With reference to the second objective, the White Paper contained plans for:

a new £1 billion a year Youth Training Scheme, guaranteeing from September 1983 a full year's foundation training for *all those leaving school at the minimum age without jobs*.[6]

The aspiration of a vocational umbrella for *all* school-leavers is not confined to the present Conservative government. Recommendations for the implementation of such provision were made both in the Fisher Education Act of 1918 and in the 1944 Education Act. Contrary to the situation in 1918 and in 1944, however, both the unprecedented numbers of unemployed amongst current school-leavers and the degree of attention drawn to young people generally by the media have so increased their profile that they are now commonly regarded as a policy priority. For some observers the government's guarantee was interpreted as blackmail. The White Paper included plans to reduce the training allowance from the then £23.50 paid to YOP trainees to £15 as from September 1983. It also proposed to withdraw supplementary benefit from school-leavers, thereby effectively making the scheme compulsory. The slow take-up of YTS places mentioned earlier may never have occurred if these plans had ever seen fruition. In April 1982, however, a report from the Youth Task Group — 'a high level working group, including representatives of industry and education', set up by the MSC to consider the White Paper proposals in detail — strongly recommended that the training allowance for the YTS should not be reduced, nor eligibility for supplementary benefit be withdrawn. In a statement to the House of Commons on 21 June 1982 the Minister for Employment, Norman Tebbit, announced acceptance of these two amendments, although there still remains a six-week reduction of benefit for YTS abstainers. Another contentious issue for the Task Group was the budget for the YTS. The government White Paper had allocated £1 billion per annum, but this was for 300,000 trainees at £15 per week. The sum was not upgraded by September 1983 when there were 460,000 anticipated places (albeit not all taken up) with an allowance of £25 per week.

The YTS offers up to one year of planned work experience and off-the-job further education and training, based on an initial and continuous assessment of participant's needs and abilities. At the end of the year the trainees will have built up a personal profile which will record their progress and achievement and serve as the basis for progression into subsequent employment or further education or training. Ultimately, YTS will be offered to all young people aged under 18 who have left full-time education. The scheme has three sponsoring 'modes', 'Youth In Society' described them thus:

Mode A: The scheme is first and foremost work related and the majority of opportunities — 295,000 — will be employer-based. These places will be delivered (sic) by a network of Managing Agents and will form the basis of Mode A provision. Managing Agents take responsibility for designing, managing and delivering all aspects of YTS provision. A Managing Agent may itself be a sponsor of a YTS scheme, or may be acting on behalf of other sponsors.

Mode B1: A further 80,000 places are provided by the sponsors of Community Projects, Training Workshops and Information Technology Centres. Here the MSC is the Managing Agent (as under the YOP).

Mode B2: The final 85,000 places will also be managed by the MSC, through a network of 'linked schemes' comprising training courses (largely in Colleges of Further Education) linked to periods of work experience on employer's premises.[7]

Modes A, B1 and B2 represent more than a pragmatic splitting of operations for organizational purposes. *The Times Educational Supplement* referred to the difference between the Modes as reflecting 'some fundamental tensions and conflicts in the ideology and practice of vocational preparation'.[8] The two main kinds of scheme are funded differently. Mode A sponsors are employers who receive a government subsidy for each trainee taken on; the employer is responsible for paying the trainee and providing on and off-the-job training and further education. Mode B1 sponsors are mostly voluntary organizations or local authorities who provide a variety of training specifically for the young unemployed. Mode B2 is run by Colleges of Further Education and some schools and provides short off-the-job training courses with work experience placements. All Mode B sponsors claim the cost of their training provision from the MSC and the MSC pay the trainees. The *TES* goes on to say that:

> The biggest difference (between the Modes) is in the ultimate motivations of the two kinds of sponsor: most employers, however public spirited, must regard the YTS as helping to provide them with better trained workers for their own needs, whatever else it does, and largely at the taxpayer's expense; while most Mode B sponsors are motivated by the same kind of objectives as teachers ...
>
> On the face of it, Mode A and Mode B ought to be potentially of equal value, both providing a foundation year of work experience, training and education with much the same balance between the three elements. But the MSC and ministers are making it increasingly plain that they regard Mode A as by far the most desirable kind of sponsorship and imply that Mode B is there, partly because it may not be possible to find enough training places with employers, and also to take care of those youngsters whom, for one reason or another, the employers don't want.[9]

From April 1983 fifty-five Area Manpower Boards were established to cover England, Scotland and Wales (Northern Ireland has separate arrangements under the Youth Training Programme). They replaced the twenty-nine former Special Programmes Area Boards and eighty-eight District Manpower Committees. The new boards 'have the task of helping to plan and promote the MSC's employment and training programmes for both young people and adults'. The YTS is overseen by a seventeen member Youth Training Board, to report to the MSC on progress made toward the YTS objectives and recommend changes if appropriate. Professional advice for the Youth Training Board falls under the aegis of a new Advisory Group. Members of this group have been individually invited to serve in 'a personal capacity'.

From an establishment perspective the YTS attacks a crisis in post-school training. Only around 50 per cent of British school-leavers have received any further training or education since the 1940s, compared to around 80 per cent in France and 90 per cent in Germany. This comparison is often cited as a cause of the relatively slow productivity growth from British labour post-Second World War. When linked to the recession and the increasing speed and impact of technological change the result is a massive increase in unemployment, especially amongst school-leavers and those approaching retirement, the former being seen as the greater problem since some unemployed youngsters face a lifetime on the dole. In the words of Tony Warren, a representative of the Leicestershire and Northants Area Manpower Board:

> The recession is producing permanent changes in the Labour market that will not disappear if and when better times come. Craft apprenticeship will never completely recover because of new technology and the relative decline of the manufacturing industries that are its base. New technology is producing a potential increase in demand for technician and supervisor level skill. The number of unskilled jobs has been very badly hit, however, and even those that exist make demands on skills of numeracy, communication, basic manual dexterity, understanding organizations etc. In particular all young workers must be adaptable enough to cope with the introduction of new techniques and several job changes during a lifetime.

The case for the New Training Initiative (NTI) derives from this. The YTS will provide a foundation year of good quality training for all school-leavers and act as a bridge between school and work (NTI Objective 2). The YTS will concentrate on non-job-specific skills and encourage adaptability and enable progression into specific skills training either through an apprenticeship system open to entry at any age and based on standards of competancy rather than time serving (NTI Objective 1), or through an expanded system of adult training and retraining (NTI Objective 3).[10]

The YTS has a legacy of a generally bad press from YOP, but another consideration around the time of the new scheme's birth were the riots of 1981, when public attention was drawn to the links between unemployment and street disorder.

This is not the place to examine whether or not unemployment can be held solely responsible for the events of summer 1981, but certainly they were linked in the popular view, guided, of course, by the media. Clive Jenkins, General Secretary of the Association of Scientific, Technical and Managerial Staff, for example, in a 'Panorama' interview, proclaimed that he 'didn't want to go on reading the latest unemployment statistics by the light of the burning buildings.' Some observed that the previously mentioned government attempt to make the proposed YTS compulsory was a direct result of the riots and a belief that 'the devil makes work for idle hands'. The May 1981 MSC consultative document had not mentioned withdrawing eligibility for supplementary benefit as the December 1981 White Paper had. The intervening period, of course, witnessed the riots. As a YOP trainee said in an interview:

> YOP ... That's Youth Off Pavements innit. That's why we're not allowed to have a holiday (from her particular scheme) this summer. ... In case we all go on a riot ...[11]

The YOP was heralded by the Holland Report in 1977 as an integration of a variety of work experience schemes for the young unemployed with the aim of 'improving their employability and helping them find suitable employment'.[12] The focus on employability was a mainstay of the MSC's pre-Thatcher policy (the YTS has witnessed a shift in underlying emphasis, but more of this later). The variety of schemes organized under the YOP's umbrella took as their theme the 'mis-match' between school-leaver abilities and employer needs. There was a reluctance on behalf of employers to take on school-leavers which reflected 'their judgment that the qualities they wanted in their labour force, the qualities associated with work experience, were not those produced by schooling'.[13] In addition the position of young workers in the job market had changed:

> The most obvious was in unemployment which for the total population had risen by 45 per cent between January 1972 and January 1977, while it had risen 120 per cent for those under twenty in the same period. This was caused by a combination of the vulnerability of young workers in an economic recession, a rise of nearly one million in the number of people in the labour market between 1970 and 1981 (estimated) and a disproportionate decline in jobs thought suitable for young people.[14]

The MSC also had an ideological role to play. Increases in youth unemployment were linked to lack of discipline and motivation. In 1977 the British Youth Council pre-empted Clive Jenkins' concern mentioned earlier:

> The MSC has ... declared its fear that the failure of young people to get a job may permanently alienate them from the world of work and from society. Not only does this bode ill for the future productivity of the country's potential labour force, but it is also likely to cause high levels of crime and social unrest.[15]

An expanding system of post-school job-specific skills training served a variety of functions:

> (It) publicly acknowledges the situation and demonstrates concern by spending public funds. It also helps to reduce the youth unemployment figures as students on YOP courses do not register as unemployed. It shifts emphasis from recognizing that a certain section of society will always be unemployed. It has the effect of withdrawing the sting from those who express dissatisfaction at a system which educates for work and produces unemployment, by pointing to efforts made to rectify the situation.[16]

A major spin-off of the 'employability' theme was the implementation of a personal deficiency model.

> The Holland Report emphasizes that unemployment amongst young people is not an individualistic problem in that 'success or failure in getting a job is often a matter of luck and frequently beyond the control of the individual ...'[17] Nevertheless a message behind much of the provision for unemployed school-leavers may be that young people's employability is a matter of training. In other words, is not the logic behind a scheme which seeks to improve employability by skills training one which clearly sees unemployment amongst young people in terms of their lack of individual attainment?[18]

The MSC was established in 1974 to 'rationalize and restructure all training and employment services provided by the Department of Employment'[19] with a staff of twelve. At first seen as a temporary response to a temporary situation it soon became overtaken by events. By 1978 it had expanded to a staff of 22,000 and an annual budget of £630 million, with the YOP as its major focus. In 1976 the MSC introduced its first Work Experience Programme at a cost of £19 million per annum. In 1979 the Thatcher government, which came to power partly on a platform dedicated to cut public expenditure, inherited a massively expanded programme with dwindling reserves of street credibility and increasing public and political interest. In 1981 £1 billion of government funds were allocated to the YTS.

Chris Thompson, a representative of the MSC's Training Division, highlighted the following aspects of the YTS as those which were 'significantly different from what had gone before':

YTS is a *training* programme. Whilst YOP did provide training in considerable numbers of schemes, the biggest single element was work experience on employer's premises (WEEP), with only about a quarter of the young people on WEEP schemes taking advantage of any off-the-job further education provision.

YTS is about *broad-based foundation* training, forming a bridge between school and work. The outcomes we are seeking are flexibility, adaptability, and a capacity to transfer skills to new and as yet unknown areas of employment brought about by rapid technological change.

YTS is intended to be a *permanent* programme, offering training to all who leave school at the earliest opportunity — the second of the three major objectives of the New Training Initiative.

YTS is to be a *comprehensive* scheme covering both employed and unemployed young people. In other words, it seeks to influence the way industry trains its own workforce, as well as the provision which is made for young people who do not have jobs.

YTS is about providing *integrated* programmes of planned work experience and off-the-job training/further education, in which the work base provides the main focus for learning and achievement is measured in terms of young people's *competence in work*.[20]

The MSC, with the support of the Advisory Group on Content and Standards, has recommended that the YTS should:

offer young people opportunities to learn in the broad areas of:

The World of Work — their role and responsibilities as a worker, the role of trades unions, changes in structure of employment etc.
The World Outside Employment —the contribution of individuals and companies to the community.
Job Specific and Broadly Related Skills — skills related to work placements and also skills related to a family of occupations.
Personal Effectiveness — trainees should be able to take responsibility for organising their own lives.
Skills Transfer — the aim is for young people to be able to move from

industry to industry, taking with them skills applicable to any job.
Occupationally Based Training — what the trainees will be able to *do*
at the end of their training.
Off-The-Job training — managing agents should say where training
will take place e.g. colleges of F.E., employer's premesis etc., and the
pattern of attendance and the training content.
Planned Work Experience — learning by doing in a set work context.
Core Areas — numeracy, communications, problem solving and
planning, practical skills and computer literacy.

Chris Thompson goes on to declare that 'the MSC is not being prescriptive about the detailed content of YTS schemes'. However in *The Times Educational Supplement* of 9 September 1983, under the headline 'Politics banned from YTS', it was reported that:

> Colleges throughout Britain may have to re-write part of their YTS
> syllabus if the Department of Employment succeeds in enforcing a
> ban on political education for trainees. A draft instruction has been
> drawn up for those providing off-the-job training which will forbid
> them to include matters relating to 'the organization and functioning
> of society' unless they are relevant to trainee's work experience.[21]

The announcement of the draft instruction brought protests from educationalists and union representatives as well as employers. The MSC's Advisory Group recommended that the guidelines should be rejected and this recommendation was endorsed by the Youth Training Board. In *The Times Educational Supplement* of 4 November it was reported that Mr Peter Morrison, the new Minister of State at the Department of Employment, had been 'persuaded to drop his attempt to ban social education from the YTS' and a new draft guideline was prepared which now prohibits:

> Action in support of a political party. Participation in marches or
> demonstrations. The printing or distribution of political or publically
> controversial material. Any action to intervene in an industrial
> dispute.[22]

The last point in the new guidelines concerning the rights of trainees in industrial disputes prompted the TUC to obtain assurances from the MSC that 'the ban on intervention in industrial disputes will not in any way prevent trainees taking industrial action at their own work place'. The MSC has contractually required trainees on both YOP and YTS schemes to be afforded employee status. This includes, in theory, the right to trades union representation, holiday and sickness cover and equal opportunities regarding gender and race according to current legislation. However, legally, trainees are *not* employees and therefore not covered under employment legislation. The MSC's contractual arrangement with employers is based on goodwill and the ability of the MSC to monitor trainees' circumstances. It may have been the MSC's history concerning YOP trainees' rights which inspired the TUC to obtain the latest assurances on involvement in industrial disputes. As Tony Warren says:

... the past record of the MSC is not such as to inspire confidence. The equal opportunities provision (within the YTS) will be particularly difficult to implement. The MSC seems reluctant to allow special schemes for the handicapped.

A recent Tribunal ruling allowing blatant racial discrimination against a YOP trainee is a salutory reminder of the dangers in the YTS.[23]

A further danger in the YTS follows directly on from one of the YOP's major weaknesses alluded to earlier — that of providing cheap labour and substituting trainees for employees. The YTS has included the notion of 'additionality' within its organization, under pressure from the TUC. Additionality hopes to ensure that employers do not appoint trainees, and thereby claim an MSC grant, in order to fill vacancies. An employer wishing to take on trainees must first demonstrate that he or she has taken on the same number of employees as were appointed in 1982. Employers are allowed to claim a grant for training sixteen year-old employees so long as that for every two employees covered by MSC grants three trainees are taken on. It remains to be seen how effective 'additionality' may become. Merilyn Moos, writing in the NATFHE journal,[24] discounts the notion of additional trainees by declaring it 'institutionalized job substitution'. She goes on to say that:

> The MSC was an institution established by a conservative-run government to centralize training for private industry, so as to increase its national efficacy. Yet the MSC has developed a false mantle of neutrality. In practice this new scheme undercuts youth and adult wages (and) apprenticeships and therefore an important part of trade-union's control over the numbers entering a skill-which the government and the MSC openly deplore as 'restrictive practices'.[25]

Both sixteen year-old employees and trainees under the YTS are paid £25 per week. This is not considered a competitive wage at sixteen years, indeed, it is considerably less than most negotiated pay rates for people of this age. Employers may 'top-up' the wage to £29.49 without National Insurance or tax liabilities. However, a direct comparison between money gained from the YTS and money from supplementary benefit claims reveals a minor incentive for taking part in the training as far as many school-leavers are concerned. A YTS trainee I spoke to in Newcastle explained his situation to me in these words:

> I would get ... I think it is £23.86 on the dole ... but then that extra quid (£1) we get here goes on transport and then you got to buy your dinners. Me mum used to make me sandwiches but she says you're working now and you can buy your dinners so even if that is just 50 pence a day that's still £2.50 a week — it's £3.50 a week transport, so there is £6 gone ... And then she says to me, 'Well, you're not on the dole — you are working so ... I want more board' Three more quid she wants than I would be paying if I were on the dole — there is nine quid gone!

Apart from the previously mentioned furore over the government gambit to make YTS attendance compulsory and the more recent attempts to directly control the more political aspects of curriculum content, specific critical reaction to the YTS centres on the aspiration to train *all* school-leavers, whether employed or not. The implication is that the YTS is not about 'improving employability' for the less able, as the Holland Report told us the YOP was. There has been a shift in underlying emphasis between the YOP and the YTS concerning an acknowledgement, finally overt but understood for years on the street, that training does not provide jobs nor necessarily provide trainees with the requisite preparation.

The government White Paper of December 1981 introduced the YTS as 'first and last a training scheme'.[26] The Task Group Report of April 1982 declared it to be about 'providing a permanent bridge between school and work — not about youth employment.[27] David Raffe has pointed out that:

> On the one hand the (YTS) could be seen as an opportunist exploita-
> tion of youth unemployment in order to pursue training objectives not
> directly related to the problem. Alternatively (it) could be seen as a
> continuation of the same policy, and the emphasis on training as an
> attempt to change the criteria for evaluation and thus to pre-empt
> criticisms should youth unemployment remain high ... possibly the
> greatest danger facing the YTS as a training scheme is that it will be
> continued to be regarded as a policy for youth unemployment.[28]

However the emphasis may be shifted towards training and away from employability, it is work which is important as far as unemployed school-leavers are concerned.

In the light of a general agreement that joining the YTS will not directly result in a job, is it surprising to find the low initial take-up of places? This raises questions of how YOP and YTS trainees view their training experience. The shift from YOP 'improving employability' to the YTS being about 'training not employment' highlights a change in policy focus, and even an attempt to challenge the personal deficit model seemingly inherent in the rationale behind post-school skills training. Inevitably the inexorable rise in youth unemployment over the past decade has also had its effect on young-ster's perceptions, as they leave school to join siblings or friends of up to five years seniority who have experienced a similar situation. Ironically it is the high level of youth unemployment which is precisely responsible for many young people being able to relate their lack of work to the general shortage of jobs and not to their personal failings. However, this is *not* to say that the status of work is losing its importance. Although high levels of youth unemployment may lessen the threat to an individual's self-image that a perception of personal deficit may have brought, those who have their expectations heightened by taking part in a training scheme still have to deal with continued unemployment. The individual may be able to rationalize his or her unemployment in terms of cause, but there still remains a problem of identity within a society which has encouraged its citizens to derive their status from work and proportions its rewards accordingly. As an unemployed ex-YOP trainee said:

... it's like ... Who am I, you know? It's like ... I'm the one in ten, except that now I'm the one in seven ... You leave school and you go on the dole, and then you go on a government scheme and then you're unemployed again ... But it's more than just 'you're not working', you know what I mean? It's *un*employed, it's like negative ... I heard this guy on the radio, talking about being on the dole, and he was saying that if he tries to sort of snap out of it, cheer up sort of thing, then people give him a hard time about not wanting to work. And he's right you know, 'cos if you're not working, and like it's through no fault of your own, then you can't say 'Who am I? I'm a fireman', and if you want to be a fireman you can't say 'I'm an UNfireman ... and if you try not to be too pissed off about it then you're a sponger or a scrounger or whatever. It's like the only thing you can be if you're not working is something negative, or even something people think is bad ... [29]

The YTS is, in the words of Mr. Geoffrey Holland, the MSC's former Director of Special Programmes, 'an unprecedented response (to) an unprecedented situation'[30]. It may be too soon to determine how effective the YTS eventually will be. It may be unfair, even, to analyze its potential from its rhetoric, and for the time being the rhetoric, of both advocate and antagonist is almost all we have to go on. There is no shortage of prognoses, however, particularly from representatives of the further education sector, who possibly feel under more threat than most of those affected by the continuing expansion of the MSC and the YTS. A lecturer gave this interpretation of the situation:

This year has seen my first involvement in YTS Life and Social Skills. I was really given little choice as to whether or not to do it — roles fall in traditional areas, and MSC courses are one of the few areas of expansion. But YTS was taken on board without much discussion amongst the staff and, it seems, without much knowledge of what would be involved for the staff. For example we now have to work in the summer holidays, because the MSC has pressured the college to have all-year-round courses ... but this goes against traditional contractual agreements, lots of people see it as the thin end of the wedge, the end of FE as was, particularly in the non-vocational areas ... At the other end the MSC is under-cutting what we can provide in this area by organizing its own off-the-job training in its own centres. It's getting un-trained trainers for unemployed kids at far below the rate for lecturers. It's almost as if courses for the young unemployed are becoming privatized — in fact I heard that next year the MSC themselves are to be privatized ... I mean, does this mean that unemployment education is to become a profit-making venture ... ?

As we have seen, past policy statements have provoked unfavourable reactions, but specific criticisms have, in certain instances, brought about changes. The system *is* able to adapt — albeit, so far, in microcosm, under pressure and reluctantly, and, no doubt, as far as many are concerned, too slowly, too late and too little. The acid test for the YTS, however, is to be found in the experience of the trainee. The most telling evaluation of policy will be theirs.

Notes

1 *The Times Educational Supplement*, 2 September 1983.
2 CROFT, S. and BERESFORD, P. (1983) 'Power politics and the youth training scheme', *Youth and Policy*, Vol. 2, No. 1, Blayden, pp. 1–4
3 *The Guardian*, 5 March 1982.
4 Moos, M. (1982) 'MSC: a wolf in sheep's clothing', *NATFHE Journal*, no. 6, London, p. 26.
5 Department of Employment (1981) *A New Training Initiative: A Programme for Action*, London, HMSO (My emphasis).
6 *Ibid* (my emphasis).
7 (1983) *Youth in Society*, 78, p. 11.
8 *The Times Educational Supplement*, 13 May 1983, p. 23.
9 *Ibid*.
10 WARREN, T. (1983) 'The youth training scheme — hopes and fears', *NATFHE Journal*, no. 3, London, p. 18.
11 FIDDY, R. (1984) 'YOP, that's youth off pavements innit' in SCHOSTAK J. and LOGAN, T. (Eds) *Pupil Experience: Views from the Receiving End*, London, Croom Helm.
12 Manpower Services Commission (1977) *Young People and Work*, London, HMSO, p. 7.
13 Centre for Contemporary Cultural Studies (1981) *Unpopular Education*, London, Hutchinson, p. 230.
14 *Ibid*, p. 231.
15 Manpower Services Commission (1977) *op. cit*, p. 12.
16 FIDDY, R. (1982) 'A curriculum for employability', *Journal of Further and Higher Education*, London, vol. 16, no. 1, p. 21.
17 Manpower Services Commission (1977) *op. cit*, p. 7.
18 FIDDY, R. (Ed.) (1983) *In Place of Work*, Lewes, Falmer Press, p. 68.
19 Centre for Contemporary Cultural Studies (1981), *op. cit*, p. 231.
20 THOMPSON, C. (1983) 'Building the bridge', *Youth in Society*, 78, Leicester, p. 11.
21 *The Times Educational Supplement*, 9 September 1983.
22 *The Times Educational Supplement*, 4 November 1983.
23 WARREN, T. (1983) *op. cit*, p. 18.
24 National Association of Teachers in Further and Higher Education.
25 Moos, M. (1982) *op. cit*, p. 27.
26 Department of Employment (1981) *op. cit*.
27 Manpower Services Commission (1982) *Youth Task Group Report*, London, HMSO.
28 RAFFE, D. (1983) 'Can there be an effective youth employment policy?' in FIDDY, R. (Ed.) *op. cit*, p. 23.
29 FIDDY, R. (1984) *op. cit*.
30 *The Times Educational Supplement*, 17 July 1981, p. 7.

FRANCE

The development of the Youth Opportunities Programme (YOP) in Britain made no bones about the relationship it sought to promote between education/ training and the world of work. Similarly in France, and contemporaneous with the YOP, measures were taken to improve the 'employability' of unemployed school-leavers. In this section Chris Pilley shows how dissillusionment with these early measures has led to 'an altogether broader philosophy and a rather different approach'. In the first chapter, however, Jean-Jaques Paul gives a breakdown of the youth unemployment situation in France over the past few years and analyzes the early responses. He makes the point that, whereas those youngsters leaving school with qualifications have a better chance of finding employment than those without, there is no evidence to suggest that the past few years of increased skills training for the young unemployed have improved their market situation. Indeed, the 'Pactes pour l'Emploi', which served as the basis for training school-leavers until the Mitterand government introduced new measures, attracted accusations familiar to critics of the YOP in Great Britain — that it provided cheap labour for employers and manipulated unemployment statistics.

In the second chapter of this section on France, Christopher Pilley briefly re-reviews the early measures before examining the changes made, which were based on the Schwartz Commission's findings and which promoted the notion that the problem of youth unemployment should not be seen solely in terms of employment policy.

The two chapters which make up this section on France provide the opportunity for an additional comparison in that, whereas Paul writes as an involved party, Pilley comments from the perspective of an interested and concerned outside observer.

Young People and Systems of Training and Unemployment: The French Experience

Jean Jaques Paul

In March 1982 a French government ruling brought into being a campaign to help the social and professional integration of young people who were leaving the educational system without qualifications. The ruling declared in its first clause that: 'Vocational training and social integration of young men and women aged sixteen to eighteen constitutes a national obligation'. The initiative was to concern the State, local communities, professional bodies, trades unions, family businesses and companies. Thus a far-reaching publicity campaign was launched with 'A trade to success' as its theme. The campaign aimed to make all more aware — including young people and their families.

This new initiative is not unique, however. The various other special measures which have preceded it need to be examined before one tackles its contents and reflects on its first year of operation.

The consideration of French strategy to encourage the employment of young people must be seen juxtaposed with the situation of these people within the job market. This will be our preliminary concern, to which the first part of this work is dedicated, the second part deals with the measures effected and a critical analysis of them.

The Development of the Situation Concerning Young People on the French Job Market

Firstly we are going to examine the growth of unemployment amongst young people in France before moving on to an analysis of the types and causes of this unemployment.

In fact only a diagnosis of this kind can encourage a critical look at the measures taken in France to combat youth unemployment.

Unemployment in France

In 1982 France was registering, within the context of the International Employment Office, 1,800,000 unemployed, which represented an unemployment rate of 7.7 per cent.

Figure 1: The unemployment rate according to sex and age

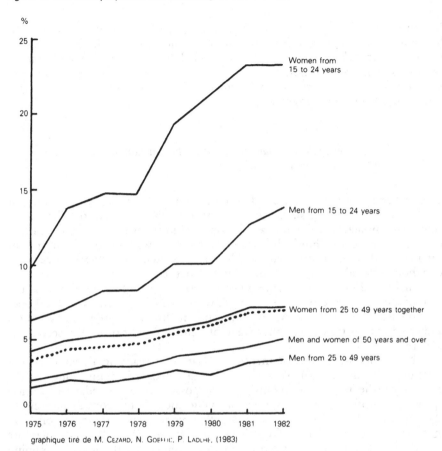

graphique tiré de M. CEZARD, N. GOEFFIC, P. LADLHE, (1983)

Source: enquête sur l'emploi.

But all workers are not subject equally to the risk of unemployment. An examination of the unemployment rate since 1975 reveals the increasing vulnerability of young people, i.e. individuals aged between 15 and 24 years. Young women appear to be particularly singled out.

However, these observations should not lead people to believe that youth unemployment in France is a problem dating from the current economic crisis. For example, it is estimated that between 1962 and 1968 the total numbers of those seeking work doubled whilst the numbers of young people under 25 in the same predicament tripled.

At the present moment 39 per cent of the unemployed are young people under 25. Two questions present themselves: are all young people affected by unemployment in the same way?; can the worsening of unemployment amongst young people be seen as a form of discrimination against them?

The following discussion will be concerned with the answers to these two questions.

Jean-Jacques Paul

Young People Facing Unemployment

It must first be remembered that young people do not represent a homogeneous population. Furthermore the concept of youth could itself be the object of debate,[1] but not to be tackled here, where we will restrict ourselves to an examination of the provision of training, at various levels, for young people in France. we will then analyze the effect of gender and qualification on unemployment.

The Change in the Standard of Educational Qualifications Held by Young People Entering the Job Market

Young people leaving the school system do not all converge upon the job market at the same time since military service and inactivity absorb fifteen per cent. In conjunction with this, almost one girl in twenty and one boy in five enter into apprenticeships when they leave school without qualifications. In total 762,000 young people left the educational system in 1979-80, 74 per cent of whom offered themselves onto the job market.

In 1980, 26 per cent of young people (30 per cent of the boys and 23 per cent of the girls) were available for work with no qualifications at all and 11 per cent possessed only the BEPC, a qualification no longer awarded today, which indicated completion of the first stage of general education in the secondary sphere.

Nevertheless, it must be mentioned that, after reaching a peak of 36 per cent in 1973, the number of unqualified young people is diminishing. At the same time the number of young people possessing a secondary education qualification of a technical nature is growing, moving up from 21 per cent to 29 per cent. Also it should be noted that young girls are more often in possession of some form of qualification than are boys. We can therefore accept the idea that there has been an improvement in the level of training amongst young people, a phenomenon which indicates that one cannot attribute the increase of unemployment within this group to its poor level of training.

Let us now consider the changing pattern of unemployment amongst young people in terms of their qualifications.

The Changing Pattern of Unemployment amongst New Entrants to the Job Market by Level of Qualification

Note that the rates shown in the following diagram are linked to the young people's situation about nine months after leaving school.

The level of qualification is a good gauge of the unemployment rate amongst young entrants to the job market. In fact the unemployment rate will decrease as one moves up the qualification scale.

So, four boys in ten and six girls in ten will be unemployed if they are

Figure 2: The influx of young workers on the job market[1] according to qualification

Sex and Year	No qualification	BEPC	CAP-BEP	Baccalauréat général	Baccalauréat de technicien	Diplôme des formations supérieures courtes	Diplôme des formations supérieures longues	Ensemble
Students or pupils 1972–1973								
Men	40	12	25	6	3	7	7	100
Women	33	13	19	12	3	15	5	100
Together	36 (43)	13 (12)	21 (19)	10 (8)	3 (3)	11 (10)	6 (5)	100
Students or pupils 1979–1980								
Men	30	10	31	7	4	10	8	100
Women	23	11	28	13	5	14	6	100
Together	26 (34)	11 (10)	29 (26)	11 (9)	4 (4)	12 (11)	7 (6)	100

Surveys on employment, March 1974 and March 1981. Table from F. AMAT (1983)

(1) The influx on the job market: these are the pupils or students in March of year N who declare themselves to be gainfully employed (not including apprentices) — or in search of work during the survey on work in March N + 1. Therefore new workers are those people who in March 1974 declared themselves to be in work or unemployed when they were pupils or students in March 1973, in the same way as those who in March 1981 declared themselves employed when they were pupils or students in March 1980. The results in parentheses include those young people who found apprenticeships on entering the job market.

(2) Sans diplome: unqualified people having completed at least 10 years of study. The age for the end of compulsory schooling is 16.
 — BEPC: brevet d'études du premier cycle
  Qualification awarded at the end of the 1st stage of general secondary education. (10 years of study)
 — CAP: Certificat d'aptitude professionelle
 — BEP: Brevet d'études professionnelles.
  These qualifications are awarded at the end of a short secondary course of vocational training. (10 to 12 years of study)
 — Baccalauréat général: Qualification awarded at the end of general academic secondary education (12 years of study)
 — Baccalauréat de technicien: Qualification awarded at the end of an academic course in secondary education with a vocational bias.
 — Diplôme des formations supérieures courtes: awarded generally two years after the baccalaureat for a short, higher level course.
 — Diplôme des formations supérieures longues: awarded for studies at a higher level for beyond two years of study after the baccalauréat.

N.B. Times of study indicated are minimum requirements.

43

without qualifications, whilst only one boy in ten and two girls in ten will be unemployed after completing studies of a higher nature (over two years of study after the baccalauréat). It is, in addition, worth noting that girls, although equally well qualified, will face unemployment more often than boys. The difference has changed little between 1974 and 1981. Furthermore, the situation has worsened most drastically for unqualified young people or for those with the lowest level of qualification. The unemployment rate of the unqualified multiplied by 3.5 between 1974 and 1981. The unemployment rate for those possessing the secondary vocational qualification (CAP-BEP) has also multiplied during the same period, by 3.5 for the boys and 4.2 for the girls.

An interesting and paradoxical fact, here, concerns the development of the situation facing young people completing vocational training. The unemployment rate is increasing most strongly both for those completing a secondary vocational qualification (CAP-BEP) and for those completing a short course of vocational studies of a higher level (formations supérieures courtes). In the light of these figures one cannot state *a priori* that a development in vocational training can help combat unemployment amongst young people.

The position that has just been described represents the month of March following the end of the academic year. The unemployment experienced by young people could then be an initial spell of unemployment, where no job has yet been gained, or a second spell of unemployment where a job has been held and lost.

To reiterate, it seems that the type of unemployment experienced will vary according to training and sex. In fact, the least qualified boys will become unemployed as much through difficulty in finding work initially as through becoming unemployed for a second time after losing work. Well qualified boys will become unemployed more through problems in finding work. As for the girls, unemployment will be experienced more than in the boys' case, through difficulty in finding a first job.

It does not seem that the growth in unemployment, either for young people or adults, can be attributed to a lack of training or to a lack of vocational bias. Perhaps therefore, rather than seeking a cause of unemployment amongst young people in poor training or negative attitudes to work, it would be better to look at how more fundamentally the structure and development of the production system have created the situations already described.

The Pattern of Occupations Entered

To ascertain to what extent the development of the production system could have influenced the situation of young people on the job market, we are first going to consider the types of occupations entered by this group.

But to begin with let us state that the increase in unemployment amongst young people does not appear to be due to a disinclination on the behalf of employers to employ them, insofar as the number of new young workers recruited annually within the total workforce remains virtually constant.[2]

Figure 3 Unemployment rate of young entrants on the job market in 1974 and 1981 by sex and level of qualification.

Sex and Year		No qualification	BEPC	CAP-BEP	Baccalauréat	Diplôme des formations supérieures courtes	Diplôme des formations supérieures longues	Together
					Qualification			
Men	1974	12	5	6	9	3	10	9
	1981	42	29	21	19	12	11	26
Rate	(1981)	3,5	5,8	3,5	2,1	4	1,1	2,9
Rate	(1974)							
Women	1974	18	16	10	10	4	12	13
	1981	63	43	42	28	13	21	39
	(1981)	3,5	2,7	4,2	2,8	3,2	1,8	3
Rate	(1974)							

Source: Surveys on employment March 1974 and March 1981

Amongst women holding an initial secondary qualification of a technical nature, 10 per cent will take up positions as unskilled workers, 24 per cent an unqualified post and 46 per cent a qualified staff post. For women holding a qualification of a higher standard (formations supérieures courtes), 12 per cent will follow a profession as a qualified staff member, and 78 per cent in lower salaried posts. The highest qualification holders will include 21 per cent in managerial positions and 11 per cent in positions of professional status.

If one compares this analysis to the situation of young job seekers in 1973, it appears that the relation between standard of qualification/standard of job has worsened after a basic secondary education. After gaining a higher qualification the opposite is true. For example, in 1973 six young men out of ten with no qualifications held jobs as unskilled workmen and practically half the boys holding a basic vocational qualification held posts of skilled workmen (38 per cent today). By comparison two-fifths of those possessing higher qualifications took up managerial posts; today they represent three-fifths.

With the girls, whereas the division between types of job remains stable after a higher level of education, various changes have affected the types of jobs entered after a basic secondary education. It is worth noting, in particular, the worsening situation for those gaining the général Baccalauréat who will be less likely to take up lower salaried posts (38 per cent in 1973 compared to 16 per cent in 1980) and more often take up posts as qualified staff (36 per cent in 1973 compared to 48 per cent in 1980).

Young workers made up 12 per cent of the 4,300,000 people recruited by employers in 1973 and 11 per cent of the 3,400,000 recruited in 1980. The problem can thus be seen to be linked straight away to the total numbers recruited. As a result, young people see their porportion of the working population decrease. In fact, from 1971 to 1981 the number of young people in the work force under twenty-five years of age has dropped from 39 per cent to 26 per cent, a reduction of a third.

If we now consider the occupations entered by young workers in 1980 in relation to their standard of qualification, we can say that generally the standard of occupation corresponds with the standard of qualification possessed.

For men, 56 per cent of the unqualified will take up positions as unskilled workmen, whilst 38 per cent of those having completed a basic vocational course in secondary education will take up positions as skilled workmen. A further 33 per cent from this group will enter positions as unskilled workmen. At the other extreme, 59 per cent of those completing initial higher studies (supérieur court) will enter middle management or technician posts and 77 per cent of those completing further higher studies (supérieur long) will enter management or professional posts.

The important link between standard of qualification and standard of job can also be seen with women's employment but they more often take up posts in the tertiary field than do men. Thus, 24 per cent of unqualified women will take up posts as unskilled workers, 35 per cent will take up posts as unqualified staff, and 25 per cent as qualified staff.

The period has seen a strengthening of competition in the search for work, with only holders of higher qualifications being spared. On the other hand, the unqualified are seeing their possibilities of finding work diminish

Figure 1: Type of work entered in 1980 according to qualification and sex (by percentage)

	No qualification	BEPC	CAP-BEP	Bac général	Bac technique	Diplôme des formations supérieures courtes	Diplôme des formations supérieures longues
Agriculturists	13	10	11	11	15		
Engineers							21 11
Technicians					27	13	
Skilled workers	18	10	38	16			
Unskilled workers	56 24	35 14	33 10	13	15		
Management posts				15		11	56 54
Middle Management				17 16	12	46 78	14 21
Qualified staff	25	18 46	53	10 48	18 63	12	
Unqualified staff	35	24	23	12 20	19		

Source: Evaluation of training-work.

N.B. In order to facilitate the reading of data only percentages above 10 per cent have been given. The figures representing boys are given on the left, those representing the girls are given on the right of each column.

and their unemployment rate grow considerably. Holders of secondary education qualifications, however, are slowing down the increase of their unemployment rate by accepting jobs of lower status.

These observations show how the question of numbers is important in describing youth unemployment.

By way of illustration we can consider the link between the body of young workers holding various levels of qualification and the number of jobs of a similar standard held by them. In 1973, 127,000 young men entered the job market who were either unqualified or in possession only of the BEPC. At this time 108,000 jobs of unqualified status were taken up by new workers. In 1980 the same group represented no more than 60,000 new workers but the number of similar jobs taken up by them had fallen to 54,000. But at the same time the ratio between the number of leavers with a basic vocational secondary education and the number of jobs requiring qualifications changed from 0.9 to 1.4. This group increased to compete with the unqualified for jobs not requiring qualifications; more often than not the unqualified were pushed into unemployment.

A parallel situation developed with the girls. As the ratio of the number of unqualified new workers to the number of similar available jobs grew from 1973 to 1980 from 1.2 to 1.4, the ratio of the number of those holding a basic vocational secondary education to the number of jobs of similar status grew from 0.8 to 1.6. At the same time the number of technician, engineer and management posts filled by new workers remained in excess of those holding higher qualifications. This situation resulted more particularly from an increase in the number of such jobs at a time of general decrease in the availability of work. For example, posts for engineers increased by 20 per cent between 1976 and 1981 and those for management by 24 per cent.[3]

Particular Occupations and Unemployment

In fact the high number of unskilled jobs within certain groups seems to contribute largely to the unemployment within these groups.

This is particularly the case for unqualified boys and girls who form an important section of semi-skilled workers, with boys completing a basic

Figure 5: Unemployment rates according to profession in March 1982

	The whole population	Under 25s
Agriculturists	3	1
Heads of Business	2	6
Managerial Staff	2	8
Professions	4	8
Staff	8	13
Skilled Workers	6	11
Unskilled Workers	12	15

Source: Employment survey

technical education in unskilled or skilled posts and girls of similar background for staff posts.

The most favoured situation, in the face of unemployment, is for those holding higher education qualifications, particularly after 'formations longues', where there has been a larger number of available jobs in the managerial field.

Without wishing to lead on to an in-depth analysis concerning the scarcity of different types of job in times of unemployment, it is worth noting the important of the influence of the State in inducing different situations at such times. In fact more than four out of ten management posts are funded by the State, local councils, and public services — compared to one workman out of ten.

The structure of employment amongst certain groups of young people may, to some extent, explain the level of unemployment amongst them — a fact underlined by the use of such groups for specific tasks within the economic system. The analysis is strengthened by the fact that young people, when they compete with similarly qualified adults, are more often the ones to remain unemployed.

Two theories may be considered in this light. On the one hand, young people are often taken on for temporary jobs — young people between the ages of 15 and 24 years providing 40 per cent of temporary workers — or for limited contract work — where young people provide 50 per cent of the staff in this area. On the other hand, the other sectors within the economy capable of employing young people are cutting back more and more, for example in areas of uncertain stability as in building, public works, car repair, hotel work, and services to individuals. Sectors possessing a more stable work force, for example energy or public administration are taking on fewer and fewer young school leavers.[4]

The economic crisis has thus been interlinked with a worsening situation for young people on the job market, largely attributable to an overall drop in recruitment. All young people, however, have not been affected in the same way. Thus, boys leaving secondary education have suffered particularly badly within the secondary sector. In this area, unqualified youngsters have witnessed both a drop in unskilled vacancies and a rise in competition from colleagues with technical training. Girls will have witnessed competition from all sides whilst waiting in line for positions in the tertiary sector which usually asks for less specific qualifications.

Confronted with such a growing assortment of problems in placing young people in the job market, the authorities have brought in, over the last ten years or so, a number of special measures that we are now going to analyze.

Measures Taken in France to Help Young People into Employment

Three periods are distinguishable in France concerning measures implemented to help young people into employment. The first period is prior to 1977. It consisted of experiments and initial attempts at programmes of greater magnitude which were to develop after 1977. 1977, in fact, introduced the beginning of the second period — a more ambitious time with respect to the body of people it dealt with — when the National Pacts for employment were introduced. Finally, the third period dates from 1981, when the Left came to power; a period marked by ambitious efforts, both in content and objectives, aimed at changing the system of education.

The Period Prior to 1977

As early as the 1950s various incentives had been taken by associations within the education field to help unqualified youngsters. From 1968 onwards L'Association pour la Formation Professionelle des Adultes (Centres for Skill Training for Adults) attached to the Department of Employment instigated pre-training courses for young job-seekers to help the least qualified prepare for vocational training within the adult sections.

The acts of July 1971 institutionalized on-going training in France and allowed these training courses to develop by providing them with a legal foundation and creating a statute for 'young people in vocational training'. From 1971 to 1975 various experiments[5] organized by the Education Department were initiated which involved 2500 trainees.[6] But in 1975 came the first widespread campaign on a national scale. Named 'Operation 50,000 youngsters', it was aimed at helping unqualified unemployed young people by offering training courses. But the haste and lack of preparation in the setting up of this scheme raised problems in the recruitment and training of the trainers, in the selection of trainees and in the guidelines for the content of training courses. This scheme, interrupted in June 1976 and restarted in early 1977, affected about 32,000 young people.

The Period 1977–81

With the economic situation worsening and unemployment rising everywhere, particularly amongst young people, the government mounted the first National Pact for employment. A scheme of unprecedented size, this first Pact affected 580,000 young people. Two further Pacts, mounted in succession, made provision for young people until 1981. The special measures underwent certain changes between the first Pact (July 1977 to June 1978) and the following ones. To begin with we will set out the final planning of the Pacts and examine their results. Then we will look at the various experiments which continued to be organized throughout this period.

The Organization of the National Pacts for Employment

Measures adopted can be classified into: (1) those offering only employment; (2) those offering both employment and training; and (3) those essentially concerned with training.

Measures concerned solely with employment In order to stimulate recruitment of people under 26 years, employers were exempted from half of their National Health contributions for a period of twelve months[7], provided that recruitment corresponded with a growing workforce.

The development of the apprenticeship system In order to stimulate the growth of apprenticeships, companies recruiting young people as apprentices were exempted from the employer's National Health contribution.

Contracts of employment/training Instigated before 1977, these were slightly modified by the Pacts. Young people were taken on as paid employees with a contract of employment which incorporated a certain time devoted to classroom training. The length of training (120 to 1200 hours) was to vary in accordance with the length of contract (six months or a year). The State contributed to training costs and exempted the employer from National Health contributions.

Practical training within companies This training within companies is aimed at 16 to 26 year olds for a period of four months (six months from summer 1980) and offers classroom training of 120 hours. The State is responsible for some of the costs.

Measures concerned essentially with training These constitute 'vocational training courses' handled by public or private training bodies, whose aim is to offer young people aged between 17 and 26, professional training for future employment — though having no direct link with such fields of employment. The young person's allowance is equivalent of 75 per cent of minimum wages.

The Results of the National Pacts for Employment

It is interesting to note that, of the growing number of Pacts, those involving recruitment incentives decreased between 1977 and 1980 — dropping from 37 per cent to 23 per cent. This can chiefly be explained by the change in

Figure 6:   Growth of Measures according to Method of the National Pacts for Employment

Recruitment incentives. Exemption of employers' NHS contributions		Help in placing	
		Work Experience	Training Course
		Practical training Employment/training contracts Apprenticeships	
Pact I 552551	36.8	50.8	12.4
Pact II 275037	20.7	59.3	20.0
Pact III 328600	23.3	63.7	13.0

Source: Department of Employment

exemptions concerning employers' contributions; in 1977 total exemption was offered but from 1981 onwards only half such exemption was offered. Within the second package it was the apprenticeships and contracts offering employment/training which were the methods seen to receive increasing numbers.

In all, the Pacts were seen to affect fewer people and lose some impact, in terms of the numbers of the working population reached. Numbers of 16–25 year olds fell from 15 per cent in 1977 to 9 per cent in 1979, and the numbers of school-leavers fell from 50 per cent to 30 per cent. These figures improved, however, within the second stage of the third Pact when 476,000 trainees were affected.

On looking at the changing characteristics of people and companies involved in these Pacts, it appears that the presence of boys grew in strength in that those recruited as trainees were better qualified, and that the role of smaller companies grew in importance.[8] The Pacts seem then to have reinforced certain selection procedures to the detriment of the least qualified young people and of women.

The special measures of the Pacts seem then to have had minimum impact on the job market for young people offering to some of them only a possibility of preparation in their initial placement. In fact, at the close of each period covered by a Pact it was not established what difference had been made to young unemployment figures. A certain number remained with companies after training courses — but they would probably have been recruited even without this training. For other young people, the training course will have provided no more than a short-lived occupation without links with permanent employment. Apart from this it must be mentioned that, contrary to fears held, there was no substitution of young people for older workers.[9]

The Pacts, then, created no more than a temporary shift in the existing pattern of youth unemployment and, in not creating any new jobs, could not check the growth in unemployment. Various experimental schemes continued to be mounted concurrent with the Pacts. These concentrated on the most vulnerable young people from a training point of view.

The Various Experimental Schemes

Throughout the Pacts, unqualified youngsters with a difficult social background were a little forgotten. Even though young people in this situation constituted 30 per cent of job seekers in the under 25 age group, 18 per cent of them, having benefited from schemes in the first Pact (1977–78), followed pre-training courses — with this rate falling to 10.5 per cent in the third Pact. The experimental schemes managed by the Department of Education were basically aimed at this group. Three groups of schemes were set up. In the first instance, between 1978 and Jaunary 1980, a pilot EEC project was inaugurated after efforts by the nine Education ministers.

Equally financed by Department of Education and EEC funds, the object was to offer young people, over a six month period, training and guidance leading to a realistic career choice. This scheme involved 500 to 600 young people. Secondly, a project was set up by an educational group, named 'Project GAEC (Groupe Actions Educatives Concertees)' with French participants, involving co-operation with Quebec, in a socio-cultural project. This venture, based in Paris, aimed at producing a comprehensive answer, in educational terms, to the problem of placing the least able people between the ages of 16 and 25. Finally, the Departments of Health, Employment and Education mounted a combined venture for 16 to 21 year olds most in need of help. Forty schemes were set up in 1979–80 and fifty-six in 1980–81.

All the schemes mounted up to 1981 aimed at improving the integration of young people and thus represent a framework for integration. When the Left came to power a new angle was sought. A new framework is, then, to emerge aiming to change the education system.

1982, the Campaign for Social and Professional Integration

Once in power, the Left began by taking up responsibility for the National Pacts for Employment, renamed them 'Programmes Future Youth' and modified certain points so as to strengthen the level of training gained. At the same time a greater effort was to be made to incorporate these measures within national economic policy.

It was at this time that the government requested a report from B. Schwartz which was to specifically deal with young people aged 16 to 21 years. The report centres around three main issues:

- the guarantee of a social and professional qualification for all young people of 16 to 18 years;
- the strengthening of youngsters' opportunities in the 18–21 age range and of greater participation in the economic and social spheres;
- the inclusion of young people in city life and the creation of a new environment.[10]

The basic principles advocated for putting the schemes into motion are: to modify the content of existing courses; to develop new techniques and promote key skills; to return to a changing teaching style; and the ratification of experience and negotiation. It was this report which was to prompt the publication of the March 1982 ruling concerning social and professional integration quoted in the introduction to this chapter and which provides the foundation of the programme in operation today. This programme has a dual aim: firstly to set up a system of support, information and guidance; secondly to instigate a framework of alternate training schemes and more thorough guidance. These two aspects will be considered now.

Support, Information and Guidance

Local communities and parishes and, in particular, public and private information and guidance agencies, were encouraged to recommend setting up, from existing provision, offices always open to the public to act as reception centres and offer information and guidance.[11] These places for meeting and exchanging information are at the disposal of all young people aged 16 to 18 years who are in need of help in their career choice or method of training. In areas where placement of young people is particularly difficult (for example areas of high youth unemployment rate), local helpers are taken on. In these areas these helpers take the place of information and guidance centres in order to concentrate on the total problem of social integration and to help young people with their plans. Whereas the information and guidance centres receive public funds automatically, the local help centres have to rely on a 50 per cent minimum input from the local communities who are responsible for their creation. This last point is important insofar as it reflects the aim of the programme to involve local communities — an innovation within the programme compared to earlier initiatives.

In the same spirit, local councils were encouraged to set up 'sixteen to eighteen' committees, destined to play a major role in helping young people and in the setting up of reception, information and guidance centres.

The Training Schemes

In considering training schemes available to young people of 16–26 years of age, we are going to set out all methods used in France today, separating those of an 'employment contract' nature from the others.

Training without an Employment Contract

Let us first consider, briefly, training schemes set up with a view to vocational training within the education system, before moving on to those aimed at young people leaving training schemes.

Within the Initial Education System

This consists of courses of a technological bias, undertaken within companies for a period of six months. Classroom sessions lasting ten weeks are also organized for pupils from 'Lycées d'Enseignement professionnel' studying for secondary education qualifications of a technical nature.

Young People Leaving the Education System

First of all let us look at the alternate training offered to young unqualified people of 16 to 18 years who are seeking work, but who possess no vocational qualification. These courses in fact represent the basis of provision offered to these youngsters.

Young people can, according to choice, commence training in one of the following ways:

— a course of training, lasting on average eight months, leading directly to a vocational qualification;

— a course involving social skills for youngsters with particular difficulties, preparing them to move on to vocational training. A maximum of ten months is allowed for this sort of course;

— a group scheme of up to six weeks duration allowing youngsters a choice of special projects.

Such schemes attract an allowance paid by the State equal to 500 francs a month for the first six months and 700 francs a month from the seventh month onwards.

Further detail is not possible on the organization of these training schemes at this time. It is worth noting, however, that the amount of the allowance offered — though more than grants offered within the secondary education sector — does not allow trainees to be financially independent. Such schemes therefore do not appear to be too strong an enticement for students within secondary education. Financial independence has therefore taken second place to the maintenance of stable training measures already in existence. It is also worth mentioning that the training programmes within the National Pacts were the equal responsibility of the host company involved and a public or private training agency. Here, this responsibility is clearly designated to the body setting up the scheme.

Finally it must be noted that similar schemes have been made available to those in the 18–21 year age group who are both unqualified and prove difficult to place. For these trainees an allowance is offered which relates to a proportion of minimum wages and is of a higher rate than that paid to younger trainees.

A fourth type of scheme called 'Youth Volunteers' is available for those unemployed aged between 18 and 26 years who are interested in carrying out a task of social value. This type of scheme consists of 'useful' projects initiated by local authorities, associations and non-commercial institutions, and aims to offer an initial work or training experience. Trainees receive an allowance from the State equal to half the minimum wage. Finally, courses set up of a certain standard or length of time leading to a qualification may be offered to young job seekers.

All schemes described so far are in operation *without* involving contracts of employment.

Training Schemes with Contracts of Employment

These schemes are of long standing, having been in existence since before the instigation of special measures for Youth Employment in 1977. The schemes centre on apprenticeships and offer opportunities to 16–20 year olds that they may follow a practical training with an employer, and a more theoretical training in an Apprentice training centre. A contract usually lasts for two years and should allow a candidate to take the CAP qualification. The employment/ training contracts, mentioned earlier, also come within this category of schemes. It is also possible for young workers under 20 years of age, to take time from their work to follow 'a training scheme for young workers' in order to pursue a training of their choice. So, like all workers, young people can benefit from legislation passed in 1971 concerning on-going training.

At the time of the introduction of the special measures the government had envisaged a number of objectives in quantitative terms, the success of which is still impossible to clarify today. In theory, 100,000 unqualified young people aged 16–18 ought to profit from these measures along with 35,000 young people in the 18–21 age group. In addition, 100,000 employment-training contracts should be issued as well as 125,000 new apprenticeships. At the same time, extra places should be made available within the Adult Centres for skills training, and technical education within the secondary schools should receive a boost.

The government has set up an evaluation programme alongside the framework of the new measures. This underlines the interest shown in the 16–18 age group. A brief inspection of this evaluation system will complete the picture of new measures introduced in France.

The Observation and Evaluation of the 16–18 Programme

This programme, involving fourteen regional teams staffed mostly with academics and co-ordinated by a central team, aims to inform those involved in the programme. A role of inspection or control is not envisaged within this programme. A final report on this evaluation programme was published in the autumn of 1983.

However, some items of information can already be presented. They refer, in particular, to the reception phase for the young people and the type of offers made to them for training courses. As far as the first point is concerned, it seems that the areas covered by the reception centres has worked well, except perhaps in rural districts. Also, the inter-institutional working of the reception centres, as foreseen by the programme, has proven itself totally satisfactory. The ways in which the centres were organized has revealed a certain number of important problems — among them in particular the one caused by the educational standards of the young people concerned. In fact, the extremely weak standard of knowledge and low competency of the young who leave the education system without qualifications puts them in the position of being unable to have access to training places without preliminary preparation. It follows that there should be a revision within the system in order to avoid the decline in standards which has already affected a good number of young people.

As to the offers of training places — it appears that there is a lack of flexibility in addressing the expectations and local economic needs of the young people, due to the fact that the training organizations have been preoccupied with providing places which fit their needs — that is to say in relation to their experience, their perceptions of pedagogy and their potential resources in both materials and instruction. Nonetheless, the instigation of a rational programme to combat the huge problems posed by unqualified school leavers has, without doubt, introduced a vitality that former programmes, of an incomplete and localized nature, had been unsuccessful in doing.

Finally, attention should be drawn to new government directions that aim to make training offers less rigid by setting up appeal procedures within reception centres, by promoting preliminary courses, by introducing bridging schemes between preliminary courses and those offering a qualification and by allowing easier movement between courses.

Conclusion

The problem of youth unemployment is a crucial question which highlights the importance accorded to youth within contemporary societies. For some years now this problem has been at the centre of thinking as much on a national as an international level. It is indeed an economic problem but one which also reflects a considerable transformation throughout society in the role and place of the family. However, we must be content, in this document, to have presented a study on youth unemployment as a consequence of the economic system itself, and how French governments have attempted to cope with this question. In conclusion, let us once more make clear the position of young people within the production system and outline some future prospects as a result of existing special measures.

It seems that the situation of young people on the job market can be better interpreted by their characteristics as job seekers than by their age; their situation cannot, a priori, be singled out from that of other job seekers and unemployed people ... We must move away from the assumption that the job market is structured on a principle of competition and complementarity among groups of job seekers, groups which are formed from the homogeneity of personalities as seen by employers; personalities which are obviously not seen in the light of a 'young-old' conflict. However, with young people forming a large part of the numbers in search of work, they are subject straight away to the quantitative and structural changes of the production system within the job market. So young people are in the forefront of the group of workers most in touch with these changes. In this context, the measures taken to help them are fully justified. But it must be remembered that all young people are not in the same situation; with those leaving the education system unqualified being restricted to the least skilled jobs, which tend to reduce in number, and which offer little stability in conditions of employment.

By way of contrast, young people leaving the education system after higher studies, due more to the numbers concerned than to the particular types of jobs offered, enjoy a more agreeable transition to working life. The measures introduced which aim to give young people a vocational qualification can be supported from a strictly economic point of view. In fact they enable young people to match the qualifications offered to the changing pattern of available jobs, and to be 'better equipped' in an inundated job market. However, when young people are particularly disadvantaged and when qualifications gained within special training courses are not yet well regarded in the job market, there is still a great risk of segregation between young people who have succeeded in school and those who have failed and have been treated in a separate supportive system. Furthermore, in order for young people to 'join in' in the training system it would appear necessary to make sure that short term jobs and unemployment are financially less attractive than training, beginning perhaps with a reform of present unemployment benefit legislation pertaining to the 16–18 age group.

On a wider scale — considering the development of more and more coherent programmes — one can question the future of the whole system of initial training. In fact the proposals can avoid transferring education as a public service to private institutions and firms — they are involved because of the urgent need according to the authorities to resolve the problems — but they can be kept under strict public control.

The political commitment to bring together numerous actors into the programme for social integration and vocational training of the young has resulted in the development of a new kind of training — with much the same effect as the laws relating to continuous training have already had. It seems, therefore, difficult to imagine a return to the old system and one must expect, rather, that the involvement of these new actors will be maintained and that the situation will be transformed by the changing face of the entire training system. It is already possible to make out the new profile, but the features are not yet discernible.

Notes

1 For example PAUL, J.-J. (1981) 'Education and employment: a survey of French research', *European Journal of Education*, Vol. 16, no. 1, pp. 95–120.
2 AFFICHARD, J. (1981) 'Quels emplois après l'école: la valeur des titres scolaires depuis 1973', *Economie et Statistique*, no. 134, June, pp. 7–76.
3 PAUL, J.-J. (1982) 'Les concepts de base et less méthodes de prévision des besoins en main d'oeuvre qualifiée. Le cas français', *IIPE*, UNESCO, September.
4 CLEMENCEAU, P. and GEHIN, J.P. (1983) 'Le renouvellement de la main d'oeuvre par les secteurs: quelles conséquences pour l'acces des jeunes aux secteurs', *CEREQ, Dossier formation-emploi, collection des études*, 3, pp. 53–74.
5 ADEP (1982) 'Jeunes sans qualification. Trois annees d'operations pilotes', Une action de l'Education dans le cadre de la Communauté Europeene, Paris.
6 GIFFARD, A. and PAUL, J.-J. (1981) 'La formation continue des jeunes: contenu et impact', IREDU, Dijon, introduced various pilot schemes.
7 In France an employer's National Health contributions amounts to more than 40 per cent of wages.
8 ROSE, J. (1982) 'Contribution a l'analyse des formes sociales d'accès aux emplois: l'organisation de la transition professionnelle', thèse pour le Doctorat d'Etat Université, Paris X Nanterre.
9 The economic assessments of GASPARD, M. and FRANK, D. (1981) 'Les effets des Pactes Nationaux pour l'Emploi sur l'evolution du chômage', *Economie et prévision*, 47, pp. 5–25, are precise on this matter.
10 SCHWARTZ, B. (1981) 'L'insertion professionnelle et sociale des jeunes', Documentation française, Paris.
11 NALLET, J.F. and LUTTRINGER, J.M. (1982) 'La qualification professionnelle et l'insertion sociale des jeunes de 16 a 18 ans', *Actualité de la Formation Permanente*, 58, pp. 37–45.

References

AMAT, F. (1983) 'L'entrée des jeunes dans la vie active. Synthèse des principaux resultats de 1'observatoire des entrées dans la vie active et des bilans Formation-Emploi', *CEREQ, Dossier formation-emploi, collection des études*, no. 3, pp. 13–52.
CEZARD, M., COEFFIC, N. and LAULHE, P. (1983) 'L' enquete emploi renovee', *Economie et Statistique*, no. 151, January, pp. 29–40.

National Strategies on Youth Unemployment

Christopher Pilley

The development of the French strategy on youth unemployment shows interesting parallels and differences with what has happened in Britain in the last ten years or so. In Britain, disillusionment at the ability of the Youth Opportunities Programme to make young people significantly more employable in the face of rapid rise of unemployment generally gave rise to an increased emphasis on the need for training. In France, disillusionment with measures taken there has led to the development of a rather different approach, underpinned by an altogether broader philosophy.

As in Britain, unemployment has risen rapidly in France since the late 1970s and reached the figure of 2 million at approximately the same time as the figure of 3 million was first reached here.

As in Britain too, unemployment in France has hit young people hard, particularly so the 700,000 young French people who leave the educational system each year, of whom nearly a quarter are without qualifications. Indeed, when the new socialist government came to power in May 1981, 16–25 year olds constituted nearly half of the total number of unemployed people and 16–21 year olds nearly a quarter.

Until the mid 1970s, employment policy had been largely indirect, and concentrated on the classical Keynesian solution of increasing demand for labour in general, by increasing demand for goods and services. In the latter half of the 1970s, however, as unemployment rose, a different type of policy emerged, aiming to act directly and selectively on the labour market and aiming mainly at those people far and away most affected — the young. Three measures were instituted in 1975. These were a system of employment premiums for young people, what came to be known as the 'Granet Courses' aimed at giving a limited number of unqualified 16–25 year olds vocational training (including four weeks in a firm) and aimed at meeting the needs of the local labour market, and the development of government assisted employment/training contracts for young people.

While these measures involved less than 10 per cent of school leavers, the development of the first of three annual 'pactes pour l'emploi' (employment pacts) starting in 1977, provided a major boost to the development of a national strategy for youth unemployment, if only because of the numbers involved. The three pacts involved between 40 and 80 per cent of school leavers and an estimated 10–15 per cent of 16–24 year olds as a whole. In each of the three pacts, 1977/78, 1978/79 and 1979/81, there were four main measures and while the exact conditions and financial resources varied, the main lines of the measures remained the same, aiming at improving the career guidance and entry into working life of young people, and, in the later pacts, certain other categories, particularly certain categories of women.

The four main measures were as follows:-

1 *Reduction of Employers Social Security Contributions*

Employers in the private sector were exempted from 100 per cent (later 50 per cent) of social security contributions for taking on young people under 26 when the result was a net increase in the number of their employees. Similar exemption from social security contributions was available to firms taking on apprentices.

2 *'Contrat Emploi — Formation' (Employment/Training Contracts)*

These offered two broad types of contract for unemployed 17–26 year olds:

(a) 'Insertion Contract': 120–500 hours of training with a guarantee of employment for at least six months.

(b) 'Qualification Contract': 500–1200 hours of training, job guarantee for one year. A subsidy was available for training to be provided either by the firm itself or by an outside training organization. Firms were also exempted from social security payments and the young person had employee status.

3 *'Stage Pratique en Entreprise' (Practical Work Experience Courses in Firms)*

Unemployed young people aged 16–26 could be recruited for four months by a firm which had to give a minimum of 120 hours training. Young people had trainee status and therefore no payment of social security charges was involved. The state provided a subsidy of 70 per cent of the national minimum wage (SMIC). The trainee received 90 per cent of SMIC.

4 *'Stage de Formation et de Preparation a la Vie Professionnelle*

Aimed at unemployed 16–26 year olds to help them choose a career or appropriate training. Lasted up to 6 months and a grant to trainees of 25–75 per cent of national minimum wage was available.

At the same time as the 'pactes', a number of more limited and experimental programmes aimed at young people with particular difficulties in entry into working life had been put into action. One of these, included within the 'pactes', was the 'stage de preformation' (pre training course) linked to the 'Stage de Formation et de Preparation a la Vie Professionnelle' described above. The 'stage de preformation', however, aimed at 16–18 year olds, was seen very much as a first step in careers guidance and introduction to working life after school. Courses lasted about four months. More experimental, however, were a number of other projects aimed at young people in particular difficulty, including a large number from immigrant groups, living in large urban housing estates and who often left school without any qualifications and for whom subsequent unemployment was seen as but one element in a cycle of related problems which pushed them to the margins of society.

New Directions

Criticism of the 'pactes' grew as it became clear that they were failing to reduce unemployment, except temporarily and that they failed to create real jobs. The 'Stage Pratique en Entreprise' in particular, was criticized as merely the provision of very cheap temporary labour to firms by the state — a huge temporary employment agency run by the state itself, practically for nothing. The influential 'Le Monde de L'Education', reviewing the three 'pactes' in 1980, described them as 'an expedient'.[1] They had temporarily reduced the level of youth unemployment but young people who already had qualifications had profited most from them. Those at the bottom of the heap had stayed at the bottom. Girls were also at a considerable disadvantage relative to boys. Small firms, in particular, had, the evidence showed, tended to use the 'pactes' as a form of cheap labour, with little incentive to keep on trainees as salaried employees after the period was up.

At least as important, however was an increasingly cynical view of the 'pactes' amongst a growing number of young people themselves who saw them as a means of massaging the unemployment figures and providing firms with cheap labour. Young people had few illusions about eventual job prospects. Particularly amongst the less qualified, the indefinite future was often seen at best in terms of a series of insecure, temporary jobs, including the provision of 'pactes', alternating with periods of unemployment.

The fear that young people were in danger of becoming increasingly alienated both from the world of work and from society in general by bearing the brunt of the economic crisis was increasingly shared by politicians — particularly of the left. It is therefore not surprising that it was reflected in one of the first actions of the new French Government which came to power on 10 May 1981 in setting up a Commission under Professor Betrand Schwartz to look at ways of improving the entry of young people aged 16–21 into adult and working life. At the same time as setting up the Commission, the new Government announced changes in the provisions of the third 'pacte' aimed at making the opportunities offered more than simply temporary ones. These changes included the replacement of the much criticised 'Stage Pratique en Entreprise' by 'Stages d'Insertion Professionnelle' with fewer numbers but also a greater emphasis on training. The Government also pushed ahead with other more general measures aimed at creating jobs, such as the reduction of the working week, earlier, and phased, retirement and longer holidays.

Both the method of working of the Schwartz Commission and its conclusions represented a considerable break with the past. Both reflected the fact that, from the beginning, the Commission saw the problem of youth unemployment in the context of an overall youth policy and the logic of this perspective implied a dialogue with young people, and the adoption of an interministerial solution, rather than one seen in terms of employment policy alone. Just as youth policy could no longer be seen solely in terms of leisure — as it had in the past — so youth unemployment could no longer be seen solely in terms of the economic sphere. Thus, counter to the practice under the previous administration, hundreds of organizations, both voluntary and statutory were consulted. Besides organizations representing young people themselves, these included organizations in youth and social work, education, trade unions, family organizations and industry.

The Commission received over 400 submissions and produced its report in little over three months during the summer of 1981. The need to recognize the inter-connectedness of entry into working life and entry into wider adult roles and more generally, to break down the distinction between the economic and social spheres, is reflected in the title of the report 'L'Insertion Profession-nelle et Sociale des Jeunes'.[2]

This broadening of the issue to include 'insertion sociale' reflects a concern, as the report itself acknowledges, 'that an increasing number of young people are becoming marginalized' and a similar concern to build the sort of society from which young people are not excluded. From henceforth, the concern with the 'marginalization' of young people is placed at the centre of the stage. It is a prominent feature in the current French government's strategy.

One aspect of this concern has been centred around the quality of work offered to young people. The fear had often been expressed that young people, especially less qualified young people, were in danger of being placed in a secondary labour market of temporary and insecure work which gave them few rights and poor working conditions. The inequalities that resulted were not just between adults and young people, but also between those young people with qualifications, who were creamed off into jobs, and those without, who alternated between temporary, insecure jobs and unemployment.

There had also been considerable discussion about the attitude of young people to work itself. In France, the feeling had grown that, as increasingly well qualified people competed for jobs previously held by the less qualified, work itself had become less and less valued as a means of self-development or social recognition. On the other hand, human relationships at work had come to take on more importance to young people than the job itself or even the wages. So while it may not be true to say — as some did — that young people refused to work, the value of work for many young people was thought to have changed significantly. There is certainly evidence that they were less willing to put up with traditional hierarchies in the work situation. They wanted more automony and, in particular, the feeling that their work had some usefulness.

Such considerations explain the emphasis in the report on helping young people to develop their own lives outside of work and on the more general improvement of the quality of their lives. For underpinning the report is the belief that successful entry into working life is, in large part, dependent on a satisfactory wider social environment. To take but one example referred to in the report, it is all very well saying that young people should be prepared to move to where the work is to be found, but whether they will move depends, in part, on satisfactory accommodation being available to them. Furthermore, young people will not just go anywhere even if they can find somewhere to live. They want leisure activities, for example, and will not be attracted to areas where there is nothing to do.

Hence the report outlined a five point plan for a broader youth policy covering housing, leisure, health, delinquency and young people's relationships with the media. The report argued that the rejection of young people by the world of work — by forcing them into unqualified temporary work or unemployment — was paralleled by rejection in other spheres of life. The report argued that evidence of marginalization such as alcoholism, drug abuse, and law breaking reflected this, and that it is also reflected in the development of gangs; and it is therefore one of the concerns of the report that young people should be able to get together without being the object of suspicion or rejection by the older generation.

More generally, the report proposed measures to help young people who wanted to 'do their own thing', whether through providing meeting places and facilities, or through helping them to travel. Giving young people a voice was also emphasized and measures to encourage young people to produce their own communications media, including local radio, were proposed. The report also saw an important role for youth workers who, by taking advantage of their links with young people, could encourage action on employment, work and the quality of life.

This new approach thus represents a considerable shift from that adopted by the 'pactes'. The 'pactes' had been based on the assumption that the gap between young people and employment could be reduced by simply giving young people a mixture of training and work experience. The emphasis on 'Insertion Sociale' on the other hand means the emphasis is more on the wider problems of young people including those in most difficulty such as children of immigrants, delinquents and young people who are alienated from society in general. The emphasis moves away from simply helping young people to get a job, towards encouraging them to take control of their own lives by helping them to become responsible adults and thus play a role in a changing society. They key to this is what is termed a 'Pedagogie de la Reussite' (a pedagogie of success) — showing young people who have not succeeded that they can succeed. This is based on the principal of 'alternance' between experience and reflection on that experience. Central to the effectiveness of this pedagogy is the belief that the whole community should become an educational resource and that 'non-educational' services and resources can themselves become educational. One important condition for this, of course, is that a wide range of agencies are involved, and orchestrated by the public education and training sector — a far cry from the employer concentrated 'Pactes'. One token of success, the report argued, is that young people should be offered a qualification at the end of the course.

A broadly similar approach for the 18–21 age group, was adopted in the report. Three main measures were recommended. One was work sharing — allowing young people to choose the amount of work they do and enabling young workers to replace older workers about to retire or to take part-time work with training. Another vital element was direct action on the job side of the training/jobs equation. Positive action was required to create jobs for young people; jobs which appealed to them and which were socially useful. These could be improving the quality of life and providing personal services or, in what has become known as the 'third sector' through financial aid to young people who wanted to create their own jobs in community business ventures or local co-operatives.

Vocational and social education had to be developed and the transition of young people to working life had to be seen as only the first step in a process of permanent education. A major long-term aim in the report was to develop the right to paid educational leave in inverse proportion to the number of years already spent in the educational system.

One highly significant recommendation in the report was to set up local agencies to make contact with young people and provide information and counselling in a single place on all the problems and issues confronting them — health, sex, drugs, housing, jobs etc. The report recommended that these 'missions locales' — involving careers advisers, industrial trainers, social and community workers and others who would work with young people them-selves and those working with young people — should each serve a community of around 100,000. The report proposed that they should adopt a policy of positive discrimination and be supplemented by similar bodies at a national and regional level. The aim would be to reduce the compartmentalization between the different services concerned with the entry of young people into working and adult life.

When it was published, the report provoked considerable interest and the government sought to respond quickly to the momentum generated by it. Within a month of its publication, President Mitterand himself announced — significantly in a speech to the National Union of Family Associations (UNAF), — that the government would respect the spirit of the report and he referred specifically to the report's rejection of paternalism and the need to listen to young people themselves.

In the months that followed, there appeared a whole series of orders and circulars outlining measures to implement the recommendations of the report.[3] It is important to note, however, that from the start, the main emphasis has been placed on the 16–18 age group, and on employment, rather than on the range of other issues of concern to young people outlined in the report. Indeed, while in the spring of 1982 a number of measures, involving different ministries were announced in favour of the 16–18 age group to be put into effect the following September, the bulk of the measures in favour of older people aged 18–25 were only announced at the very end of that year.

The order of 26 March 1982, involving seven ministries, states flatly that 'The professional qualification and social integration of 16–18 year olds is a national obligation', involving not only the government, but also local authorities and other public bodies, institutions of learning, voluntary orga-nizations and professional trade union and family organizations as well as industry. The aim was to 'guarantee a professional qualification for young people aged 16–18' and to establish 'the legislative base for the first stage of an ambitious programme which should lead to a situation where, in 1985, no person in this age group will seek to enter the labour market without validated training'.

The aim was therefore clear: all young people who were beyond the school leaving age of 16, but not yet at the age of legal majority, must have the opportunity to continue education and training so long as they have not gained an educational qualification. In the longer term, the aim was that there should be no unqualified young people.

In terms of methods the order adopts the principle outlined in the Schwartz report and, like Schwartz, firmly sets itself against making training the responsibility of firms, as was generally the case in the 'pactes'. From now on, training was to be the main responsibility not of firms, but rather of the whole range of agencies within the community — including local authorities, public bodies, teaching establishments, voluntary organizations, professional bodies and trade unions as well as firms, though it was recognized that the technical lycees (Lycees d'Enseignement Professionnelle) would have a dominant role. While involving other ministries, including youth and sport and education, a co-ordinating role in the plans for 16–18 year olds was to be undertaken by the Ministry of Vocational Training.

The main measures aimed at 16–18 year olds adopt a broadly two stage process. Following the Schwartz report's recommendation for 'Missions Locales', great emphasis is placed on making contact with young people and providing them with information and counselling, as a precondition to the provision of any sort of training.

1 Contact, Information and Counselling

Permanences d'accueil, d'information et d'orientation
Nearly 900 contact points for information and counselling have been set up within existing organizations in an area such as Job Centres, Youth Information Centres and Centres for Information and Counselling run by local authorities etc. In practice, however, most are situated in town halls. Their job is to advise unqualified and unemployed young people aged 16–18 years.

'Missions locales'
Contrary to the recommendation of the Schwartz report, these have not been established throughout France and in most places a more limited role is undertaken by the 'Permanences d'accueil'. However, about sixty have been set up on an experimental basis particularly in deprived areas and these do have the wide-ranging remit proposed by Schwartz. 'Missions Locales' are concerned with a wider range of young people than the permanences — all young people over 16 — and have a much wider remit concerning themselves with the whole range of problems young people have in the entry into adult life — besides getting a job, housing, health, etc. Furthermore, they have an on-going contact with young people, acting as an intermediary between the

young person and the training organization, and providing support where necessary during training and helping young people find jobs after training.

2 *Training Courses*

Following a process of information and counselling (or in the case of the 'Missions Locales' concurrent with this) young people move towards a course aimed at giving them a qualification. There are two routes to this. Some young people will go straight on to the 'action de formation alternée de qualification' — involving a mixture of on-and off-the-job training, while others will take an intermediate path. On the one hand they can go to an 'action de formation alternée d'insertion sociale' or, if they are not yet clear about what they want to do and are therefore not yet ready for either of the other two options, they can undertake a short 'stage d'orientation appro-fondie'.

All these courses are organized through a contract signed between the state and educational and other training institutions, including local author-ities, LEPs, voluntary organizations and private bodies. After discussion each young person also signs a contract with the training organization outlining the details of the course and the rights and obligations of the trainees. In addition, particular stress is placed on the training of trainers and special funding has been made available for all this. The details of the courses are as follows:

'Stage d'orientation approfondie'

These courses are aimed at helping unqualified and unemployed young people to decide on their vocational plans and assist their wider integration into society. Any type of agency is eligible to set up these courses, including local authorities, social and community work agencies, educational institutions and public or private training agencies, though periods in firms or other places of employment form part of the course. The courses last four to six weeks (120–180 hours).

'Action de formation alternée d'insertion sociale'

These courses are aimed at unemployed young people aged 16–18 who have left school without a qualification and who are experiencing particular difficulties in their transition to adult and working life. The courses thus aim to help people in this situation to resolve the problems they find themselves in and to take their place in the wider society, as well as to clarify their own career choices. Courses are limited to fifteen young people and rely on a mixture of individual and group work methods. Great emphasis is placed on relating training to the needs of the individual young person, and the periods in the work situation aim to familiarize the young person with working life, through undertaking particular tasks, and help him or her to decide on a career which could lead later to a qualification, rather than to teach specific skills. The courses last up to ten months and can be set up by a wide range of organizations providing they have traineres with appropriate experience for this kind of work.

Christopher Pilley

'Actions de formation alternée de qualification'
These courses are aimed, unlike the 'pactes', at providing to unemployed unqualified young people a recognized qualification leading to a job as well as encouraging integration into adult life. The courses last six to twelve months, or up to two years if a 'stage d'insertion' is taken first. Thirty to 50 per cent of the time is undertaken in the work situation. A wide range of organizations can organize courses including local authorities, training units of firms, adult education and community development agencies and they can do this on their own or in conjunction with others. It is the responsibility of the organization setting up courses to find the most appropriate placements in the work situation. Only organizations providing temporary work are specifically excluded.

Young people on all these programmes receive an allowance of 550 francs a month for the first six months, and 700 francs after this.

Measures Aimed at Young People up to the Age of 25

While the emphasis during the first eighteen months of the new government was on the 16–18 age group, particularly the least qualified section of the age group with wider problems of entry into adult life, at the end of 1982 the government announced measures in favour of older young people between the ages of eighteen and twenty-five. They fall into three main categories:

1 *The development of opportunities within the educational system for the age group.*
The government has announced two main ways of doing this:

(a) an increase in numbers in professional and technical education including opportunities for those who want to get back into education to gain a qualification;

(b) the development of alternance training for people who already have qualifications.

2 *Helping the entry of young people into working life.*
While rejecting those elements of the previous 'pactes' which were felt to provide firms with cheap temporary labour, such as reductions in social security charges or 'stages practique en entreprise', the government announced that the 'contrat emploi-formation', which had been a feature of the pactes — would continue, with additional, shorter and less intensive provision for those young people who had already received appropriate training to help young people apply that training in a work situation — what is called 'contrat emploi — adaptation'. The government also announced measures to develop job sharing which could help to bring young and older workers in the same job.

3 *Guidance and counselling*
The third category of measures related to improved career guidance and counselling for young people and measures to encourage young people to

develop their own employment initiatives. The development of career guidance, counselling and training during the period of national service was to be encouraged.

The one measure aimed at 18–26 year olds that had been announced at roughly the same time as measures for 16–18 year olds — the 'programme de jeunes volontaires' is to continue. This programme is currently run by the Ministry of Youth and Sport, though other ministries are to be encouraged to set up parallel programmes. The programme provides work in the community and environmental improvement work for between six months and one year. Young people are paid 50 per cent of the national minimum wage by the state and expenses are also paid to sponsoring organizations, usually voluntary organizations or local authorities. While a training element is provided, the main objective of the programme is not so much to provide jobs but rather to help with confidence building amongst a category of young people and to give them a first experience of work.

The French government's strategy on youth unemployment thus puts a firm emphasis on a more global approach to the problem of youth unemployment, putting it within the more general context of entry into adult life and integration into wider society. Recognizing that the problem of unemployment is only one of a series of often interlocking problems suffered by large sections of France's young people, the emphasis has been placed on those young people suffering from these multiple forms of disadvantage and on helping them to overcome them through the development of the new methods characterized by the 'Pedagogie de la Reussite', based on the principle of 'alternance'.

This approach has been reflected particularly in the setting up of the missions locales and in the growth of 'stages d'insertion' to help young people get rid of a sense of generalized failure and withdrawal often linked with violence and a desire for social recognition. Nevertheless, the strategy recognizes that no course alone can provide the answers to the problems of the most disadvantaged young people without wider action on the general environment, both physical and social, in which they live and action has been forthcoming on this. For example, the Ministry of Youth and Sport has put forward proposals, following Schwartz, for the provision of small scale meeting places for young people to meet and generally do their own thing, and the government has also set up a National Commission on Community Development Housing Schemes.

It has been recognized too, that the strategy requires particular qualities of staff working with the young people, both at the information and counselling stage and at the training stage and thus the training of trainers has particular importance, particularly in giving effect to the 'Pedagogie de la Reussite' and considerable resources have been made available for such training.

A full evaluation of the strategy must wait until 1985, since by that year the aim is to ensure that all young people are qualified. Nevertheless, at the time of writing, less than one year after the strategy was put into effect, a number of questions can be raised. Firstly, devaluations of the franc and subsequent austerity measures since the heady days of May 1981 have put the fight against unemployment somewhat into the background. Nor have they spared the programmes for the young unemployed which have been scaled down for 1983/84 compared with the previous year.

It is also true to say that the strategy outlined in the Schwartz Report has suffered dilution in other ways. In particular, concern has been expressed about the extent to which the present arrangements for making and providing on-going contact with young people will really be effective. The Schwartz Report had put considerable emphasis on operating close to young people and the 'missions locales' were seen as having a quite pivotal role as a single intermediary between young people and the organizations concerned with their entry into adult and working life. They were intended to be flexible, small scale units — attractive to young people and because prominent and visible, politically important in mobilizing the wider public's awareness of the reality of life for young people. The fact, therefore, that only about sixty areas have such units — rather than the whole country — must count as a watering down of the original strategy proposed by Schwartz. This is particularly so in view of the fact that the 900 'permanences d'accueil' with a more limited remit are mostly in a single room hidden in public buildings such as town halls. The danger is that, far from being flexible they will be relatively bureaucratic and not really in touch with the reality of young people. Furthermore, the crucial role that Schwartz saw for those organizations closest to young people — for example youth work organizations — both at the contact stage and at the training stage, appears to have been somewhat downgraded.[4]

Important in the strategy too is the need for genuine collaboration between a wide range of agencies at all levels, particularly at the local level. One notable example of such collaboration is to be found in the Paris region, through the setting up of local support networks bringing together a wide range of interests. These include the Ministries of Labour, Education and Health, local authorities, employers, housing, intermediate treatment organizations and the Ministry of Youth and Sport. These networks have clearly been useful in encouraging an interdepartmental and interdisciplinary examination of how each agency deals with young people and how they can better work together.[5] However, this is not the situation everywhere.

Ultimately, it is recognized that the government strategy cannot guarantee a job to the young people who pass through its programmes. The aim, however, is to give those without a job a better chance and, by concentrating on the wider social, cultural and emotional questions confronting young people, perhaps to help them better to deal with the stresses that result from unemployment itself.

Notes

1 DUMONT, J.-P. (1980) 'Les pactes pour l'emploi. Un expedient'. *Le Monde de L'Education*, November, pp. 20-2.
2 SCHWARTZ, B. (1981) 'L'Insertion Professionelle et, Sociale des Jeunes — Rapport au Premier Ministre', available from La Documentation Française, 29–31 quai Voltaire, 75340 Paris, CEDEX 07.
3 A dossier giving details of those circulars is available from Centre INFFO, Tour Europe, Cedex 07 92080 PARIS LA DEFENSE.

4 See for example 'L'Education — hebdo' no. 7, Supplement *L'Education Magazine* (1982) 'Les 16/18 Ans' 4 November.
5 See Prefecture de la Region d'Ile de France, Mission Economique et Sociale and Groupe Regionale d'Appui Pedagogique (1981) 'Guide Practique pour la Mise en Place des Actions d'Insertion des Jeunes', available from Prefecture de la Region d'Ile de France, Mission Economique et Sociale, 21, Rue Miollis, Paris.

GERMANY

As with the papers which made up the previous section, the two contributions on Germany provide more than one comparison. The section on the German Federal Republic, by Volker Koditz, gives 'a guide through the tangle of schemes' which have comprised that country's responses to the problem of youth unemployment. Koditz writes from the perspective of someone involved in the evaluation of the European Community's Pilot Programmes on Transition. His paper was first published in the book by Hans Petzold and Wolfgang Schlegel[1] but was translated specifically for this collection. Frank Bacon's contribution deals with the contrasting experience of the German Democratic Republic and is written from the point of view of an observer. Sadly, Dr. Bacon died during the production of this book.

The situation in the German Federal Republic is not dissimilar from that already described in Britain and France, at least as far as effect is concerned, although the differing political motivations of the various Lander add an additional layer of complexity. Koditz describes the potential 'shunting yard' effect of the compulsory Tenth Educational Year for vocational training, where completion of the set courses qualifies many youngsters for little more than unemployment, unskilled labour or more courses. It is interesting to note that the German Federal Republic has recently introduced a 'work experience' scheme as an innovation within its vocational provision and an import from Britain. Thus, what Koditz describes as 'the labyrinth of measures', has introduced 'a new path through the maze', and one which is already criticized for hiding statistics and providing employers with cheap labour. Across the border in the German Democratic Republic circumstances are very different. Here, according to Frank Bacon, is 'a nation which suffers only from a labour shortage', although there are readily discernible similarities in the ten years of compulsory schooling in both East and West Germany. There are also parallels to be drawn between the motivation behind the GDR's system of vocational preparation in the later years of schooling and the intentions of the YOP and the YTS in Britain. The differences emerge in the levels of youth unemployment for each country. Vocational preparation takes on a less controversial guise where the major problem still seems to be one of which field of work to prepare for.

Volker Koditz

Note

PETZOLD, H. and SCHLEGEL, W. (1983) *Qual ohne Wahl: Jugend zweschen Schule und Beruf*, Frankfurt am Main, Verlag Jugend und Politik.

The German Federal Republic: How the State Copes with the Crisis — a Guide through the Tangle of Schemes

Volker Koditz

Some Introductory Remarks Concerning the German System of Education and Training

Compulsory education in Germany begins at the age of six. Primary school lasts for four years (six years in Berlin) and is followed by a variety of lower secondary education (Sekundarstufe 1). The distribution of children to the different forms of lower secondary education depends on the achievement level they have reached in the primary school (and sometimes an entry examination).

The Hauptschule is the lowest level of lower secondary education and lasts five or six years depending on the Lander. In Berlin, for traditional reasons, it lasts for four years. The Hauptschule is orientated towards immediate entry into the labour market for unskilled young workers or apprentices. It is considered mainly as a working class or foreign worker's school and, as far as public opinion of its achievement level is concerned, also more and more as a 'Restschule' — a school for low achievers.

Attempts have been made, particularly within Lander governed by the Christian Democrats, to change the image of the Hauptschule over recent years. Selection procedures at the end of primary schooling have been made stricter and, in order to increase the chances of Hauptschule-leavers obtaining places in full-time vocational schools, the amount of work experience schemes and forms of controlled work experience within the Hauptschule has been increased.

The Realschule — in former times also called the Mittleschule. This lasts up to the tenth year of schooling. Originally, it was the school which was orientated above all to the services sector, especially for girls. School-leavers are either going to an apprenticeship in commerce etc. or to a full-time vocational school. With the worsening situation in the labour market (or the lack of apprenticeship places) the Realschule increasingly takes on the traditional functions of the Hauptschule, particularly in urban areas. In the countryside it has the function of providing social mobility — in urban areas this is taken on by the Gymnasium.

The Gymnasium is the traditional route to higher education, however, due to the labour market situation (which also applies to the academic professions) and the lack of apprenticeships, the Gymnasium increasingly has the function of finding apprenticeship places. Recently, new forms of higher level apprenticeship schemes for Gymnasium leavers have been created — Berufsakademie.

There have been recent reforms which have led to a greater degree of differentiation within the last three years of attendance at the Gymnasium. Students are now able to specialize more, in contrast to the traditional concept, and choose some main subjects where courses are held in a more university-like atmosphere. For several reasons these reforms were criticized; in my opinion the main reason for the criticisms was the move away from the traditional concept of a general 'maturity' related to the final examination. In principle the Abitur still gives access to all forms of higher education, but in practice 'numerus clausus' devalued the function of the general entry certificate. University-based entry examinations are only discussed for the medical profession.

The Gesamtschule (comprehensive school) was the big reform of the early 1970s, mainly a project of the Social Democrats. In the Lander governed by the Social Democrats it is offered as another type of education — alongside traditional forms. Closely related to the discussion and the concept of the Gesamtschule is the comprehensive fifth and sixth year, which works differently in different Lander — ranging from some curricular similarities during the course of these years, to a common course for all pupils.

The Vocational Training of Germany is characterized by two main features:

(i) the majority of young people go through a dual system apprenticeship scheme, which provides all sorts of traning — including training for the services sector — and lasts for one-two or two-three years;

(ii) vocational training within full-time vocational schools is traditionally of only minor importance — training for nurses etc. Due to the problems of the labour market, especially for girls, it is increasing in importance, but mainly as a 'waiting' situation for an apprenticeship — like in the case of the one year Berufsfachschule.

The Lander governments have reacted to the problem of youth unemployment in several ways:

(i) the discussion of a tenth compulsory year at the Hauptschule, with special vocational preparation courses. Discussion was mainly focussed on whether or not this should happen in the Hauptschule or in the vocational school — a Vocational Preparation Year. The tendency in the Christian Democratic Lander is to leave the Hauptschule with nine years and have the vocational year in the vocational school. In the Social Democratic run Lander the tendency is to have a ten year Hauptschule plus a vocational year in the vocational school;

(ii) basic vocational training: the purpose of this course in the vocational school was originally in order to increase the quality of the dual system vocational training. At first many employers were reluctant to count this year as a first apprenticeship year, but increasingly attitudes have changed, and nowadays in some professions, youngsters will only be taken on when they have had such a course. But very often this course is only considered to be a 'waiting situation';

(iii)   the already mentioned BVJ (Basic Vocational Preparation Year) has been introduced in the Lander as a hedge against unemployment for all young people without a job, or without an apprenticeship place. The quality of these courses appears to be generally quite poor;

(iv)   besides the educational authorities schemes there are schemes emmanating from the Employment Authorities (Bundesanstalt fur Arbeit — the equivalent of the MSC). This institution runs a basic vocational training course (of nine–twelve months) which is quite similar to the BVJ and aims to give young people some kind of basic qualification and some vocational preparation. The other courses run by the employment authorities are more orientated towards ESN people. The courses are situated in private firms or are run by commercial training firms or voluntary organizations — eg the church etc. The Bundesanstalt is only the financing body in these circumstances.

How the State Copes with the Crisis: A Guide through the Tangle of Schemes

The state reacted to the development of the vocational training system in the years following the mid-1970s in three different ways:

(i)   by giving up any attempts to improve the quality of vocational training and cutting back existing reforms step-by-step, thus encouraging those firms which had apparently become uncertain as a result of the policy reforms to show greater willingness to offer training;

(ii)   by generous direct and indirect subsidies of training places. Behind this policy was the hope of stimulating industry and commerce through financial incentive and making training a more desirable prospect.

(iii)   by swift introduction of a whole range of schemes to prepare the young for a vocation, coupled with an extension of compulsory schooling for the young unemployed. The official aim: to increase the chance of a training place by providing specific vocational training.

Most important here is the emergence of a relatively independent field in education which lies between the end of school life and the start of working life. It equals a far-reaching structural change to the vocational training system and offers the key to understanding the actual development and becomes therefore the main point of discussion in this chapter.

First though we shall look at the two other attempts the state made to overcome the crisis.

Cut-Back of Reforms and Subsidy Policies for Employers

The failure of the vocational training reforms together with the passing of the AplFG (a law designed to promote the creation of training places) marked a new trend in the state's vocational training policies. All strategies were now purely quantitatively oriented towards securing training places for the young unemployed.

The nucleus of this new vocational training policy was, and still is, to encourage employers to offer training, either through financial stimulus or through the abolition of regulations which apparently made the employers uncertain and less willing to make training places available. This led to a step-by-step cut-back of already existing reforms and a final abandoning of long-term reforms in vocational training. At the same time an impenetrable network of subsidy schemes evolved to secure (additional) training places or employment for young people.

The following examples, of which one could list even more, show this clearly.

Example: Making Training Places Available

The AplFG contained, as a last remnant of the original reform, plans for a funded financing of vocational training — a regulation which made it possible for the state to request contributions from those employers who did not take part in the training programme in order to finance additional training places. This levy of 0.25 per cent of all yearly wages and salaries could be claimed if the availability of training places dropped below 12.5 per cent above demand.

Although prerequisites for such measures existed continually since 1976, the regulation was not once put into use (compare table 1).

Table 1: Availability of and demand for training places

Year	Training places available	Training places requested	Overlap
1976	517,100	526,700	−9,600 = −1.9%
1977	583,500	585,000	−1,500 = −0.3%
1978	621,600	625,800	−4,100 = −0.7%
1979	677,287	660,452	+16,785 = +2.5%
1980	694,605	667,355	+27,250 = +4.1%
1981	642,700	627,492	+15,208 = +2.4%
1982	651,000	667,000	−16,000 = −2.4%

The government abandoned the implementation of this 'instrument for emergencies'[1] with the justification that it was hoped 'that employers would in future display sufficient enthusiasm that the legalised training levy would not have to be raised'.[2] In the meantime the need has become even greater but the 'training levy instrument' does not exist anymore. In December 1980, on request of the union controlled Länder, the Federal Constitutional Court declared the AplFG unconstitutional for technical reasons (an abuse of the independence in matters of education and culture).

In the new AplFG, which was passed in 1981, there is no longer any mention of a financing regulation, despite the fact that the Federal Constitutional Court had actually recognized in its judgment on the AplFG, the constitutional possibility of financing through a levy.

Example: Trainer's Suitability Regulation

This regulation too is a relic from the time of training reforms. It was passed in 1972 with the aim of improving the quality of training and to commit 'instructors' to undergo a test of the quality of training given, within a specified period of time.

Under pressure from industry all instructors with training experience amounting to ten years or more were exempted from this test and, in addition, the deadline for the aptitude test was postponed until 31 December 1984.

Finally, the Bundeskabinett (Federal Cabinet) decided to exempt from the aptitude test, those who had been training for five years continuously, or for six years altogether, provided they had given no cause for complaint.

Example: Youth Employment Protection Law

At the beginning of 1976, the Bundestag (Parliament) passed, with only a single vote against, a new law (JAschG) for the protection of young people in employment. This new law — which was celebrated as an improved protection for working youth — contained several special regulations which in practice weakened the, till then, existing protection law. For example, it became much easier to use young people for piece work or to require them to work on Saturday, Sunday, Bank Holidays or night shifts and, in addition, the possibility of employing youngsters had been considerably extended by introducing relevant special regulations. But even then, there still exists a campaign, mainly by the Christian Democratic Parts (CDU) controlled Länder and the various commercial associations, to abolish the JAschG altogether because of its apparently discouraging training regulations.

A majority of the CDU-controlled Länder in the Bundesrat (Upper House of Parliament) eventually passed a bill which envisaged a more flexible structure for the daily working hours of the young — effectively to make it possible to bring forward by one hour the start to the working day and to extend daily working hours to eight-and-a-half hours.

Example: Compulsory Attendance[3] at a Technical College (CATC)[4]

In the FRG, until a few years ago, all young people up to the age of 18 who did not pursue secondary education had to attend a technical college whether they were employed or being trained. In all Federal Länder, since about 1976, there gradually emerged regulations which in particular exempted unemployed young people from this compulsory attendance at a technical college (CATC). Most frequently, though, there appeared regulations which revoked the compulsory attendance for those who had no training place after either one year of Basic Vocational Training (BGJ) or one year of Vocational Preparation (BVJ) — or — after one year of any of the other vocational preparatory schemes. In some of the Federal Länder decrees were passed whereby educational authorities could release unemployed young people on request from the CATC. The intention behind this is clear: in this way the employment of such young people would become more attractive to the potential employer. More and more firms have taken advantage of this by asking young applicants to request release. The regulations within the various Länder with regard to the CATC are documented in the appendix to this chapter.

Example: Special Training and Work Contracts for Young People

A whole network of subsidy schemes to promote training places and employment for the young emerged parallel to the systematical cut back of reforms.[5]

The almost random distribution of funds, without control over quality, is characteristic of these subsidy policies. This has led to misuse. It meant that firms often requested subsidies for training places or employment which they would have made available in any case (Mitnahmeeffect/'take-with-it effect'). The so-called 'special training and work contracts'[6] in Nordrhein-Westfalen are an especially obvious example for this.

They were intended, by definition, to serve those young people who were ready for employment but who had not yet completed training. During the one year period under 'supervisory and protection' contract young people spent eight hours per week in a CT, three hours weekly training under supervision at their place of employment and the remainder — twenty-nine hours — being engaged in productive work. To this end, in 1976, the Land Nordrhein-Westfalen subsidized wages based on 60 per cent of the wage rates (that is to say the usual local remuneration for two six-month periods) and in addition employers were granted a sum of DM 2000 as a 'signing on fee'. Under the agreement employers were not obliged to offer young people employment or a training place, neither did there exist any control measures to protect young people from being dismissed before they had completed the one-year period. In fact, after an investigation, it was discovered that a number of employers had dismissed young people after only a few weeks — but not before they had collected their grants. As a result, the guidelines of the agreement were changed and employers were now obliged to make available training places to young people who had successfully completed their intro- ductory year. To guard against early dismissal, measures for repayment of grants were tightened. The result was that instead of the expected 10,000 applications by employers only sixty were in fact made.[7] (Compare Wennin- ger, 1979).

In Hessen employment of young people out of work has been subsidized since spring 1982. It is feared though that the success of this scheme will amount to nothing more than employers using young people under 20 when in need of unskilled labour. New places for training or employment are not created. At best, there may occur a shift in the age structure of the unskilled and unemployed.

Advertisement:
Hint for the Day: Youth Unemployment
Financial Aid

Employers who are based in Hessen and who are willing to take on unemployed youngsters who have no vocational training, may claim in addition to the grant from the employment authorities a further allowance of DM 3000. The Land Hessen has made available 2 million DM to assist attempts by the employment authorities to integrate unemployed people into gainful employment. The incorporation of these young people becomes more and more difficult as there is little employment offered for them.

The employment authorities will grant subsidies in addition to the initial 'training allowance' and the 'signing on fee' on condition that any youngster, at the time of being employed, should be under 20 years of age. The training allowance is paid in two instalments.

Offers of employment or training places should be made to your local employment authorities who will be pleased to supply you with any necessary information.

While the original reform plans of the Socio/Liberal Coalition government intended to reduce the number of young people without a vocational training contract, *i.e.* employed as untrained and unskilled labourers, attempts have been made since 1975 by the Länder to make such employment again more pallatable and thus reduce the problem of unemployment. This became obvious with the introduction of the subsidy schemes mentioned above and especially by the clandestine abolition of the CATC (Compulsory attendance at a Technical College[8]).

It is difficult to assess how far the measures have had the hoped-for effect. Officially, it is stated again and again, that the number of young people attending a CT without vocational training contracts is decreasing — *i.e.* in the Vocational Training Report 1983. However, there is no mention of the fact that a steadily growing number of young unskilled workers have been released from the CATC and therefore, would not appear in any of the technical colleges' statistics.

Extension of Compulsory Schooling and Vocational Preparation: The Tenth Educational Year as a 'Collecting Point'

The main focus of the state's educational and job market policies to overcome youth unemployment and the lack of training places was, and still is, the swift extension of compulsory schooling and the introduction of vocational preparation as a 'collecting point' for potentially unemployed school leavers. Thus emerged in recent years a veritable tangle of measures in vocational areas enmeshing more and more Mainschool[9] (Hauptschule) and Special School leavers. Even the conference held by the Ministers for Education and the Arts could shed no light on the manifold forms of organization in the various Länder. All measures have in common, at least so we are made to believe, the focus of increasing the chance of a training place for affected young people by providing specific vocational training and by compensating for educational or social weaknesses.

The existing general and vocational *compulsory* schooling system has meanwhile absorbed all measures for extending schooling and for vocational preparation under the term 'Tenth Educational Year'. This means that in most of the Bundesländer, schooling is automatically extended by one year for those youngsters who, after finishing their general schooling, are not continuing with secondary education or who have not been able to find a training place.

This ruling especially affects pupils from main and special schools who, at the end of their nine years of schooling have not yet found a training place. The extended compulsory full-time education may be any of the following:

— one year of basic vocational training or
— one year of vocational preparation or even
— continuing with a tenth year at a comprehensive school, main-school, or special schools (where such classes may be available) or
— one year of any of the opportunities for vocational preparation recognized by the Federal Institute for Employment[10]

This way of organizing the Tenth Educational Year in Hessen seems to be repeated in similar form in all of the other Bundesländer — though perhaps the various measures may go under different names. In most of the Bundesländer the Tenth Educational Year is mainly oriented towards vocational schooling (TC) and has therefore little to do with the original idea of the tenth school year, the extension of general compulsory education by one year. To make this clearer there follows a short account of how the tenth general educating school year developed into the Tenth Educational Year. As early as 1970 the Bildungsrat[11] (Council for Education) requested a tenth generally educating school year as part of its plan for a new structure — the abolition of the four-tier school system (Gymnasium oriented towards higher education; Realschule offering an intermediate level; Hauptschule providing a minimum level of general education and the Special School for the disabled including ESN) was then for the first time clearly defined. Under the final Vocational-Education Reform Plan of 1973, the tenth school year was to be integrated into the future comprehensive school. All pupils would attend school together for ten years and in the eleventh year, unless they were entering for Abitur (after the thirteenth year), they would receive basic vocational training as provided by the Basic Vocational Training Year (BGJ). However, even then, employers and their associations and the CDU/CSU[12] (Christian Democrats) rejected decidedly the idea of a 'comprehensive' tenth school year.

The rejection of 'academic schooling' in favour of 'economically oriented basic training for the more practical minded young people' (a recommendation by both the Institut der Deutschen Wirtschaft[13] (DIW) and the Minister for Education and the Arts for Baden-Württemberg and Rheinland-Pfalz,[14] already appeared as catchphrases in the conservative education reforms of the mid-1970s. Employer's associations classed the increasing problem of youth unemployment more and more often as a one of young people being 'not sufficiently motivated' and sometimes as being 'unwilling to learn'.[15]

The educational crisis led the Socio Liberal government to make three compromises which were of great importance to the subsequent development of the tenth school year. Under pressure from employers and the CDU/CSU they were eventually implemented:

1   In 1976 labour market policies and financial pressures took over from socio-educational arguments as the reason for an additional school year. 'Feasible and cheap reforms for the transition stage from school to employment' now became the catchphrase for new reforms.

2   As the integration of the comprehensive school as secondary school

for all was blocked by several of the Bundesländer and after extending again and again its 'experimental status' the idea of a unified secondary school system was dropped ('postponed'). The tenth school year that was to be incorporated into the comprehensive system was now to become an extension to the mainschool.

3   The third 'compromise' was to shift the tenth school year to *vocationally oriented* institutions. The tenth school year, in the sense of offering an extension to general education, had thus become the only alternative to the Vocational Preparatory Year (BVJ) and the Basic Vocational Training Year (BGJ).

This development resulted in barely concealable contradictions between Socio Liberal and union programmatics and those that were politically realistic with regards to the tenth school year. Socio Liberal demands were for a tenth school year for all pupils under the postulates of uniformity, equality and interchangeability within the education programme. But as the crisis in the educational system became more acute and the employment situation more desperate, inequality and a hierarchical set-up formed the background for the transition stage from school to employment: *Under the common seal of 'Tenth Educational Year' more and more pupils were being graded and reoriented before the start of any kind of vocational training.*
The following overview will show how the various measures with regard to the Tenth Educational Year are being individually implemented.

How Is the Federal Institute for Employment Helped by the Measures?

Vocational preparatory measures for the young unemployed are nothing new. Already in the 1960s the employment exchanges offered courses to young people who were unsuccessful in securing a training place — despite the great number of free training places at the time. They were unsuccessful 'because employers rejected them as vocationally immature'.[16]
The character of these measures changed drastically, however, with the fast rise of youth unemployment and the lack of training places. The number of course participants tripled in only two years: whereas in the educational year 1973/74 the number was 13,905, by 1975/76 it had reached 38,838. With the introduction of vocational preparatory schemes (especially the BVJ) numbers dropped steadily but rose again when measures were introduced to integrate young foreign people (MBSE), to over 30,000 by the end of the 1970s. (Table 4 at the end of the chapter will give a clearer picture of the quantitative development of the various measures.)
Courses which were introduced as a result of the AFG[17] 'legislation to promote employment) are being financed by the Federal Institute for Employment (BA) and implemented by independent organizations (associations, the Church, employers' associations, unions, private schools, etc.). Here it is important to differentiate between *six types of measures*, varying in their aims and therefore also in content and method.
Supportive Courses (F-Lehrgänge); courses to improve integration

(LVE); basic training courses (G-Lehrgänge) G1, G2, G3; and measures to aid vocational and social integration of young foreigners (MBSE).

The *Supportive Courses* are, according to the criteria of the Federal Institute for Employment, intended for those youngsters who 'are neither physically nor mentally ready for vocational training but who would eventually, by attending these courses, reach the required level of maturity'.[18]

Participants are introduced, if possible, into five different areas of vocation 'by means of 'practical work instruction' courses of four to six weeks. During the third part of the course one vocational area will be identified for future training and instruction in that area intensified'.[19]

In these courses the importance of obtaining so-called extra-functional qualifications in areas such as 'responsibility, care, punctuality, consistency, ability to take stress, order, cleanliness etc.' is particularly stressed.[20]

The *Courses to Improve Integration (LVE)* quite definitely begin a 'step lower' than the Supportive Courses. They are intended for young school-leavers 'who will probably not be able to cope with the demands of vocational training and who are not ready for the transition into employment — that is to say, an occupation in a workshop for handicapped people — but who may well become so'.[21]

These courses are intended mainly for school-leavers from special schools and mainschools without leaving certificates, to prepare them for 'simple vocational occupations'. Accordingly the 'instruction curriculum ... contents are to be carefully directed towards actual availability of such occupations'.[22]

In a brochure published by the Labour Exchange Frankfurt for school leavers 1983, it is said, very simply, that the LVE 'in general prepares young people for future occupation'.[23]

The *Basic Training Courses* were introduced in 1974 and are divided into three different groups, the G1, G2 and G3 courses.

The *G1 course* is intended for school leavers 'who are not able to pursue their hoped for vocation because of lack of suitable training places' but who have reached the required level of maturity for employment.[24]

This course basically duplicates the first year of Vocational Training but — unlike the BGJ — is not taken into account against any possible vocational training period later.

The *G2 courses* were intended for school leavers 'whose applications for training places are refused because of their unsatisfactory school results'.[25]

Instead of attempting to rectify these deficiencies the courses were planned 'to instruct participants mainly in practical skills in such areas as may later offer employment or training places on the local job market'.[26]

The G2 courses were abandoned in 1982.

The *G3 courses*, in number the most significant of the Basic Training Courses, make their intentions even more obvious. Their definition is to offer courses 'for unemployed young people who — irrespective of any decisive factors — are classed as unsuitable for vocational training.'[27]

Those attending are instructed in 'practical vocational skills' and are taught basic 'knowledge of conduct, industrial health and safety standards'[28] which, as F. Braun points out, may at best increase their immediate suitability for employment.[29]

The most recent pre-vocational measures are those introduced by the

Federal Institute for Employment to encourage vocational and social integration of young foreigners (MBSE). They were introduced in 1979 with that particular group in mind and have as their official aim 'increasing the likelihood of securing a training place or employment and are designed to provide vocational instruction, skills instruction, teaching of language and general education'.[30]

The focus though is on vocational preparation (100 hours = 60 per cent). Youngsters should acquire knowledge of three different vocational areas.

The MBSE is of special importance to young foreigners since, after completing such as course, they are issued with a work permit.

Vocational Preparation — Terminological Juggling?

It will already have become apparent that the term 'vocational preparatory measures' is misleading, at least for part of the courses provided.

In reality — as their definition, aims and course curricula show — a great number of young people are being prepared for either skilled or unskilled occupations. A survey of the Bundesinstitut für Berufsbildung (BIBB)[31] shows that in 19 per cent of the Supportive Courses (F-Courses) and 65 per cent of the Courses to Improve Integration (LVE) 'according to the respective directors of the schemes, young people are being mainly prepared for unskilled occupations'.[32] It is only too apparent what the career prospects are for those young people: a steadily growing number do not receive vocational qualifications after a year's course and are then either employed as unskilled workers or become unemployed.

Young people within the MBSE programme are most affected by this. In 1980/81, 11 per cent secured a training place, 33 per cent employment and 43 per cent became unemployed[33] Despite all the various measures introduced by the Federal Institute the number gaining recognized training contracts dropped steadily from 61 per cent in 1971/72 to a mere 21 per cent in 1980/81.[34] *That means that more than three-quarters of the annual number of almost 50,000 young people taking part in one of the various schemes have to face a downgrading to unskilled worker or unemployment.*

Privatization and Competition among Agencies

All measures so far described are carried out by independent agencies under guidance from the Federal Institute. The local Labour Exchange then handles the allocations for the various courses. It is rare to find, in any one place, all of the different courses available and young people are, irrespective of their individual needs, assigned to courses which happen to be available in that particular area. In addition, it is barely conceivable that labour exchanges would be in a position, after only a short interview 'to fit youngsters into the categories "suitable for training" or "unsuitable for training"'.[35]

Besides this often arbitrary way of selecting and assigning young people to the various courses, disturbing tendencies are becoming more and more apparent among some of the organizers. For them the implementation of such measures has already beome a reliable source of income — their efforts are geared towards gain. This has become even more critical since 1981, when allocation of the various measures went on principle to the lowest bidder, irrespective of qualitative considerations. Employers' associations, private schools and established organizers by far out-run other bidders in the competition. First, they usually already have fully equipped workshops financed by the Federal Institute for Employment when funds were still readily available. Secondly, they often work with low paid personnel (i.e. unemployed teachers), and their savings in salaries are considerable compared with other organizations. Thirdly, they have managed to establish a special relationship with the Labour Exchanges over recent years.

All these factors lead to a secure monopolization by certain organizations.

More and more often small organizations and representatives who have to rely on self-help are left standing. Without 'friends in court' they have no voice, and yet, it is they who usually have more immediate contact with young people and show integrity in their pedagogical achievements.

As the possibilities for Labour Exchanges to control the quality of courses are extremely limited and in practice rarely taken advantage of, it is not surprising then that this leads to misuse.

The Union for Education and Sciences is obviously also of that opinion as the following extract from an article from the *Frankfurter Rundschau* (19 March 1983) will show:

GEW[36] Against Privatization of Vocational Education

Getting Young Workers Without Paying for Them

Taking as example the 'measures to improve social and vocational integration of young foreigners' (MBSE), the GEW representative Albert Schobbe made clear at Friday's press conference in Frankfurt, that his union was opposed to the 'obvious privatisation' of the vocational education sector. According to Schobbe the MBSE is a perfect example of how enterprises exploit the present educational crisis to their own ends.

The most dubious outcome for the GEW is that the very same employers who shirked successfully from making available training places could now cash in on public financing while filling their vacancies with young people they don't have to pay for. That this is lucrative is obvious from the intensive advertising by the Educational Association of Employers in Hessen, who tried, by writing to schools, to 'redirect' pupils away from the tenth school year and into joining the private workshops.

Once there, so it is feared by the GEW, and young people firmly in the hands of the employers, no public control measures can protect them from being at the mercy of totally unsuitable instructors and firms who may very well have been established for the very purpose of creaming off public money.

At the next meeting of union representatives in Friedberg next

Thursday the GEW in Hessen intends to set in motion an offensive against the privatisation of vocational education.

The Basic Vocational Training Year (BGJ) — Adjusted to Suit Labour Market Conditions

The Basic Vocational Training Year (BGJ) — also called Basic Vocational Schoolyear — became a focal point for the vocational education reforms.[37]

It was — according to the structures proposed by the Educational Council — to follow a tenth general education school year and offer, in terms of schooling, vocational instruction on a wide basis. The BGJ became thus an important link between vocational preparation/choice of vocation on the one side and specialized vocational training in the dual system on the other. The essential aims of the initial reforms were:

- to make it easier to decide on a vocation by 'staggering' the choice,'
- despecialization of the first part of vocational education (aim: basic education with regards to vocational areas);
- an integration of general education and vocational content.

This would ensure a more flexible and long-term usability of qualifications and that skilled workers would be employed within their field of interests. Since the decision by the Bund-Länder-Kommission in 1976 to expand the BGJ to 120,000 places by 1982, it has become the most important of all the vocational schemes.

However, the aims and content of the BGJ contradicted, right from the start, the vocational training interests of individual firms. In particular, the instruction in wider vocational fields and its basic qualifications and the expansion of a general education under the state's supervision (at a TC) met with bitter opposition. To fight this, firms rallied all their powers under the slogan 'against the undermining of the proven dual system and turning vocational training into academical courses' — and the question whether the BGJ was *acceptable in any way* became the main point of all discussions.

Although the Ministers of Education and the Arts decided in 1973 in a general agreement concerning conditions of employment that young people, after attending the BGJ, should be taken straight into the second year of a vocational training contract, a great number of firms refused to take the one year of Basic Vocational Training (BGJ) into account. By 1978 this had the following effect: in most vocational areas only half of the BGJ counted towards the training period. At the same time basic instruction in the wider field of vocations was narrowed down, therefore reducing the areas of choice. Meanwhile the situation has become so serious that most of the young people give up any claim, after having completed the BGJ, for the year to be taken into account — in order to get a training place. This means that in practice young people choose to leave without a leaving certificate, often before the end of the year, or they may choose a training place in an area other than that which the BGJ had prepared them for — in both cases forfeiting any claim for the year to be taken into account. The simplest way though, seems to be not to mention at all to the potential employer that a BGJ has been attended.

Volker Koditz

Today, the BGJ can rightly be called an *'example of the reversal of the intentions of education policies'*[38] Increasingly, young people attend the BGJ only because they cannot find a training place and because the extension of compulsory schooling forces them to complete a Tenth Educational Year. The main problem for the success of the BGJ lies in the lack of training places as there is no guarantee of specialist training in the dual system as a follow-up to the BGJ and so young people are once more forced to search for training places. Although many young people give up readily any claim for the BGJ to be taken into account, less and less are able to find a training place after completing the BGJ. The BGJ — originally thought of as a forward looking step towards qualitative improvement of the whole vocational education system has, *with increased youth unemployment, become a stop-gap in the dual system.*

In addition to the BGJ in its 'scholastic' form, there still exists in various Bundesländer, the so-called cooperative Basic Vocational Training Year (BGJ-k). This was created on the initiative of industry and commerce and is conducted within the dual system of vocational training. Young people complete the practical part of their training in firms and in addition generally attend a technical college twice a week.

The BGJ-k was obviously created in competition with the BGJ. As it provides an even narrower basic vocational education (in 'vocational fields') than the 'scholastic' BGJ, it is able to meet the qualification demands for individual or branch specified vocations. Usually, even before they start attending the BGJ-k, young people have to decide on one or a few closely connected occupations and there is even less question of the ability to choose from the wider field of occupations than with the BGJ. When looking through the various occupational areas the BGJ-k offers it becomes apparent that there is a proportionally high increase in two-year training contracts producing inferior qualifications. The major share of the BGJ-k is taken up within the 'Textile and Clothing Industry' the 'Building and Wood Industry' and the 'Metal Industry'.

The great advantage of the BGJ-k is that it offers contracts to young people for the whole of their training period i.e. also for their specialist training. However, firms are only then obliged to retain young people for the second year if they have successfully completed the BGJ-k. In terms of numbers compared with the BGJ-s, the BGJ-k is of less importance, although it predominates in individual industrial regions and Bundesländer.

In 1981/82, 94,245 pupils attended the BGJ and of that number 16,695 were in the BGJ-k. One can forecast a further increase during the next few years because of the rising lack of training places. (See figure 1 illustrating the development.)

No national survey has been made to give proportional evidence of the transition from the BGJ into training. One can assume though, that in 1982 the majority of those who successfully completed the BGJ managed to find a training place. Since then the situation has become drastically worse: *in practice, at least half of the young people who have completed the BGJ find themselves on the street.*

Figure 1: Development of both types of the Vocational Training Years

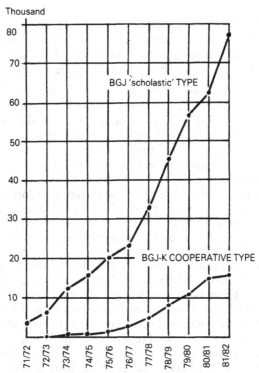

The Vocational Preparatory Year (BVJ) — The Grey Area of Unskilled Worker Production

Since 1975 technical colleges have offered the so-called Vocational Preparatory Year (BVJ). In some of the Bundesländer it is possible for youngsters without training to combine the BVJ partly with the Tenth Educational Year — an alternative way of completing the extended compulsory schooling period. (More details of the regulations in individual Bundesländer appear in the appendix.)

At a conference on 6 September 1973 held by the Ministers of Education and the Arts, a general agreement on conditions of employment led eventually to the so-called 'Special Version' (Sonderform) of the Basic Vocational Training Year for specified target groups. Within it special provision is to be made 'for young people for whom a Basic Vocational Training Year would be lacking in content . . .'[38]

With growing youth unemployment though the BVJ's objectives changed. Both the Federal Ministry for Education and Sciences and also employers originally defined the BVJ as a preparatory measure for vocational training. By compensating for general educational weaknesses of pupils who complete their main or special schooling without a leaving certificate, it was intended to make integration into the dual system or rather the Basic Vocational Training Year possible. Officially the aim is still the same today.

The Labour Exchange Frankfurt writes in its pamphlet issued for school leavers in 1983.

> The Vocational Preparatory Year is intended to further pupils to the point where they can recognize their vocational potential and abilities and are able to start training or are able to attend the Basic Vocational Training Year with reasonable expectations for success.[39]

However objectives have shifted long ago. Already in 1976 the Department for Education and Social Sciences of the Employers' Associations in West Germany demanded that the special forms of the Basic Vocational Training Year, i.e. the BVJ, 'should not be part of basic vocational training but rather be pre-vocational — that is to say, vocational preparatory measures of very elementary level which cannot, in many cases, be counted towards specific vocational training'.[40] The Ministry for Education and the Arts of Rheinland Pfalz finalized the BVJ's changed objective by formulating it as: 'the minimum objective of the Special Form of the Basic Vocational Training Year is for participants to reach a level where they are able to 'earn their living'. It is therefore most important to provide instruction in basic practical skills which relate to a wide occupational field'.[41]

In Bayern the BVJ is known under the name of Basic Vocational Training Year for Young Workers' (BGJJ) and in Bremen as 'Occupation Preparation Year' (AVJ). Such formulations make the shift in objectives very clear. No longer is the BVJ intended as an *introduction* or *preparation* to vocation but rather as a *substitute* for vocational education. This is made even clearer by its curriculum content which is geared towards the qualification requirements of unskilled workers. Virtues like 'staying power', order and diligence are on top of the list of the re-oriented BVJ. Although the teaching of such content has been shown to be extremely difficult — pupils are 'tired of school' and not easy to motivate — there is no doubt that the official intention is to keep the BVJ as a 'tool' to turn out unskilled workers. Again this is made evident by yet another 're-arrangement' of regulations: To enable industry to make optimal use of 16 and 17 year old unskilled workers 'on offer' all the Bundesländer meanwhile implement the three years of 'compulsory' attendance at a technical college in a very relaxed and flexible manner. Young people who have no training place after completing the BVJ are automatically or on request released from the compulsory attendance at a technical college (see appendix).

Already in 1978 the IG Metall[42] claimed that legislators 'in individual cases give in to pressure by employers for cheap and readily disposable unskilled workers'.[43] Meanwhile, there can be no more question though of individual cases. At present 50,000 young people attend the BVJ and the number is steadily rising (compare table 2 for quantitative development).

Although there are no exact figures available for the transition into a training situation everything seems to point to young people's chances being pretty low. By 1976 the Ministry for Education and the Arts concluded with regards to the re-orientation of the BVJ: 'The success rate for a meaningful integration into working life is about 80 to 90 per cent ... the major part end up in some secondary occupation in the production or service industry'.[44]

In an estimate for the year 1979/80 the BIBB suggests that half of the young people leaving the BVJ go straight into being employed as young unskilled workers, 30 per cent actually find a training place and that 20 per cent continue with the BGJ or attend a technical college for specific vocational instruction.[45] These numbers are now out of date. At present one has to assume that no more than 10 per cent of young people having completed the BVJ succeed in securing a training place.

The BVJ becomes even more problematical because of the stigma that is attached to those attending it. Whereas the BVJ was initially intended for 'school leavers without mainschool leaving certificate' it now caters for 'educationally disturbed young people', youngsters who are 'unfit for training' or even 'handicapped'; this shift seems to repeat itself within other vocational preparatory measures organized and financed by the Federal Institute for Employment:

> 'The Vocational Preparatory Year admits young people who ... because of physical and/or mental development are not capable of entering into a vocational training situation.'[46]
> 'The first objective of the special form of the Vocational Preparatory Year is to try to make employable young people who are educationally disturbed or handicapped.'[47]

The BVJ's lack of prospects and its stigmatization has natural consequences in every day school life: numerous teachers and academics talk about the daily experiences with the BVJ as bringing extreme pressures to teachers and students and over-burdening them. Even an official investigation initiated by the Federal Government and the Land Nordrhein-Westfalen comes to this shattering conclusion. '... one could not say that the 'Year' had been a success', and worse than that 'we are talking about a pedagogical catastrophy with as yet unknown consequences'.[48]

The Tenth Mainschool Year — Improved Chances?

The Tenth Mainschool Year came into being — as described at the beginning of this chapter — when a tenth school year was requested within the comprehensive school system. Right from the beginning, the CDU controlled Länder and also the employers' associations had protested against this request which was presented as part of the overall educational policies of 1973. The tenth school year for *all* made way for the Tenth Education Year.

The form the Tenth Educational Year may take varies within the Federal Länder. The tenth year can be completed either at a Mainschool, at a technical college or there may be a choice between either mainschool or technical college. It often is only obligatory for those pupils who, after their ninth year at school have not yet found a training place (regulations of the various Federal Länder in the appendix). In Hessen, for example, the Tenth Educational Year can by choice be completed either at a technical college (BGJ, BVJ) or as a tenth year at the mainschool.

The Labour Exchange Frankfurt writes:

> The tenth year at the mainschool offers the possibility to extend general education for young people who have completed their main

schooling but who have not yet found a training place and who want to continue to improve their general education. The focus here is on practical instruction (i.e. Job Related Training/Polytechnik) and an intensive preparation for working life and adulthood.[49]

The *Hessische Teacher Journal*[50] made the following comments to the introduction of Tenth Mainschool Year:

> What is supposed to be taught in the tenth? The eighth school year is an extension to the seventh, the ninth an extension to the eighth and now the tenth is to extend the ninth? It cannot be done that way. We desperately need a new concept for education after the seventh schoolyear. Without that, what good is the availability of a tenth? Our mainschool is not equipped to teach anything but reading and writing — vocational preparation — don't make me laugh![51]

The Tenth Mainschool Year is especially criticized for its so obvious selection techniques. In Nordrhein-Westfalen there are now graded leaving certificates A and B awarded after the Tenth Mainschool Year.

Already in the ninth year 'good' pupils receive special attention in the form of 'intensified instruction' (especially in foreign languages) which then allows their selection into Set A of the Tenth Mainschool Year. This grading then leads to a leaving certificate of higher qualification than the general leaving certificate. The level reached after the tenth year for Set B corresponds more to the old Ninth Mainschool leaving certificate — Set B being intended for the low ability pupils. In Hessen pupils have a further choice. They can complete their Tenth Mainschool Year at either 'Secondary Modern Level' or the 'Extended Mainschool Level' and receive equivalent leaving certificates or as Set B suggests with the 'old Ninth Mainschool leaving certificate'.

The GEW–Berlin protested against this further discrimination within the Mainschool:

> With regard to social integration the most detrimental pedagogical measure is that, true to the idea of selection, the weaker pupils are separated from those who are believed to be academically more able.[52]

What this means in real terms to pupils is described here by a researcher in education from Lower Saxony:

> A repeated selection of academically stronger pupils for the tenth year at 'Secondary Modern Level' leads already in the ninth year at the Mainschool to competition and pressures on achievement ... The victims are the 'simple' Mainschool pupils who 'don't make it' or are left behind — they feel like nothing on earth — failures because they were either too stupid or had been too lazy.[53]

Over 80,000 pupils attend nationwide the Tenth Mainschool Year (see table 2 for quantitative development). Figures for successful transition into a training situation are not yet available. Until the beginning of the eighties half of those having completed the tenth year could count on a training place. Since then the situation has worsened. Reports of experiences show that attending

(Bubble: 'To be able to assess you all fairly, we ask you all to undergo the same test: please climb the tree!')

(Picture: Free Enterprise welcomes the young generation.)

the Tenth Mainschool Year at best improves chances of a training place for those who were able to complete it with the 'higher qualifications' (extended mainschool certificate etc).

An Overview of the Pre-vocational Education System

After the relatively detailed presentation of the individual measures to extend schooling, that is to say vocational preparatory measures with regard to the Tenth Educational Year, the following will look at the pre-vocational education system as a whole.

First a diagram showing the quantitative development of the various measures:

Table 2: Quantitative Development of the pre-vocational education system

Year	Type of Measure		10th Main-school Y.	BA Courses	Total
	BGJ s/k	BVJ			
73/74	12.616	4 516		12.967	30.099
74/75	17.108	6.145		23.606	46.859
75/76	21.546	13.030		35.934	70.510
76/77	25.757	24.751		34.553	85.061
77/78	37.904	29.541	33.004	31.777	132.226
78/79	52.993	44.797	38.012	27.276	163.078
79/80	67.305	48.854	42.935	38.769	197.863
80/81	77.960	46.091	57.598	33.963	215.612
81/82	94.245	46.582	82.841	35.100	258.768

Source: The figures are taken from the yearly 'Vocational Education News' published by the BMBW (BVJ; BVJ), the monthly 'Official News' published by the Federal Institute for Employment and the 'Statistical Publications of the Ministers of Education and the Arts Conference'.

It becomes apparent from the table that the number of young people making use of the extended schooling, or rather the vocational preparatory measures, has, from 1973 (before the onset of youth unemployment) until the early 1950s increased ten-fold. From the approximately 700,000 young school leavers at secondary school level I[54] (Special School, 9 years at Mainschool or Secondary Modern) who apply for training places nearly 300,000 are simply being sent to school for another year or rather to attend one of the vocational preparatory courses. If one takes the proportional average of those who succeed with the transition into a training situation as a basis for individual measures then one can roughly estimate that only a third (perhaps more after the BGJ and the Tenth Mainschool Year, but considerably less after one of the Federal Institute's measures or the BVJ) will in this roundabout way still manage to secure a training place within the dual system. That means in other words that at present — and this is steadily increasing — nearly 200,000 young people leave school and are unable to gain any further vocational qualifications. *Every fourth youngster who leaves school after reaching secondary school Level I and who does not continue with further full-time secondary education, (i.e. grammar*

Figure 2:   The pre-vocational education system and the transition figures of those who attend

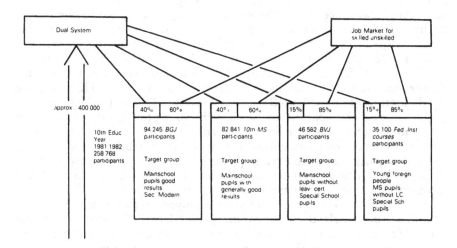

Secondary School level i
Approximately 700.000 youngsters leave each year with secondary school level 1 without
continuing with secondary schooling, that is to say that they are looking for training places
within the dual system
Approximately 400.000 secure a training place more or less immediately. The remainder is
placed, as illustrated into the various vocational preparatory and school extending schemes

*school or full-time vocational training) is, without participation in the dual system of
the apprenticeship scheme, downgraded to unskilled worker.*

The above diagram makes this more coherent. To make the system
explicit it had to be somewhat simplified and generalized. In practice it is
much more complicated and presents young people who are faced with the
task of finding their way through with something that looks like a veritable
labyrinth of measures. It begins with the fact that regulations with regard to
the Tenth Educational Year vary from Bundesland to Bundesland. In addition,
although individual measures are offered to certain target groups (compare
diagram), they are not always available as alternatives. In practice young
people often end up in a scheme that happens to be available in their area or
where there happen to be vacancies.

There is also a possibility to attend some of the courses consecutively. For
example, more and more young people change over from the BVJ to the BGJ.
This, though would not fall within the compulsory schooling period of the
Tenth Educational Year but be voluntary. For some young people this may be

the only alternative to being unemployed or their last hope of eventually securing a training place.

A further point which makes the pre-vocational education system even more complex is 'selection', whereby varying qualifications are being awarded; so for example after the Tenth Mainschool Year where pupils may aim either for the secondary modern leaving certificate or the extended mainschool leaving certificate. Some of the schemes designed by the Federal Institute for Employment offer courses that also lead to a mainschool leaving certificate. In a similar way after successfully completing the BGJ and in some of the Länder after the BVJ mainschool qualifications may be granted.

Further confusion is caused by the various distinctions of the schemes themselves. Hessen for example has, for the education year 1982/83 divided the BVJ into BVJ-A and BVJ-B courses. The BVJ-B though, which offers no qualifications at all, seems to cater mainly for young foreigners. Finally, there is the most recent substitute for vocational-training with resulting qualifications and possible employment namely one year of 'work experience'. The aim of this particular scheme by employers, is to offer young people who at the age of 18 have not yet found a training place or who are unemployed 'temporary insight in and experience of working life in general'[55]

This probationary year for young unemployed people seems to have been imported from England, where young people have been working on this scheme for years, without guaranteed wages or employment being guaranteed. In practice, the 'work experience' year is just another path through the maze and does not lead to qualifications or employment. As most young people, by the time they reach 18, will have completed one of the various pre-vocational courses the 'work experience' scheme (which is an employers' initiative) can only have two aims. Firstly, to cover up the hopeless prospects for an increasing number of young unemployed. Under this scheme they disappear for a whole year from any unemployment statistics. Secondly employers gain under the label of 'work experience' cheap labour together with the possibility of further selection after the year is completed: young people may complete their year of work experience and then — as a reward — be perhaps employed as an unskilled worker.

This evaluation of the 'work experience' scheme is not 'unqualified' as the various guidelines under which it is implemented will demonstrate. Offers for 'work experience' places are made by employers on condition that:

— all costs are met by the Federal Institute for Employers;
— employers will not be committed to offer employment after the year;
— no detailed job description for the year has to be given.

To the last point employers quite openly made the following comment 'detailed job descriptions would be totally unpractical for a "work experience" scheme and would not meet the individual needs of young people'.[56] The IG Metall[57] comments on the 'work experience' year: 'This initiative by employers is a long term way of getting round the policies for a training place and qualifications for all . . .'[58]

A 'Career' in Schemes within the Labyrinth of the Tenth Educational Year

When speaking of a labyrinth of measures then this does not only refer to the multitude of confusing versions of the vocational preparatory schemes. In practice, more and more young people are 'cheated out' of any hope; once they have accomplished the tasks that are set for them during their vocational preparatory year they are often once again advised by respective institutions to consider yet another form of vocational preparatory measures. For example, should young people after successfully completing the Vocational Preparatory Year not find a training place then they are frequently moved on to the Basic Vocational Training Year — again without any guarantee that a training place would follow. This kind of 'shunting yard' where young people are pushed from one scheme to another destroys any kind of concept of a 'vocational future'. Teachers of the various schemes of the Tenth Educational Year often report that their pupils learn one thing quickly and that is that their individual efforts — successes like gaining the mainschool leaving certificate or mastering basic vocational skills — are of no use: at the end there are always better qualified applicants for jobs or training places.

Although this disillusion continues more young people attend at present several of these schemes one after the other. Often it is not the hope for a training place at the end but rather the fear of being unemployed — the reaction of their parents relatives or contemporaries. Teachers from technical colleges and social workers describe the unbelievable 'careers' of individual pupils. Official reports or figures are not available though.

We have chosen as examples the histories of two pupils from a small town in Northern Hessen and would like to illustrate their paths through the maze of compulsory schooling, its extension, and the various vocational preparatory measures.

A technical college lecturer describes Erika's and Bernd's careers.

A Long Way Round to the Supermarket

Erika, at 15 completes mainschool with good results (2.00 = B). Influenced by her sister, who is five years older, and who works in an insurance company nearby, she would like to make her career in business or commerce. As she lives in a rural district she is prepared to travel daily 30 km to the next town for her training. Her sister advertises for her three times in the local paper. Erika sends twenty-four applications, always with negative results. Many firms point out to her that she would need at least 'secondary modern level' or some basic vocational knowledge for her to begin training.

As Erika has not been able to find a training place by the start of the summer holidays, she now has to attend the tenth compulsory year. She would prefer to do this as a Tenth Mainschool Year, hoping that she might get her Secondary Modern Leaving Certificate — but in her catchment area there is no Tenth Mainschool Year available. In the whole of Hessen there are altogether only 1000 places.

Erika is now forced to complete the Tenth Educational Year in one of the schemes offered by the Technical College. As her results from the mainschool are good she is accepted for the BGJ. She is also lucky as they offer her a course in 'Commerce and Administration'. Faint hopes for a future career as 'Industrie-Kaufman/frau'[59] rise again.

She works diligently during the year and completes second best. Already, while attending the BGJ, she applies for training places but without success. Under pressure from her parents and now also from her sister she applies for places in vocational fields other than 'hers'. through personal contacts of her mother's she finally gets a training place as 'sales assistant' in a local supermarket. She has to though — and this is made quite clear to her — forfeit any claim for the BGJ to be deducted from her training period. Erika has to — at 17 with basic knowledge in 'commerce and administration' — complete the full training period as a sales assistant.

Compared with other people in her village she has been lucky, although she had never wanted to train in that particular area at all.

Vocationally Trained to Become an Unskilled Worker

Bernd and Erika went to school together. For several years he had lived in a home — his parents are divorced — but during the last years at mainschool he lived with his father and stepmother. While at school his conduct had caused great problems and he only just managed to complete school with a certificate. Teachers though admitted that he was very able but did not always apply himself nor show the right level of interest. That he was indeed able became apparent through his hobby as a radio enthusiast. Here he also found recognition among his school friends. Having only just 'scraped' through school he is not able to find a training place. He has to complete the Tenth Educational Year in BVJ where the vocational field assigned to him is 'metal processing'.

Although Bernd is not able to improve greatly his shortcomings, especially in mathematics, because of the catastrophical class conditions thirty-nine pupils and only fifteen workshop places) — he learns from his every-day school life that: he has to give up his dream of becoming a radio or television technician. Both teachers and parents explain to him how hopeless it is to hang onto that dream.

The Labour Exchange suggests that he should in addition attend the BGJ. Bernd though feels aggressive towards school and prefers to be unemployed rather than to spend one more year at school with still the same outcomes — no prospects. Bernd's situation becomes public through a newspaper article. The firm that employs his father promises to help. He is offered a place as unskilled worker in the building yard — under the condition that Bernd asks for release from the CATC (Compulsory Attendance at a Technical College). As this is no problem in Hessen (compare appendix) Bernd gets his place.

He is 17 years old, has attended school for ten years, is a radio enthusiast and now an unskilled worker in a building yard without vocational qualifications and without any prospects.

On a Skewer

'. . . the GEW tells me how much apprentice wage I have to give you. One of the reasons why so many of you young people are not able to find training places is that this wage is very high.

But continue to apply yourself at school. Make yourself known at the Labour Exchange. Look at newspaper advertisements and listen round. Why not advertise yourselves — and don't give up straight away. All that is good does not come easily you have to work for it. I wish you luck . . .'

> This is a letter the firm
> 'Metallbau Scriot Schweissfachbetrieb'
> Munchen wrote in answer to approximately
> forty applications for a training place.

Published in the *Frankfurter Rundschau*, 19 April 1983.

APPENDIX

Regulations concerning compulsory attendance at Vocational Institutions (CATC) in the 'Länder' of the Federal Republic of Germany.

Baden-Württemberg

The 'ruling concerning the length and completion of the CATC' of 4 December 1981 states under 11.5:

> Pupils who have attended a full-time vocational School for at least one year or who have completed the first stage of full-time training are released from CATC . . .

This means that, anyone who has not, after the BVJ or the BGJ, found a training place, does not need to attend a vocational training institution, in other words is available on the job market as unskilled labour.

Bayern

The 'law concerning compulsory schooling' states in its revised version of 3 September 1982 under section II, article 14 (2):

> Attendance at a Vocational Training Institution is no longer compulsory if the Education Authority concludes that further attendance is unnecessary because of previous vocational schooling. This applies especially to young people who have previously — voluntarily — attended, and successfully completed one of the special forms of the Basic Vocational Training Measures for young employees . . .

This means: that if an employer will only take on a young person as unskilled worker under the condition that he or she does not attend a vocational training institution, the Education Authority will conclude that the young person concerned no longer needs to attend a vocational training institution.

Rheinland-Pfalz

The 'law concerning schooling in Rheinland-Pfalz' of 6 November 1974 states in Article 48(2), 3:

'Released from further schooling are those who ... having successfully completed the Basic Vocational School Year or the 10th schoolyear at a Mainschool, Secondary Modern or at a Grammar School, and who are not engaged in a vocational training situation.'

The Basic Vocational School Year is in effect the BGJ and includes automatically the BVJ as special form of the BGJ.
Further in Article 48 (2), 4:

Also released are those who are, in the opinion of the Educational Authorities, sufficiently educated.

Saarland

The compulsory schooling law in Saarland states:

4   From CATC released are those young people who, having regularly attended the BGJ or its special form, the BVJ, at a Vocational School or at another institution recognized by the State as being of equal status and who are not engaged in a vocational training situation ...

Schleswig-Holstein

The 'law concerning schooling in Schleswig-Holstein' of 2 August 1978 states in Article 41, 3-4:

The CATC ends before the in Article 40 stated period (i.e. age of majority) when the concerned ...
3. has successfully completed the BGJ, or another full-time school year at a Vocational Training Institution, or has completed any other full-time course recognized by the Ministry of Education and the Arts as being equivalent and is not engaged in a vocational training situation.
4. is, according to the Education Authorities, sufficiently educated.

Berlin

The compulsory schooling period in Berlin is ten years. The 'revised law concerning schooling Berlin' of 20 August 1980 determines to whom the CATC applies. Article 14 (2) states:

'Those who after general compulsory schooling are not engaged in a vocational training situation according to the Vocational Training Regulations, or who are not in employment or are continuing with higher secondary education, are obliged to attend — in their 11th year — a Basic Vocational Training Course ...'

This means: Young people who cannot secure a training place, either become unskilled workers without any right to further education or have to continue schooling for an additional year (by attending the BGJ).

Bremen

The 'law concerning schooling in Bremen' of 4 October 1982 states in its ruling on CATC for young people without a training place (Article 35):

(4) Compulsory schooling ends for young people who have success-fully completed a vocational training course according to Article 17, 5 (meant here are the BGJ, BVJ or other vocational preparatory measures introduced by the Employment Authorities) or a full-time course lasting at least 2 years.

Hamburg

Article 27 of the schooling laws of 17 October 1977 for Hamburg states succinctly:

(4)   The Education Authorities can, in individual cases, release from compulsory schooling
3.   young people without training contract;
4.   young people having completed a course at a full-time vocational school (Berufsfachschule);
5.   foreign or stateless young people.

Hessen

The law concerning compulsory vocational schooling of 30 August 1978 states under Article 2(2) and (3):

(2)   Young people who are not engaged in a training situation according to the regulations concerning vocational training, can, on

request, be released from CATC if proof of a minimum of eleven years of schooling can be given. The decision whether to release young people from CATC is to be made by the Head of the appropriate Vocational Training Institute.

(3) If the under section 2 stated conditions (i.e. eleven years of general schooling) are not met, the local Education Authorities decide (preserving the right to revoke this decision), whether in individual cases previous schooling justifies an early release from further compulsory schooling. Here age and social conditions of the young people are to be considered.

This means: that in Hessen, too, young people without training contracts are, after having completed their tenth (compulsory) schoolyear, released from CATC if they can, only under that condition, secure employment as unskilled workers.

Niedersachsen

The Act of 27 February 1980 with regard to 'the introduction of a one-year full-time training course for young people without training contracts as from 1 August 1980' states:

1. All young people who from the end of the schoolyear 1979/80 onwards
   — are being released from school and
   — have not completed their 12 years of general compulsory schooling and
   — who are not directly engaged in a training situation, have to complete a further part of their compulsory schooling by attending a full-time vocational course for at least one year. Young people who leave school at the end of schoolyear 1979/80 or later can only apply for employment after having completed general compulsory schooling or after at least one further year of full-time vocational training.

This can be interpreted that compulsory vocational schooling can be met by attending the BGJ or the BVJ.

Nordrhein-Westfalen

In the 'revised version of the Compulsory Schooling Law' of 2 February 1980, Article 11 states:

(3) Compulsory vocational schooling ends
   b) when, after 11 years of schooling, the concerned has completed a one-year, full-time course at a vocational school or an equivalent vocational training course at a recognized institution and is not under training contract with an employer.

(4) CATC also ends before the in section 1 and 2 stated period (18th

year of age or after completing vocational training) if the Minister of Education or the by him lawfully authorized Education Authority concludes that previous schooling makes further attendance at a Vocational School unnecessary.

Notes

1 ENGHOLM, the then Secretary of State and later Minister for Education, 1980.
2 SCHMUDE, Minister for Education, 1980.
3 Usually one day a week (see introduction).
4 Part-time vocational school (Berufsschule) in the dual system, offering courses similar to part-time courses at technical colleges in England.
5 Illustrated in more details in PETZOLD, H.-J. and SCHLEGEL, W. (1983) *Qual ohne Wahl*, Frankfurt am Main, Jugend zwischen Schule und Beruf, pp. 185–6.
6 Comparable to the 'stages en entreprises' in France and Belgium.
7 Compare WERNINGER (1979).
8 Compulsory part-time attendance up to the age of 18 at a technical college means in general attending a vocational course one day per week and the remaining four days on-the-job training. There are also en-block courses at central vocational institutions for 'rarer' professions such as glassblowers, etc. .
9 See introduction.
10 Labour Exchange Frankfurt (1982) p. 19.
11 The Bildungsrat was abolished in 1976.
12 CSU (Christliche Soziale Union): Bavaria's Christian Democratic Party.
13 Institut der Deutschen Wirtschaft: Employers' Research Institute.
14 BUNK, G. and ZELDER, R. (1976) *Das Berufsgrundbildungsjahr*, Cologne.
15 Illustrated in Institut der Deutsche Wirtschaft (1979) *Jugend mit Zukunft*, Cologne; see especially chapter entitled 'Zur typology gegenwärtiger Jugendgenerationen', p. 53.
16 WIETHOLD (1981) p. 718.
17 The AFG is the key law for the Bundesanstalt. It is concerned with all its activities, ranging from vocational counselling and guidance to training schemes for the unemployed, retraining, unemployment benefits, employment subsidies and to various instruments of vocational integration of the disabled.
18 Federal Institute for Employment, quoted by BRAUN, F. (1979) 'Wie jugendliche Arbeitslose für unqualifizierte Arbeit ausgebildet werden', in LENHARDT, G. *Der hilflose Sozialstaat*, Frankfurt, p. 291.
19 *Ibid.*
20 *Ibid.*
21 *Ibid.*, p. 292.
22 *Ibid.*
23 Labour Exchange Frankfurt (1982) p. 40.
24 Federal Institute for Employment.
25 *Ibid.*
26 *Ibid.*
27 *Ibid.*
28 Federal Institute for Employment, quoted by BRAUN, F. (1979) *op cit.*, p. 296.
29 *Ibid.*
30 Labour Exchange Frankfurt (1982) p. 40.
31 Bundesinstitut für Berufsbildung: Federal Institute for Vocational Training.
32 Vocational Training Report (1981) p. 66.
33 Compare Institut für Arbeitsmarkt und Berufsforschung (1983) p. 1.

Volker Koditz

34 Compare Drexel, I. (1983) 'Problemgruppen des Ausbildunsstellenmarktes, unter-
   wertige Wege ins Erbwerbsleben und einige gesellschaftliche Konsequerizen' in *IG*
   Metall Finanzierung der beruflichen Bildung, Schriftenreihe der IG Metall, Frankfurt,
   p. 111.
35 Wiethold (1981) p. 718.
36 Union for Education and Science.
37 The vocational education reforms are discussed in more detail in Petzold, H.-J. and
   Schlegel, W. (1983) *Qual ohne Wahl*, chapter 1, p. 21.
38 Quoted in the chapter by Braun, F. and Drexel, I. (1979) 'Bewältigung des
   Ausbildungsplatzdefizits durch Sonderausbildungsgänge?', *Demokratische*
   Erziehung, 1.
39 Labour Exchange Frankfurt (1982) p. 20.
40 Bunk, G. and Zedler, R. (1976) *op cit.*, p. 51.
41 Kultusministerium Rheinland-Pfalz (1976) *Schriftenreihle Schulversuche zum Be-*
   rufsgrundbildungsjahr, Zwischenbericht, Mainz.
42 Metal workers' trade union.
43 Preiss in *Frankfurter Rundschau*, 26 October 1978.
44 Kultusministerium Rheinland-Pfalz (1976) *op cit*, p. 202.
45 Compare Jugendpressematerialien (1981) p. 16.
46 Minister for Education and the Arts for Hessen (1982) p. 9.
47 Halbergerhütte GmbH? Entwurf einer Handreichung für die einjährige Ausbildung
   zum Giessereiwerker nach §48 BBiG, Brebach o.J.,
48 Spiess, et al. (1982) 'Das Berufsvorbereitungsjahr in NRW. Abschlussbericht der
   wissenschaftlichen Begleitung zum Projekt' Verhaltensbeeinflussung, Erziehung-
   sstrategien im BVJ in Nordrhein-Westfalen, unveröffentliches Manuskript, July.
49 Labour Exchange Frankfurt (1982) p. 23.
50 Published by the GEW trade union in Hessen (see page 104).
51 Hessische Lehrerzeitung (1977) *Für und wider ein zehntes allgemeinbildendes Schul-*
   jahr, Heft 11, Frankfurt.
52 GEW, p. 9.
53 Goos, H. (1977) 'Von der Sackgasse zum Nadelöhr' *Pädextra*, no. 10.
54 Level reached after completing compulsory education.
55 Federal Employers Associations.
56 BDA (Federal Employers' Associations Aufruf Aktion 'Jugend and Beruf 1983').
57 Metal workers union.
58 IG Metall.
59 Certificate on the level of 'skilled worker'. The training is within the dual system
   and lasts three years.

References

Arbeitsamt Frankfurt (Hg) (1982) *Schulische und betriebliche Ausbildungsmöglichkeiten in*
   Arbeitsamtsbezirk Frankfurt am Main, Frankfurt.
Balon, K.-H. et al. (1978) *Arbeitslose: Abgschoven, diffamiert, verwaltet*, Fischer-
   Taschenbuch, Frankfurt.
Berufsbildungsberichte, Werden jährlich von der Bundesregierung in Federführung des
   Bundesinstituts für Berufsbildung und des Bundesministeriums für Bildung und
   Wissenschaft erstellt.
Bundesanstalt für Arbeit (Hg): MatAB 4/1979.
Bundesministerium für Bildung und Wissenschaft (Hg) (1979) Gutachten zum 10.
   Bildungsjahr. Werkstattbericht, no. 17, Bonn.
DJP-Jugendpressematerialien (1981) *Jugend ohne Arbeit*, Heft 1, Gelsenkirchen.

ENGHOLM, B. (1980) 'Verzicht bleibt umstritten', *Frankfurter Rundschau*, 20 December.

GEW-LANDESVERBAND BERLIN/fachgruppe Gewerbliche Schulen, Informationen, 10/79.

HANESCH, W. and SINGLE, U. (1977) *Weg von der Strasse für ein Jahr Focus-Verlag*, Giessen.

HOMANN, U. (1981) *Die Diskussion der Schulpflichtverlängerung in der BRD 1949–1979 — eine annotierte Bibliographie*, Max-Planck-Institut für Bildungsforschung, Berlin.

IG METALL (1983) *Stellungsnahme zur Arbeitgeberinitiative zur Nachqualifikation von jugendlichen Arbeitslosen, unveröffentlichtes Manuskript*, March.

Institut für Arbeitsmarkt und Berufsforschung (1983) 'Verleib von MBSE-Teilnehmern' in *IAB-Kurzbericht (intern) vom 11.2.1983*.

Jugend mit Zukunft (1979) *Podiumsdiskussion des Institut der deutschen Wirtschaft*, Cologne.

KLOAS, W. (1979) 'Berufsstartoribleme und Massnahmen zur Berufsvorbereitung und — Ausbildung von Sonder — und Hauptschulabgängern' Bendesinstitut für Berufsbildung, Berichte zur beruflichen Bildung, Heft 17, Berlin.

LENHARDT, G. (Hg) (1979) *Der hilflose Sozialstaat*, Suhrkamp-Verlag, Frankfurt.

OFFE, C. (1977) *Opfer des Arbeitsmarkts*, Luchterhand-Verlag, Darmstadt.

Päd, extra — Themenheft (1977) *Schüler auf der Wartebank*, Bensheim, October.

PETZOLD, H.-J. (1981) Schulzeitverlängerung: Parkplatz oder Bildungschance? Päd extra-Buchverlag, Bensheim.

SCHMUDE, J. (1980) 'Ausbildungsabgage vor Gericht' in *Frankfurter Rundschau*, 12 March.

STRATMANN, K. (Hg) (1981) *Das Berufsvorbereitungsjahr — Anspruch und Realität*, Schroedel-Verlag, Hannover.

WENNINGER, G. (1979) 'Zur Effektivität von Beschäftigungshilfen für arbeitslose Jugendliche' in LENHARDT, G. *Der hilflose Sozialstaat*, FRANKFURT, S. 314 ff.

The German Democratic Republic: The Other Germany — Planned Economic Security

Frank Bacon

This chapter seeks to provide a glimpse of the other side of the coin by considering policy and provision for ensuring the largest and most highly productive labour force possible in a nation that suffers only from a labour shortage, the German Democratic Republic (GDR). It is not intended as a defence of Marxist-Leninism but aims to be a factual account based on personal experience and investigation.

To understand the undoubted success of the GDR it is necessary first to look at its birth and the conditions in which it was born. It is commonplace to speak of the German Federal Republic — West Germany — as a nation that recovered well and rapidly from defeat and devastation at the end of World War II, to refer to the German character, its ability for hard work, sound organization and tight planning. The people of the GDR are no less German and share all the qualities attributed to that race. Without doubt, the GDR is the most opulent of all Eastern bloc countries. To walk the streets of, say, Leipzig and see the well-stocked shops, or to spend an evening in a crowded restaurant or night club and observe the free-spending patrons, are quite different experiences from similar activities in Leningrad or Cracow. The success of the GDR has been achieved in little more than thirty years, from a daunting start.

The eastern provinces of old Germany were occupied by the USSR in 1945 and what was left of them after the cession of land to the USSR and Poland was small indeed, amounting to some 42,000 square miles, or approximately two-fifths the size of West Germany. The post-war Russian occupation zone contained only a very small industrial region, in which about half the industry and most of the power generating capacity had been destroyed. All that remained was one blast furnace, an old-established textile industry and some optical and precision instrument manufacture. There were few natural resources but a vast rural area, the tenant farmers of which had a very low productivity record. Even before the war the population of Germany's eastern provinces received some 45 per cent of its agricultural products from the western region and by 1946 eastern productivity was only about 40 per cent of what it had been in 1936. It was, moreover, calculated that almost half the agricultural machinery had been destroyed in the war. The land occupied by the USSR was incapable of feeding its people.

The USSR occupation forces, then, were faced with a very serious situation and they responded by taking over without compensation the estates of all Nazis and war criminals and all other estates in excess of 250 acres. Nearly a quarter of a million farm labourers and resettlers were given plots of land, implements and livestock, and about half that number of smallholders were given additional land. The aim, however, of all Allied Powers was to resuscitate the economy as speedily as possible and to establish some form of indigenous authority to which full power might eventually be handed. Naturally the USSR looked for groups with sympathetic political views, which might come together to form a provisional government. Following the surrender of May 1945 the Soviet occupation authorities had immediately allowed the formation of anti-fascist groups. By June/July a number of political groups had emerged: the Communist Party, the Social Democratic Party, the Christian Democratic Union and the Liberal Democratic Party. These agreed on a joint action programme and, with Soviet suppport, began to get production going again.

In April 1946 the Communist and Social Democratic Parties united to form the Socialist Unity Party of Germany (*Sozialistische Einheitspartie Deutschlands — SED*) and, with its associated parties in the united front, began to set up organs of government. When the SED held a referendum in Saxony-Anhalt, where much of the industrial potential was concentrated, an overwhelming majority opted for confiscation without compensation of all Nazi-owned businesses, a decision that was very soon executed throughout the Soviet zone. Thus a nationally-owned sector of business came into being and quickly achieved some outstanding production under very difficult conditions. At this period Germany was in theory still a single nation under Four Power occupation but the currency reform enacted in the three Western zones in June 1948 left it with two distinct currencies and from that time the demarcation line of the Soviet zone effectively became a state border. When, in May 1949, the political parties in the three Western zones adopted a constitution for a federal republic, the division of Germany was completed. On 7 October 1949 the Council of the United Front Parties in the eastern zone met in Berlin to reconstitute itself as the provisional government of the GDR, to which the Soviet Military Government transferred all administrative responsibilities. So the GDR was born, with a National Front government, whose aim was to bring about full democratic control as quickly as possible. In October 1950 a general election was held, in which the SED, with the support of its associated groups, came to power, where it has remained. Contrary to popular belief, the GDR is not a one-party state and its Constitution guarantees the existence of several parties. Its parliament, the People's Chamber, has deputies from the SED, the Christian Democratic Union and the Democratic Farmers', Liberal Democratic and National Democratic Parties. There are also deputies from four national organizations that came into being in 1946–47 in the wake of the formation of the SED: the Confederation of Free German Trade Unions, the Democratic Women's League, Free German Youth and the League of Culture of the GDR.

The newly-elected Government went quickly to work and not unnaturally adopted Russian procedures. Thus, in 1951 the first Five Year Plan was launched, with the aim of developing the economy. There were two main strategies — the first, to establish a metallurgical industry; the second, the expansion of the heavy engineering industry. Aid from the Council for Mutual Economic Assistance (of the USSR and its sister nations) had already enabled the establishment of power and machine tool industries and a major bloc of light industry. At the same time the administrative structure of the country — the old German *Länder* system — was found to be too clumsy and slow-working to meet the rapid expansionist policies being pursued by the central government. In 1952, therefore, the five *Länder* were replaced by fourteen *Bezirke* or counties and this facilitated the management of the reconstruction effort.

On the agricultural front, although land had been taken into public ownership, its working had continued in the hands of smallholders and even though the number of farmers was much greater than formerly, production had not greatly increased. It appeared that farms were too small to afford modern machinery and in order to make them more economic, farmers were encouraged to form cooperatives. The first of these came into being in 1952 and received modern agricultural machinery from the USSR. Once new industries had been established and agrarian reforms initiated, all round advance was almost automatic. By 1960 all farmers were linked into cooperatives and production had increased greatly. Numbers of self-employed craftsmen had also formed cooperatives and under the second and third Five Year Plans (1956–65) efforts were made to involve all private tradesmen in the national effort, an arrangement being made whereby retail trade was pursued on a commission basis. During this period, too, the State progressively participated in private firms, as a transitional stage towards full state ownership. It is interesting to note that the Government did not take any drastic steps to achieve public control but was content to initiate movements and to allow them to progress largely at their own rates, relying on their successes to encourage others and indeed it was not until 1972 that the State finally bought up remaining private business interests. Indeed, it is still possible to employ up to nine people in a private business; around two per cent of the total workforce consists of self-employed persons, wholesale and retail traders and freelance workers generally.

During the second and third Five Year Plans there had been a concentration on the creation of new industry, the extension and modernization of existing industry and the re-equipment of vast segments of it by application of new scientific and technological developments. At the end of the period the nation was well established in many industrial areas: power generating machinery, chemical plants, shipbuilding, semi-conductors, control engineering, television manufacture and petrochemicals, the last having been built up virtually from scratch.

All this development had obviously called for well qualified professional people and educated workers and the demand was met by changes in the educational system. In the earliest years of the GDR education had continued largely on the old German pattern. Even that had not been easy; something like 28,000 out of a teaching force of some 39,000 had been closely involved in Nazi activities and were unacceptable in the post-war period. They were replaced by some 40,000 new teachers, people from many backgrounds, who received professional training on an in-service basis. At the same time the greater proportion of university teachers were similarly replaced and special courses instituted to prepare people without secondary education for university entrance. In spite of these early difficulties, the GDR did not hesitate to make further changes in the education system necessary to support the expansion of the national economy. In the early fifties the system was remoulded and numerous technical and other specialized colleges established, to facilitate the provision of men and women able to lead and to participate intelligently in modern business and industry. It was recognized that economic success depended upon sound education, vocational preparation and training. Teachers of all kinds and at all levels were recognized as guardians of the nation's future, a position of high regard that they still retain, even to the extent, uniquely, of enjoying special tax privileges.

As industry had developed it had continued to be organized in separate units, each factory and plant operating in isolation. From 1963, however, cooperation was encouraged and the fourth Five Year Plan (1966–70), with a view to increasing efficiency, initiated a unification process under which separate factories were organized into large complexes. At the same time, for the intensification of production and the more economic employment of modern equipment, the agricultural cooperatives began to work in larger groupings.

The population of the GDR was comparatively small and has shown the declining tendency of some other European nations. It is today almost seventeen millions, the people of working age numbering 10.6 millions and being almost equally divided between men and women. It is, therefore, obvious that the working population was readily absorbed by the increased economic bases, both industrial and agrarian, and that it was necessary for women of working age to participate in gainful employment. At the same time, the growth and intensification of industry and the ever fresh scientific and technological innovations demanded that young people should be better educated and receive such vocational preparation and training that would enable them to participate fully when they came to work. In 1965, therefore, the education system was completely reorganized by the passing of the Integrated Socialist Education System Act, an act that has been so successful in the achievement of its aims that it remains, with few subsequent amendments, in force today. With virtually all people of working age at work and with young people well prepared for it, further economic growth was clearly dependent upon improved efficiency and the fifth Five Year Plan (1971–75) emphasized the need for a more intense use of resources, largely through modernization schemes and a number of strategies to that end were evolved. Workers, farmers and intelligentsia alike were encouraged to exercise initiative and useful suggestions — duly rewarded — were immediately incorporated into working procedures. This encouragement to become innovators is now an established feature of the GDR. The latest available Government statistics claim an annual benefit from utilized innovations of some 5000 million marks (in a national income of some 200,000 million marks). The growing crisis in Western Europe at the beginning of the 1970s put some strain on the GDR (some 25 per cent of its trade was then with capitalist nations — it is now 33 per cent) but greater industrial efficiency was achieved and between 1971 and 1975 manufacturing output grew by 6.4 per cent. Indeed, in anticipation of an increase in national income, a social welfare programme had been initiated: accelerated production of consumer goods, half a million new dwellings and large sums to be spent on education, health, culture and social services generally. Retail turnover increased in the same period by 20 per cent and personal incomes by 27 per cent.

People, then, had a considerable incentive to maintain their levels of efficiency in working, essential in a nation where the workforce was fully employed and where a labour shortage was appearing. The Sixth Five Year Plan, therefore, continued the policy of obtaining a more intensive use of existing facilities and resources, thus obtaining higher productivity at lower cost, better use of fixed assets, improving quality standards and advantage from every aspect of scientific and technological advance. Similar cost-benefit improvements were looked for in service industries. The sixth Five Year Plan (1976–80) took further account of the possibilities by providing for an increase of 130 per cent in industrial productivity, to be achieved by 1980. That was equivalent to the work calculated to be performed by 125–130,000 workers, who were estimated to be needed in the economy but who would not be available.

Consultation at all levels is a mark of GDR philosophy. The State Planning Commission, responsible for the Five Year Plans, acts in close cooperation with economic bodies and individual enterprises and so is enabled to coordinate all envisaged projects, to lay down annual targets and to direct special tasks to be achieved by individual plants. Works managements and trade union committees discuss targets with the workforce, so that every worker knows what is expected of him and how his work fits in with that of his colleagues. Under the name of 'Socialist emulation', competition is encouraged; industrial enterprises vie with each other for the best production efforts, though they are expected to exchange information and to cooperate when necessary. Thus it is that in less than forty years the GDR has pulled itself into the world's top ten industrial nations, with some 8.7 of its seventeen million population at work, a remarkable proportion by any international standard. Remarkable, too, has been the improved productivity. It has been calculated that in 1970 it took sixty-two people in manufacturing industry to produce a million marks of national income; today it is claimed that this amount is produced by about thirty-five workers. Behind this success, of course, lie appropriate rewards — but productivity must come first, justified on the grounds that it is one of the irrefutable principles of socialist economics that only such wealth as has been produced can be distributed. It is worth noting here that, contrary to popular Western belief, the GDR does not claim to be a communist state; it sees itself progressing towards an advanced socialist society, leading to a gradual transition to communism. Certainly in its procedures there is a considerable measure of pure German pragmatism.

Life is not entirely without restriction; the visitor is struck by the small number of private cars on the roads although the latest available statistics claim an average of thirty-nine cars for every 100 households. The GDR has no natural oil resources, the whole of this commodity being imported from the USSR, but the careful Germans take no more than is necessary. Oil and petrol go primarily to manufacturing industry and essential transport. But this is just about the only restriction that the foreign visitor may observe or experience.

On the other hand, public transport of all kinds is remarkably cheap and efficient. It is, of course, not easy to check official claims about industrial development, national income, social progress and the like but the GDR today presents a very different picture from that of, say, fifteen years ago. Even to the casual observer it is obvious that people generally are cheerful and prosperous. Shops are stacked with goods and seem always to be full of customers. Places of entertainment are well patronised by well-dressed and free-spending people of all ages. If the proof of the pudding is in the eating, the eating in the GDR is excellent.

It has been noted that the GDR quite early realized that economic success depended upon sound basic education and vocational preparation and training. By the late 1950s it was clear that if there were to be continued economic improvement, popular education had to be reorganized. After some national debate the People's Chamber, in December 1959, decreed that a general polytechnical school system should be introduced within five years. This resulted in the Integrated Socialist Education System Act of 1965, designed to meet national needs as the fourth Five Year Plan was commencing and involving a marked change from the traditional German system. As industry developed, at a considerable pace, and as scientific and technological innovations were incorporated into manufacturing processes, the need for well-educated and well-trained workers became ever more pressing, particularly as the small population neither provided a large reservoir of potential workers nor allowed for lengthy apprenticeships. Two things were necessary: the one to provide a sound yet not unduly lengthened general education and preparation for the world of work; the other to continue to encourage married women to undertake full-time work.

The new education system, therefore, was based on a common school, the *Polytechnische Oberschule* or ten-year general polytechnical school, which would educate all young people between the ages of six and sixteen, have a wide-ranging curriculum of general education and a measure of vocational preparation. If, however, women were to go to work in any large numbers, it was necessary to make adequate provision for the care of children under the age of six. A comprehensive kindergarten system was set up to cater for children between the ages of three and six. Below this tier of child care and pre-school education were creches for children under three years of age, though mothers are encouraged to care for their children at home during the first year of life. In these ways it was hoped to encourage mothers to work, and to prepare all young people for future work in advanced industries. At the same time provision had to be made for the future intellectuals — the professional people and the leaders of the nation. Obviously these would need an advanced general education as a prelude to college and university. For them the *Erweiterte Oberschule* or extended school was established, to continue general education for a further two years, at the end of which the students would take the *abitur* examination, the traditional entry qualification to higher education. It was considered that in these ways all young people would be prepared for work in manufacturing, agricultural or service industries but that thereafter some few would be able to progress to the professions and to positions of leadership. It was clear that at the age of sixteen there would have to be some form of selection but it was considered that any trend towards social divisiveness would be avoided if all were to undertake some form of vocational preparation during attendance at the ten-year school. The added advantage would be that industrial and other leaders and professional persons would have had some early insight into the lives and working conditions of the vast majority of people. The universities and colleges to which extended school students would progress had been subject to some expansion and reformation in earlier years. They continued now with small reforms designed to meet more closely the needs of the somewhat differently educated students whom they would be receiving in the future.

There was, too, an educational backlog. The period immediately following World War II had been one of initial chaos and then of gradual growth, almost from scratch, in education as in industry. As already noticed, the dismissal on ideological grounds of the greater proportion of the teaching force created a great shortage of qualified and experienced teachers, a shortage made good by recruitment of novices who had to learn teaching skills on the job, frequently with classes of up to fifty children. The education of young people in the early days of the GDR obviously had been less than the best. With the early struggles and the need for rapid expansion of industry, the education even of those at school just prior to 1965 had been in varying degrees deficient. In 1965, therefore, there were many people, young and middle-aged, who had not had the opportunity of achieving their full potential. Provision had to be made for them, so that by improving their educational status they might become better informed and more efficient workers. A system of continuing education was strengthened and expanded, a trend that has continued, so that workers might have opportunities of keeping abreast of scientific and technological developments and so that young people who might have experienced failure at some point in their education or who were, in the classic phrase, late-developers, might have opportunities of overcoming earlier problems. It is a tribute to the planning that preceded the 1965 Act that this complicated system has proved to serve well its intended purposes. The main strategy, however, is to be found in the ten-year school and its curriculum. All children who are not handicapped must, from the age of six, attend this school, the curriculum of which is standard throughout the country. The school is divided into three stages: lower (first three years), middle (second three years) and upper. A reference to Table 1 will indicate the curriculum content by subject and length of study and how these change in successive stages and years.

Vocational preparation is considered to be a most important school function. The aim is that by the age of 16/17 (when most young people will leave school) every pupil will have acquired some industrial skills, an awareness of what it is like to work in industry, some knowledge of the relationship between work and the national economy, and an idea of the key role that each worker plays in his workplace and as a citizen. This introduction to the life of the majority of citizens is deemed to commence as soon as a child starts school; manual training is undertaken for one hour weekly in the lower stage and for two hours weekly in the middle stage. Manual training, of course, has long been a feature of English education (at least for boys), even though now more commonly called woodwork and metalwork, or even technology. It is, however, doubtful whether (after the earliest days perhaps) it

Table 1 Timetable for the Ten-Year School

Subject	School year									
	1	2	3	4	5	6	7	8	9	10
German	10	12	14	14	7	6	5	5	3	4
Russian	–	–	–	–	6	5	3	3	3	3
Mathematics	5	6	6	6	6	6	6	4	5	4
Biology	–	–	–	–	2	2	1	2	2	2
Physics	–	–	–	–	–	3	2	2	3	3
Chemistry	–	–	–	–	–	–	2	4	2	2
Astronomy	–	–	–	–	–	–	–	–	–	1
Manual Training	1	1	1	2	2	2	–	–	–	–
Gardening	1	1	1	1	–	–	–	–	–	–
History	–	–	–	–	1	2	2	2	2	2
Geography	–	–	–	–	2	2	2	2	1	2
Civics	–	–	–	–	–	–	1	1	1	2
Drawing	1	1	1	2	1	1	1	1	1	–
Music	1	1	2	1	1	1	1	1	1	1
Sport	2	2	2	3	3	3	2	2	2	2
Technical Drawing*	–	–	–	–	–	–	1	1	–	–
Socialist Production*	–	–	–	–	–	–	1	1	2	2
Productive Work*	–	–	–	–	–	–	2	2	3	3
Total weekly hours	21	24	27	29	31	33	32	33	31	33
Optional extra subjects:										
Needlework	–	–	–	1	1	–	–	–	–	–
Second foreign language	–	–	–	–	–	–	3	3	3	2

* Vocational preparation subjects taken during half-day release to industry

has been seen as a preparation for work, but the fact remains that it is a means of acquiring manual dexterity or that it is, in a more grandiose German phrase, an introduction to industrial arts skills.

From the seventh school year vocational preparation commences in real earnest. Manual training in school is replaced in the final four years by what is called polytechnical education. This has three essential elements: technical drawing, an introduction to socialist production and productive work. For this instruction children are released from school for half a day each week, when they attend special technical schools, where they are taught by trained specialist teachers, who are assisted by supervisors and skilled workers from industry. It has been noted that wherever possible, as part of the national economic plan, industrial units have been formed into large complexes and in each local area one or more of these are nominated to provide the facilities for polytechnical education — the teaching rooms, laboratories, workplaces, materials and, of course, the teachers' skilled assistants. In agricultural areas, in scattered industries and where industrial units are small it is customary to establish special polytechnic centres, where work facilities are provided. Some such special centres are provided by municipalities. In rural areas the centres may provide residential accommodation, the young people attending for blocks of instruction rather than for the weekly half day.

Figure 1:   *The Integrated Socialist Education System*

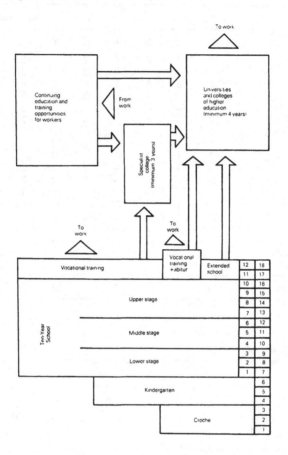

During school years 7 and 8 technical drawing and socialist production are studied for one hour each week. The introduction to socialist production is designed to make young people aware of the principles on which the national economy is based and the vital role that each worker plays — the need for high competence and high levels of efficiency at work and so the fact that their own future efforts will regulate the levels of their earnings. These subjects are accompanied by two hours of productive work; what the pupils then see around them and what they pick up from the skilled workers who help to supervize them effectively reinforce their theoretical learning. During the final two years of compulsory schooling, socialist production matters are studied for two hours weekly and productive work undertaken for three hours. This half day release for polytechnical education is not allowed to interfere with general education — all schools are open for five-and-a-half days each week. The productive work undertaken by the pupils is always a necessary part of the work of the parent enterprise. It is usually undertaken in special pupils' workshops, though where there is adequate safety the young people may even work alongside the adult workers. The emphasis, then, is on the production of marketable goods. One may observe youngsters producing, for example, perfect electrical components, or visit a school in which the chairs have been made by upper stage pupils. Nor are these skills acquired in any parrot-like fashion; adequate theoretical knowledge is first inculcated. An inspection of text books, worksheets and other available material always indicates a satisfactory relationship between theoretical learning and productive ability. For the final two years in particular there are national outline programmes for productive work, intended to ensure that roughly similar work attitudes, skills and experiences are acquired in spite of differing industrial conditions. The aims of this vocational preparation are generally to enable pupils to obtain a high level of practice-related instruction, acquire fundamental technological and economic knowledge and general working skills, see for themselves the extent to which workers have a say in their workplaces, and gain an insight into the roles of trade unions and other social organizations in industry. Though aimed at somewhat younger people, those aims are perhaps not very different from those of our own Youth Training Scheme. As to the production of marketable goods, the German belief is that optimum educational effect is achieved only if the work situation is as real as possible, a belief that lay behind our own Youth Opportunities Programme and which has been carried over into the YTS. This form of vocational preparation during school life is seen (as indeed the GDR Minister of Education has said) as an advance investment for good and effective vocational training after school. What pupils learn from theory and practice, and the incidental learning acquired from the workers who help to supervize them, are integrated with learning in other subjects of the school curriculum and complemented by Civics, which is studied for one hour weekly from the seventh school year and for two hours in the final year. Civics is in fact an introduction to Marxist-Leninist theory, the study of which helps to underpin the principles of socialist production, the general working procedures and the functions of trade unions in relation to high competence and efficiency at work, as mainstays of national (and so of personal) prosperity. The general aim is that by the time young people leave the ten-year school they will have fairly clear pictures of their own future roles and importance as citizens and workers.

By the time that the majority of youngsters leave school, in their seventeenth year, they have acquired a fairly good idea of what it is like to be 'at work' and they are ready to engage in much shorter apprenticeships than would otherwise have been necessary, an important factor in a country where every available worker is needed. It is worth nothing that in our own country, as a result of the Youth Training Scheme and proposals by the Engineering Industry Training Board and similar bodies, shorter apprenticeships now form an important matter for discussion. In the GDR, then, the 90 per cent or so who have not been selected for extended general education are ready to change their vocational preparation for apprenticeships and vocational training. The need for efficiency and competence at work are considered paramount in all areas and two years' preparation is required by law for every kind of work, whether for the electrical engineer, or trawler deck-hand, or hotel waiter, or bank clerk. The system is effective; even the most casual visitor may see this in the standards of hotel service.

Since industry of all kinds is predominantly in the hands of the State, jobs can be closely related to national needs at any time and the number of apprenticeships becoming available in each type of work is known in advance. There is in each locality a vocational guidance centre (*Berufsbetriebzentrum*), which, during the final school year, circulates all leavers with details of the apprenticeships that will be available in their area at the end of the school year. Pupils are then free to apply for apprenticeships of their own choice, though they are advised to state at least two alternatives, and the applications are sent to the relevant employing units. In the GDR state-owned enterprises do not appear to be any less discriminating than private employers. Where the number of applicants exceeds the number of places, they seem to look primarily for candidates of good educational achievement, good health and good personal qualities. It is claimed that something over 80 per cent of school leavers obtain apprenticeships of first choice and that less than 1 per cent refuse the first offer of employment. Since economic growth appears to be around 4 per cent per annum these do not seem unlikely figures. Where young people are in doubt regarding which applications to make, the guidance centres will provide detailed information about the various types of available work, and illustrated briefings are available to individuals and groups. This is not to say that the authorities have no problems in guiding young people into suitable employment. It is freely admitted, for example, that too many girls wish to become beauticians, hairdressers and shop assistants and that too few make first choice of technical work. In an attempt to alleviate such problems, vocational guidance commences early in school life, at first informally through subjects like geography, in which local industries are explained. The partnership between school and industry occasioned by polytechnical education also helps to widen children's horizons. Even so, not all problems are removed. Apart from the desires of some girls, some parents seek to influence job choice. Guidance centres recognize that they have 'league tables' of what they consider desirable jobs and urge their children to seek apprenticeships for those at the top. Cooperation between guidance centres does ensure that details of apprenticeships in other parts of the country may be made available, so that, for example, the young man in an inland town is not precluded from seeking work in shipbuilding or in sea-faring. It will, however, be obvious that, in spite of tight manpower planning, even in a country with a small population total success cannot be maintained. It is readily admitted that whilst the nation generally has a manpower shortage, certain areas of work are overmanned and a degree of job change is encouraged. Enterprises short of labour are ready to retrain older workers and it is a function of the vocational guidance centres to advise people who are seeking a change of work.

Once established in their apprenticeships, young people are required to undertake vocational training and to continue some aspects of general education. For the bulk of young people the training and education take place in apprentice schools attached to the various industrial enterprises. The system is not dissimilar to the British practice of releasing apprentices from work, on day-release or block-release to colleges of further education. In the GDR, of course, this training and continued education are compulsory for all and indeed are under the control of the State Secretariat for Vocational Training. The curriculum follows patterns readily recognizable in this country; on average one-third of the teaching time is spent on theoretical topics and two-thirds on practical instruction. There are, of course, variations according to the needs of the trade; the theory/practical ratio of the apprentice tailor, for example, is 1:3, that of the budding data processor 1:1. In the continued general education Civics and German Language are compulsory subjects. There are variations from the standard two-year apprenticeship. Gifted students who are not selected for extended education (the proportion varies between seven-and-a-half and ten per cent per annum) may be allowed to extend their apprenticeships to three years during which they study concurrently for the *abitur*. They are then in the position of being able to enter higher education at some future date and there is thus a reservoir of people ready to take up higher posts, a safeguard against any miscalculations in the annual selection for extended education. It appears that many teachers in vocational training establishments have come up through this route, qualifying first as skilled workers and subsequently obtaining a degree and teacher training. At the other end of the ability scale account is taken of those who have not been successful in the ten-year school. For those who have succeeded in every grade up to the eighth, certain jobs are reserved, including those of fitter, turner, grinder, gardcer, forester, decorator, garage mechanic and post-office worker. For them, according to ability, the apprenticeship period varies between two-and-a-half and three years. For those of even lower ability there are special courses lasting between one and two years to enable them to acquire minimal skills for such jobs as domestic helps, dressmakers, confectionery workers, store-clerks and assistant cooks. Whatever the nature of the apprenticeship, there is, of course, now a guaranteed job at the end. Article 140 of the GDR Labour Code requires that 'at least six months before the expiry of the contract of apprenticeship the enterprise is obliged to offer the apprentice a job in the enterprise corresponding to the vocation in which he has been trained'.

Whatever their job, many opportunities for further education and training are available to all workers. College courses are parallelled by distance learning programmes directed from regional centres based in universities. The *Volkshochschule* (People's College) organization offers evening and weekend courses at many levels and in many subjects, non-vocational as well as vocational. Much useful work is also undertaken by URANIA, a learned organization concerned with the popular dissemination of knowledge in the natural and social sciences and technological fields. In need of labour, the GDR makes all possible efforts to increase efficiency and to intensify production. Further education and training, therefore, are encouraged. Article 145 of the Labour Code notes that continuing education courses 'enable employees to raise the efficiency of their work and to take a creative part and show greater expertise in running the enterprise'. Article 150 of the code makes it clear that

> the enterprise is obliged to support employees taking part in basic and further training schemes by such measures as allowing them to arrange their working hours in the most suitable way, granting them leave of absence, mentor arrangements, exchanges of experience, refunding of personal expenses and other suitable measures . . . Good

showings by employees ... are to receive moral and, as far as the enterprise's possibilities allow, material recognition.

Thus the GDR seeks to use to optimum advantage its limited work force potential. Back in 1950 the country's first Prime Minister said that 'the state we have created is not a bed on which one can loll about'. It seems certain that no one has lolled about; that this new country has managed to win and retain a place amongst the world's top ten industrial nations in less than forty years is remarkable enough. That it has maintained full employment and achieved continually increasing living standards is praiseworthy. As to the ways and means by which these successes have been achieved and whether they depend more from socialism or from Germanic character, the reader must make his own judgments.

References

First Hand Information Series (1978) *The School Function of our Schools* (a speech by Dr Margot Honecker, Minister of Education), Berlin, Panorama DDR

First Hand Information Series (1980) *Policies Which put People First*, Berlin, Panorama DDR

First Hand Information Series (1981) *Introducing the GDR*, Berlin, Panorama DDR

First Hand Information Series (1981) *Learning for Living*, Berlin, Panorama DDR

First Hand Information Series (1981) *Vocational Training for Today and Tomorrow*, Berlin, Panorama DDR

Heitzer, H (1981) *GDR: An Historical Outline*, Dresden, Verlag Zeit im Bild

(1982) *Statistical Pocket Book of the GDR*, Berlin, Staatsverlag der DDR

Beiträge zur Produktiven Arbeit der Schüler, Berlin, Volk and Wissen Volkseigener Verlag

Detailed information about continuing education and training opportunities is best obtained from local and regional German language prospectuses, published prior to the beginning of each academic year, for example:

Lehrprogramm: Volkshochschule (published in every large town and district)

Weiterbildung Programm (published by universities)

Hochschul Fernstudium (published by the Central Office for Distance Learning of the Ministry of Higher Education and available through the regional centres)

NORWAY

The following chapter by Ian Charles is the only contribution from Scandinavia to this book. The Norwegian experience occupies an interesting position within the accounts offered in this book. It reflects some of the attitudes to vocational education more usually associated with Eastern Europe in a country with one of the highest per capita standards of living and one of the lowest unemployment rates in the West. Albeit at a rather tentative level, the Eastern connection is to be found in the prestige traditionally given within Norway to manual and craft labour. The Steen Committee, which is responsible for the current structure of vocational education provision, makes efforts to reduce any status differential between 'blue' and 'white' collar training and tries to promote a willingness amongst youngsters to consider a wide range of occupation. Thereby attempts are made to avoid over-subscription for some vocational areas, and shortages of labour in others. This is not to say that there is no hierarchical structure to the job market as perceived by youngsters, nor is the threat of unemployment not taken seriously. There is, however, a relatively low number of unemployed school-leavers. Part of the reason for this is to be found in the policy measures taken to absorb youngsters in further education. These are measures which have been in effect over the past decade. Further education in Norway, although not compulsory in a legislative sense, is 'an offer you can't refuse' mainly because, as Charles puts it, 'there is no incentive for the unemployed school-leaver *not* to continue his or her education'.

The Norwegian Solution: Further Education, An Offer You Can't Refuse

Ian Charles

So far this decade, unemployment has risen in Norway to a comparatively low level in relation to other Western countries. Since the 1960s the Norwegians have been preparing for the current technological revolution, and specifically the problem of youth unemployment, through a radically restructured further education system.

Norway emerged from the 1970s into an almost unique position in relation to her allies and trading partners in the West. Since the oil crisis of 1973 other countries have experienced high inflation, recession in industry and an alarming rise in unemployment. Mainly through the discovery and exploitation of a vast quantity of North Sea oil in relation to a small population,[1] Norway has become one of the wealthiest countries in the world. Across the population as a whole, registered unemployment stood at an average of 1.7 per cent in 1981, the most recent year for which figures are available.[2] In theory, unemployment among the 16–19 age group is still only 'structural'. It will be shown that this relatively comfortable state of affairs owes itself principally to the establishment by 1976 of what is effectively a universal comprehensive further education system in the 16–19 sector. While in Britain for instance, the education system has had to modify and adapt very rapidly to accommodate schemes such as the Youth Opportunities Programme and its successor the Youth Training Scheme, Norway had already built this facility into the framework of its further education system by 1974.

Brief Historical Background

The Norwegians have a long history of educational provision, and the first upper-secondary schools corresponding to the modern concept of a college of further education date back to the 12th century.[3] Attempts to establish compulsory basic schooling began in 1739, but little progress was made before the dissolution in 1814 of the 300 year-old Danish controlled Union between Norway and Denmark, when Norway was freed from the Danish tradition of a 'tied' peasantry. The Primary School Act of 1827 was the first positive step towards universal educational provision. The system progressed over the following century, despite setbacks resulting from high emigration in the later

19th century and the effects of the two World Wars. During the 1950s the compulsory education system was progressively standardized nationally, so that by 1959, with the passing of the Primary School Act (amended in 1969), nine years' compulsory schooling became established nationally. Under the previous primary system, pupils[5] had the option at the age of 14 to go on from their primary (7-14) school to either a two-year 'junior grammar school' (realskole) or a one or occasionally two-year 'continuation school' (Framhalds-skole) for a less academic education. This was not dissimilar to the grammar/ secondary modern system in England, although the selection age was different. These two types of school were incorporated into a nine-year (7–16) fully comprehensive system by the Acts of 1959 and 1969.

Parallel to the establishment of universal primary (7–14) and lower secondary (14–16) education, a number of upper-secondary (16–19) schools had developed. The most common of these was the 'gymnasium' (gymnas), equivalent to a sixth-form college. Here pupils were offered an academic general education in preparation for university or professional entrance. Other schools existed to provide training in commerce, technical subjects, crafts and so on. Unlike the English technical college, these schools were generally devoted to one vocational area only, such as building or mechanical engineering. Normally, but not always, these schools were administered by county authorities (fylker) as opposed to the compulsory sector, for which the municipal authorities (kommuner) are responsible. Although the kommuner were understandably legally required to provide a primary/lower secondary school system within their boundaries, no such obligation existed for the fylker to make any minimum level of further education (upper-secondary in Norwegian parlance) provision. Meanwhile all higher education in Norway was and still is directly funded by central government.

Integration and standardization of primary and lower-secondary education was completed nationally by the early 1960s, and from this time onwards attention became focussed increasingly in government and educational circles on similar reform of the 16–19 sector. During the planning and subsequent execution of this reform a framework was created for further education which so far has covered the needs of the school-leaver.

Reform of Further Education: The Planning Stage

From the mid 1960s, various committees were set up to represent the interests of all the parties concerned with further education, including technical and vocational teachers, schools and employers. The brief was to consider the ways and means by which an integrated 16–19 system could be established and organized. By far the most important and influential of these was the School Committee of 1965 (skolekomiteen av 1965), which was convened by the Ministry of Church and Education. It later became known as the Steen Committee (after its chairman, Reiulf Steen), and will be subsequently referred to by that name in this chapter.

The Steen Committee published three reports, in 1967, 1969 and 1970. Whether by good fortune, prophetic wisdom or simple common sense, the reports identified the future requirement of a more 'flexible' work force, and asserted that this would have to come about via an extension, albeit on a voluntary basis, of the comprehensive education already received by pupils over the compulsory nine-year period. Young workers of the future, it stated, would need to be given 'transferable' skills in addition to a specific training, and the notion of a 'job for life' was obsolete. Headings were used such as 'Educational problems in a society in a state of rapid change'.

The three reports ran to over 500 pages. As early as 1965, the Steen Committee recognized the need to consider a 'wholistic' programme of education and training for school leavers:

> In a modern society technological and scientific progress lead to great and rapid changes in working life. Traditional jobs disappear or change in character, and new jobs and industries spring up in the course of a relatively short time. Our further education establishments — both grammar schools and technical schools — give in a way the appearance of a society with a more static employment situation than that which we nowadays experience. Modern production processes make constant demands on theoretical expertise in a steadily increasing number of industries.[5]

The above extract is taken from the introductory pages of the first report of the Steen Committee. Acknowledgement of the relationship between the education system and changing technology and employment demands appears consistently throughout all three reports. By the third and final report, the role of the education system is stated in more direct terms with regard to future changes in technology and its effect on society. For instance:

> Modern society becomes, at a rapid pace, increasingly complex. We make enormous technological progress and achieve an increasing power over Nature. Our body of knowledge increases in every area of life ... both economic and social patterns are constantly changing ... nothing of this is irrelevant to the School. Its primary task is to give the younger generation the appropriate knowledge and training to prepare them for what they need to work and participate in our existing society; and at the same time help them to develop the understanding and foundations to equip them to meet the multifarious problems that future society will confront them with ...[7]

The language and implications of the Steen Committee's reports, dating back over eighteen years now, are echoed in statements made today in Britain about the nature and purpose of new training initiatives for the unemployed school leaver. The architects of school reform in Norway had, it turns out, made a precise analysis of the problems and challenges facing a future generation of school leavers seeking work. Furthermore they had identified early on the need for a redesigned post-compulsory school system as the answer to the problems which would arise out of the technological revolution.

The Steen Committee Recommendations

By the time of the publication of its third and final report in 1970, the Steen Committee had recommended the following, in the light of probable future developments:

All 16–19 education should be integrated administratively into one type of comprehensive upper secondary school, to be known as a 'further education' (videregående) school.

These new schools should be established and administered by the county authorities, who would have the right to decide the form in which the schools in their districts would be organized (ie split-site or purpose-built combined).

With control of all 16–19 education by the county authorities, there should be a legal obligation on each authority to provide a place in a further education school for every eligible 16 year-old.

Experimentation and Legislation

Before the publication of the second and third reports, the gist of the Steen Committee's recommendations had been 'leaked' fairly consistently, and the various agencies concerned with implementing and designing the new system were already carrying out experimental work in selected schools.[8] These schools were operating a reformed curriculum, and by 1973 some purpose-built schools were already in existence.[9]

A Parliamentary Report was presented in May 1970[10] entitled 'On the Reform of the Grammar School and the Development of the Further Education School'. A reform of the further education system along the lines of the Steen Committee's recommendations was debated in Parliament from November 1971. A Bill was presented in December 1973[11] and became law in June 1974.

The Upper-Secondary Act of 1974 came into effect in June 1976. It was phased in over a five-year period, partly to allow the county authorities time to finalize plans for re-organization in their respective districts, and also to allow existing pupils to complete their further education under the old system. All 16–19 education was covered by the Act, with the exception of the 'Folk High Schools'[12] and certain forms of in-service training run internally by public corporations such as the railways and post office.

An all-through 'single school' system (ethetsskole) was an ambition in Norway over 100 years ago, and was expressed by the pre-eminent Norwegian educationist of the nineteenth century, Hartvig Nissen. Interestingly, much of his philosophy developed after observations of the Scottish folk school system made during visits in the 1840s. Thus the establishment of universal nine-year compulsory schooling through the 1959 Act made the subsequent reform of further education almost inevitable. The 1959 Act made possible common entry criteria for further education. This is made clear in the Steen Committee reports, and later in the 1974 Upper-Secondary Act itself. In the opening paragraph it is stated:

Ian Charles

> This Act applies to upper-secondary (16–19) education, which builds
> on the basic (compulsory) school ...[13]

Throughout the text of the 1974 Act lies the implication that further education or training upon leaving compulsory school should not be regarded as a 'desirable' option but as an essential component of the education and personal development of every 16 year-old. With the passing of the 1974 Act, it was anticipated that within a few years virtually every school-leaver would complete at least one year of further education and/or training. The National Council for Innovation in Education[14] saw the 1974 Act as a de facto raising of the school-leaving age without any legally-enforced compulsion:

> The National Council for Innovation in Education assumes that approximately 90 per cent of this age group will apply for this option ... the pupils should be allowed to choose their course of study

The New System

From the time the 1974 Act came into effect in the summer of 1976, every 16 year-old has had the right to a further three years' general education and/or vocational training. The main entrance requirement is the successful *completion* of nine years of compulsory school. In certain cases, pupils are accepted without this requirement at the discretion of the local county school board. Formal examinations at secondary level were virtually abandoned by 1975, so the new 16–19 videregaende schools are to all intents and purposes open-entry:

> The normal condition of entry to upper-secondary education is that one should have completed the nine-year basic school. Other pupils may be accepted in accordance with further regulations issued by the Ministry of Church and Education.[15]

Furthermore, choice of subject or vocational training is also free, subject to availability of places. This will be covered in more detail later:

> On entry the applicant's preferences for a line of study and for optional subjects shall be taken into consideration as far as possible ... a pupil accepted at an upper-secondary school shall — as far as possible — be able to continue his education there for three years, or more if he has chosen a line of study which requires a longer time ... if a pupil encounters difficulties over following his chosen course, the school shall endeavour to identify and provide another course appropriate to his needs. If this proves difficult, the county school board will try to arrange a suitable course for him at another school either within or outside the county.[16]

So in theory at any rate, every school-leaver is provided with a place in a further education establishment for up to three years or more, and that place should be for a course of education/training of his or her choice. Figures for entry to further education show that the first objective at any rate — capacity to absorb the entire 16 year-old population — has largely been achieved. In 1965, when the Steen Committee was first convened, 62.7 per cent of the 16 year-old population entered further education for at least one year. A gradual rise after that, accelerated after the passing of the 1974 Act, led to a figure in 1980 of 83.2 per cent, the latest year for which figures are available.[17] Allowing for the small percentage in any age group who for one reason or another (such as a severe physical or social handicap) cannot be accommodated in a regular educational institution, and the pupils who choose to attend folk high schools, the Norwegians are very close indeed to a universal cull of all eligible school-leavers into further education. For 17 year-olds entering a second year of post-compulsory education or training the figure remains high (70 per cent in 1980). More than half the eligible population is still involved in a third year (55.8 per cent in 1980). When these figures are compared with those for unemployment over the same period, and taking into account the existence of National Service for all men, it will be seen that the reformed further education system has until now at any rate absorbed quite effectively the potential surplus of 16–19 year-olds on the labour market.

The Points System for Entry to Further Education

Although the total number of further education places may have been sufficient to date, the second aim described above to give pupils a free choice of course *as far as possible,* is resolved through a lottery which takes place every summer in each county. Every applicant earns a number of 'points', and where demand for a particular course exceeds supply, places are filled by applicants with the greatest number of points. Those who are unsuccessful are immediately given bonus points for the subsequent year's intake should they be particularly committed to a certain course. More commonly, unsuccessful applicants will be more likely to accept an alternative course for one or two years, with the possibility of a relative straightforward transfer later to their original choice. This is facilitated by the modular nature of courses, described below. Points are earned principally for successful completion of nine years' compulsory schooling, but can be supplemented by various other criteria, which include: time spent at home caused by having to look after a child or handicapped person; industrial experience gained by the small minority who have found employment immediately after leaving compulsory school; men who have already completed National Service; and so on. The points system means pupils are allocated a place by the county authority, not by the individual school. Particularly in the case of pupils seeking academic further education this system has helped to remove the inequality of standards caused in the past by heavy competition for places in schools with a 'good' reputation. Nowadays, Norwegian 16 year-olds are normally far more concerned with what they study than where they study.

In practice, obtaining a school place is no problem. Achieving one's first choice of course is dependent very much on geographical circumstances. Traditionally the large urban areas, and particularly the capital Oslo, have been very well endowed with the old 'grammar schools', and less so with vocational establishments. Generally the reverse is true of less populated areas.[13] This has resulted in the situation where in the cities, pupils seeking a vocational training find themselves allocated a place for general education, and in rural areas academically able pupils may have to settle for a vocational course. Although under the 1974 Act county authorities are supposed to make provision according to local demand and the wishes of the individual, this inequality exists today and will continue for some time to come. The reasons are economic; in principle, the 1974 Act represents a radical — some might say revolutionary — transformation of provision for the school-leaver. However, the county authorities have had to implement this new system from the standpoint of the facilities existing in their districts at the time the Act was passed. Some building of new schools and considerable expansion of existing ones did take place fairly rapidly after 1976, and in some cases had already taken place in anticipation of the new law.[14] But for the most part, the initial phase of the reform has been, in terms of school places, principally concerned with the administrative integration of the different educational institutions. To a certain extent, the imbalance before 1976 of courses and subjects has not changed, just as the extension of comprehensive secondary education in England in the mid 1960s resulted in many 'split site' schools.

Curriculum Reform and Course Structure in the New Schools

The apparent freedom of choice for pupils expressed as an aim of the 1974 Act but largely unfulfilled over much of the country nearly ten years later is a source of disappointment and frustration to many school-leavers who are theoretically eligible but in practice unable to pursue the course of their choice. Up to a point, however, corresponding reform of course curricula and the introduction of a 'modular' system of foundation courses has helped to accommodate the potential mis-match of pupils' aspirations and abilities with the courses available.

Together with integrated further education schools came a completely revised course structure. All pupils now take a one-year 'foundation' course in general education or a vocational area, which is followed by a second and sometimes third year of more advanced study. In addition to this standard model, and of increasing significance in the light of current employment and technological trends, is the so-called 'two-year combined foundation course' (2-årig grunnkurs) which combines general and vocational education in a unique way made possible by the administrative reforms embodied in the 1974 Act. In detail, the three choices available to school-leavers under the new system are as follows.

Foundation Course in General Education

This replaces the first year of the old 'grammar school' three-year course, and is the most popular of the three foundation options. It is self-contained and a certificate is gained at the end of the year. Pupils wishing eventually to enter higher education or undergo professional training will proceed from the foundation year to a second and third year of general education, specializing in one of various areas, including languages, natural sciences, social sciences or aesthetics. Under the old system, specialization began in the first year; the new foundation year is common to all pupils, and contains elements of all the specialisms in addition to a common core of subjects such as mother tongue and physical education. There is also a series of 'study electives', such as musical instrument tuition or a second foreign language. The new foundation year differs from the previous system in three important ways. Firstly the modular structure means that pupils are credited independently for *each year* of study, and can leave the system at the end of the first or second years with a valid qualification. Under the old system, it was necessary to complete three years before a certificate was awarded. Secondly a pupil is now able to delay his or her choice of specialized study for a further year, offering in the first year the chance to sample a broad range of subjects at a more advanced level than that experienced in secondary school. Thirdly, and of increasing value in the context of matching pupils' educational backgrounds to a volatile labour-market, the self-contained nature of the foundation course makes possible in many cases a direct transfer to another area of study later on with full credit allowed for study already completed. Since the entry requirements for higher education have also been liberalized in recent years to the point where the main criterion is successful completion of three years' further education, irrespective of what form this takes, the new course structure can be of great value to pupils who find themselves taking a longer time to discover their potential. General education has always been a popular choice for school-leavers in Norway, and if anything its popularity has increased since the 1974 Act. At that time, approximately 30 per cent of school-leavers chose general education. The latest available figures show that the proportion has risen considerably to 71,513 out of a total intake of 151,777.[20] Much of this rise, however, may not be so much concerned with the 'popularity' of general education as the inability of county authorities to provide sufficient places in vocational education to meet the demand. Since obtaining employment in Norway without completing at least one course in further education is virtually impossible, it is likely that a large number of pupils are taking the foundation year in general education because they are unable to find places for vocational courses. As mentioned above, this is especially true in urban districts. In addition, school-leavers have to compete for places with people returning to education during their working life. These mature pupils will be more favourably placed in the lottery, since their industrial experience will earn them extra points.

Foundation Course in Vocational Education

As with the general education foundation year the foundation course in vocational education is divided into three parts: a core of compulsory subjects, specific training in one vocational area, and a choice of study electives. Again, the successful completion of this year is a qualification in its own right, but also qualifies pupils to proceed to a second and possibly a third year of more specialized vocational study. Under the 1974 Act, all kinds of further education and training carry equal weight, so a pupil who completes the equivalent of three years of vocational education is similarly placed with 'academic' pupils vis-a-vis entry to higher education. This is important not only because it makes the new system non-discriminatory between academic and vocational study, but also because the inherent flexibility offers a wider choice to pupils as they emerge from three years of further education. This is in marked contrast to the situation in England, where there is often a greater deal of prestige attached to more 'academic' qualifications such as O-levels and A-levels compared with recently-introduced qualifications which are frequently viewed with suspicion by employers and higher education institutions.[21] Again, this foundation year is far less specialized in the new schools. For example, electrical engineering was previously split from the outset into 'heavy' and 'light' (electronic), and pupils had to choose their vocation immediately upon entering technical school. Now the choice is deferred for a year; there is a common foundation course in electrical engineering. In the future, specialization may be deferred even longer; experimentation is currently taking place with a two-year foundation course, with the aim of producing the maximum versatility among the future workforce in a constantly changing industry. Pupils enjoy the advantage of not having to be committed at too early a stage to a particular vocation, and have the opportunity to experience a wider vocational preparation, while observing current trends in the respective industries.

From case studies carried out by the author during 1981/82 in three Norwegian further education schools[22] there was clear evidence that a large number of vocational pupils are not greatly impressed by the opportunities potentially offered by this extension of their 'basic' education; most of those interviewed claimed they had already made a career decision, and generally saw this extension of their further education as a means of keeping them off the labour market for a longer period. Although much of the ideology expressed in the Steen Committee reports and the 1974 Act itself are 'pupil centred', emphasizing the value to the individual of being able to defer a career decision, there is no doubt that the reform of further education has been of great benefit to the country as a whole in helping to keep unemployment down to a minimal level among the 16–19 age group. A small and very gradual rise in unemployment to an average of 1.7 per cent of the total labour force[23] has been achieved only because of the corresponding rise in the numbers of people entering (and remaining for longer in) further education. So emergency measures along the lines of the Youth Training Scheme in England have not yet proved necessary in Norway; the regular further education has since its reform in 1974 been structured to cope with extended education and training for an otherwise potentially unemployable 16–19 population.

The Two-Year Foundation Course (2-årig grunnkurs)

Of the three foundation options available under the new system, this development may well be of great significance in the years to come, although it has not yet met with the popularity originally anticipated by the Steen Committee. It is a programme of study which owes its existence entirely to the administrative reforms embodied in the 1974 Act, and predates the concept of combining theoretical and vocational education which has been promoted by the Further Education Curriculum Research and Development Unit in England.[24] The course fits into the new system as shown in the centre of the Figure 1 below.

During their two years' foundation study, pupils spend 50 per cent of the time studying general education (following the same curriculum as the one-year general education pupils) and the other 50 per cent on a vocational course (again comparable to one followed by one-year foundation course vocational pupils). Choice of vocational area is theoretically free, but in practice most schools for timetabling reasons may be able to offer only a small selection of vocational courses for combination purposes. At the end of the two years, pupils have the equivalent to one year's qualification in both general education and the chosen vocational area. In addition to this double qualification, pupils have three options if they wish to continue their education:

(a) to enter the *second year* of the general education programme;
(b) to enter the *second year* of their chosen vocational area; or
(c) in certain circumstances pupils may take a combined 'supplementary' year in either general or vocational study. In effect, this supplementary year is a compression of two years' regular advanced study, and requires a high level of ability and motivation; very few pupils are considered capable of succeeding with this option.

Figure 1

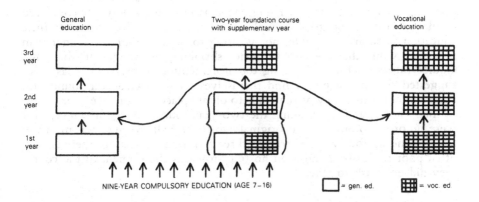

So for the overwhelming majority of pupils taking the two year foundation course, the choice if they wish to continue will be between option (a) and option (b). Thus in all probability these pupils will spend four years in further education as opposed to the three they would have spent had they initially opted for a single foundation course. The idea of a combined course was suggested in the first report of the Steen Committee in 1965, pointing out several advantages of the scheme from the pupils' point of view. They are given the opportunity to experience two different study disciplines at an advanced level before having to choose the one which suits them better; this also helps them to defer any career decisions for a further year. Pupils eventually opting for a vocational career will have benefitted from a more extensive general education than they would otherwise have received, which could assist them when and if they need to undergo any form of further education later in life, or retraining in their chosen careers; this is apart from the value in terms of their personal development. Similarly, pupils choosing the 'academic' path will have had the value of some practical training, of no small benefit again in terms of career and personal development. Norway has always pursued a tradition, in common with many East European countries but in contrast to most Western states, of celebrating the value of manual labour and crafts. The two-year foundation course represents this ideal, attempting to break down the imbalance and social barriers between 'blue' and 'white' collar society. The importance of this was noted by the Steen Committee, which stated that modern conditions require a more open and flexible attitude towards different kinds of work; indeed the absence of this willingness to consider a wider range of options may be a major reason for the shortage of suitably skilled applicants for training in certain industries in England during periods of high unemployment. Despite tradition, there is nonetheless in Norway today a degree of inflexibility among school-leavers, and it is too soon to predict how far the expansion of numbers taking the combined course will contribute towards eradicating this problem. Currently the two-year foundation course accounts for approximately 20 per cent of all foundation course pupils; this figure has remained stagnant for two years, after a rise of 14 per cent since its inception in 1977.[25] A probable reason for this is that with unemployment now rising, albeit at a relatively slow rate compared to many Western countries, school-leavers are concerned to complete their education as soon as possible, not wanting to be in school any longer than necessary while they see job vacancies shrinking in number all the time. Course tutors interviewed during the aforementioned case-studies last year suggested that many pupils find themselves taking a two-year foundation course only because they were unable to obtain places for the one-year course of their choice, and were taking the two-year course under sufferance, as it were, in order to pursue their original choice after all. Because this means in effect spending four years instead of three in further education, there is very often poor motivation and even hostility towards the element of the course they did not wish to take.

Norwegian Society and the Education System

In helping to keep youth unemployment at minimal levels over the last few years, the part played by the reformed further education system cannot be overestimated. In England, recent attempts to attract unemployed youths into the further education system have had to be made with the offer of a training allowance paid by the Manpower Services Commission, due to the historical expectation among large numbers of the working-class population that children should earn a living as soon as they are legally entitled. Without the training allowance currently offered, it is likely that many more school leavers would opt to claim unemployment benefit rather than pursue full-time study in further education. The Norwegian experience is quite different. There is a long tradition among all social classes of supporting children throughout their education, whether or not they are 'obliged' to attend school. At the age of 19, anyone wishing to pursue his or her education is automatically entitled to receive a low-interest loan from the State, regardless of the level or duration of study. Up to that point, it is universally accepted that children are supported by their parents. Consequently, there is no provision for the payment of unemployment benefit to 16 year-olds if they are eligible to attend a further education institution — as virtually all of them are. It costs nothing to pursue a course of further education in Norway; there are no course fees, all materials are provided, and there is a travel allowance paid where appropriate. So there is tremendous pressure on school-leavers to continue their education, not merely from a 'positive' viewpoint (counselling, parental pressure and so on), but also from a negative one; that is, there is no financial incentive for the unemployed school leaver *not* to continue his or her education. Although a large number of 16 year-olds would be very pleased to enter the world of work immediately, that option is effectively cut off.

All men must undergo National Service. For those who enter the military, the period of compulsory service is one year; the 20 per cent who are conscientious objectors are allotted duties in a civil capacity, such as hospital orderlies, kindergarten assistants and so on, and their period of service is eighteen months. Although in any event no government in Norway since World War Two has shown any sympathy towards repeal of National Service, it would be even less likely to be considered at present; the existence of National Service keeps a substantial number of men away from the labour market all the time.

Education is and has always been a major area of interest and concern in Norway; the other sectors (adult, higher, special and nursery) not covered here, have all undergone significant reforms and expansion in recent years, parallel to the most significant reorganization, which has been in the primary, secondary and further education sectors. This interest crosses political boundaries to a considerable extent; thus the switch to a Conservative administration in the election of 1980 after more than forty years of Labour domination has not significantly altered educational direction to date. Some administrative reorganization has taken place in the civil service sections responsible for education[26] and the work of the National Council for Innovation in Education has been cut back. Despite all this, however, it is fair to say that in Norway the value of education as an investment in the future is recognized by all persuasions in society, government and the media. An increasing problem in Norway today is caused by the fact that the majority of the 'dissidents' in respect of education are the pupils themselves, and much research is currently being carried out into school-refusal, school phobia and what the Norwegians call 'school tiredness', the hostility towards school after nine years at primary/secondary level, which has quite likely been preceded these days by several years in a kindergarten. Curriculum reform at further education level has not kept pace with structural reform, and attention will undoubtedly need to be focussed on this in the near future. It is likely that a degree of 'work experience' will need to be included in more vocational courses in order to overcome this problem of lack of motivation. This was recommended recently at the annual conference of the Norwegian equivalent to the C.B.I. (Norsk Arbeidsgiverforening).[27]

During the early 1970's there was a shortage of unskilled and semi-skilled labour, which was overcome to an extent by immigration. This was halted almost completely in 1975, and without any colonial tradition, Norway has no obligations or commitments towards any other country with the exception of Denmark, Sweden and Finland, with whom there are no restrictions. This is a two-way process though, and net immigration is now very low in Norway.[28] The birth rate is quite low, and there are no dramatic 'bulges' of 16 year-olds looming on the horizon. The major unknown, therefore, is the size of the job market in years to come. It would seem that, for the time being at any rate, the further education system will cope with the needs of the school-leaver. But pressure is increasing for the reasons described above, with society as a whole seeking an extension to the period of education, and a reduction sought by many disaffected 16 year-olds. A compromise, almost certainly, will be found through more imaginative curriculum planning and the development of work experience inculcated into regular vocational courses. Despite these problems, however, the Norwegians have either by good foresight or good fortune reformed the structure and provision of further education in time to put up some resistance to the problems caused by a shrinking job market. It remains to be seen whether this reform will be adequate in the event of the economy suffering any major setbacks before world conditions in general improve again.

Notes

1 4.1 million as at 1 January 1982 (NOS Statistical Yearbook 1982).
2 NOS Labour Market statistics 1981.
3 Norwegians generally translate the 13–16 sector as 'lower secondary' and 16–19 as 'upper secondary'.
4 These were the cathedral schools in Christiania (now Oslo) and Trondheim.
5 The word 'pupil' in Norway refers to anyone who is studying at primary, secondary or upper-secondary (further education) level, regardless of age. The word 'student' is used only to describe someone undergoing higher education. This nomenclature is followed throughout the chapter.
6 Instilling 1 (1965) *Om Det Videregaende Skoleverket Fra Skolekomiteen av 1965 Kirke Og Undervisningsdepartementet*, p. 6.
7 Instilling 111 (1970) *Kirke Og Undervisningsdepartementet*, p. 55.

8 DOKKA, H.J. (1981) 'Reformarbeid i Norsk Skole', *NKS-Forlaget,* Oslo. p. 181.
9 Norway has a national curriculum in all subjects and types of school; the National Council for Innovation in Education (Forsoksradet) was able to co-ordinate research and experimentation through legislation passed in 1953 for this very purpose.
10 St. meld. nr. 91, 1969–70.
11 Ot. prp. Nr. 18, 1973–74.
12 An almost uniquely Scandinavian phenomenon, folk high schools are small, private further education boarding schools financed by foundations often associated with religious groups, trades unions etc. Nowadays they frequently take pupils who for social or psychological reasons have not adjusted to conventional schooling. Although a fascinating concept, the folk high schools by virtue of the very small numbers attending them, are not relevant to the subject of this chapter.
13 Act of 21 June 1974 'Concerning the Upper Secondary School', kirke-og undervisningsdepartemente, p. 1.
14 This organization is the equivalent of the Schools Council in England.
15 Act of 21 June 1974, *op cit* para. 7.
16 *Ibid* para. 18.
17 NOS Statistical Yearbooks 1965 and 1982.
18 Despite a concentration of approximately 1 million around the three major connurbations (Oslo, Bergen and Trondheim) the remaining 3 million population is scattered throughout the most sparsely populated country in the west (30 people per square mile).
19 Some 'model' schools such as Bjorkelangen and Romerike were completed in the early 1970s as part of the experimentation recommended by the Steen Committee.
20 NOS Statistical Yearbook.
21 For example the Business Education Council (BEC National and General) awards.
22 The case-studies referred to were carried out in connection with a PhD thesis at Elvebakken videregaende skole in Oslo and As videregaende skole in the town of As.
23 NOS Labour Market Statistics 1981.
24 FEU (1978) *A Basis for Choice,* DES.
25 St meld. nr. 22 (1979–80), kirke — og undervisningsdepartementet, 1980.
26 Until 1982 all primary, secondary and further education was under the Ministry for Church and Education. Further Education has since been separated from the former and instead combined with higher education.
27 'Aftenposten' 7 June 1983.
28 4071 (NOS Vital Statistics and Migration Statistics 1980).

NORTH AMERICA

The United States of America

As far as statistical evidence concerning youth goes, and within these pages there are comments from those who do not believe that this is a great distance, it should be borne in mind that 'youth' does not represent a homogeneous entity. Young people, although often grouped together for statistical purposes, can be obviously differentiated further into sub-sections including class, gender and ethnicity. This is a theme encountered in previous chapters and one to be developed in the following chapter on youth unemployment and work programmes in the United States of America.

Close to the time of the introduction of the Youth Opportunities Programme in Britain and the Pactes pour l'Emploi in France, the USA Congress legislated for the Youth Employment and Demonstration Projects Act (YEDPA) which 'established a well-funded focus on the problems of those youth with especially high rates of unemployment'. As in Britain and France the government responses to the problem of youth unemployment encompassed a variety of schemes under the umbrella of one Act. Again with chronological similarities in Europe — particularly in Britain, YEDPA was superceded in September 1983 by the Job Training Partnership Act (JTPA). There are further comparisons to be drawn between the JTPA and the British Youth Training Scheme (YTS). The JTPA, like the YTS, emphasizes training. They are both products of a conservative administration which came to power within the lifetime of the previous measures. They both suffer from restrictions in funding. Hamilton and Claus offer an analysis of the earlier responses to youth unemployment, they give an alternative interpretation of the situation as they see it, and an insight into how the most recent legislation approaches the problem.

Canada

At a time when even the archetypical youth labour market job at the fast-food counter is at a premium, when entry level jobs with prospects for skill acquisition and promotion are either disappearing in the wake of major technological changes or are being filled by experienced workers whose jobs have been declared redundant, at a time when most job vacancies are filled by people who already hold jobs in that particular field; in times such as these, reducing the problem of becoming established in the labour market to a question of 'choosing' an occupation that 'fits' an interests, aptitudes, and temperaments profile actually *increases* the probability that students will leave school ill-prepared to deal with the harsh realities of the social and economic conditions that will confront them.

This is the argument put forward in this contribution from Canada by Don Dippo. Dippo identifies a trend within the current thrust of career development programmes in Canada — that of 'talent-matching'. This is an aspect of career development which emphasizes 'commodification', or the enhancement of the saleability of labour by transforming people into more marketable goods. He gives an assessment of the suitability of this approach — and, importantly, its underlying ideology — for dealing with the problems faced by school-leavers in the current economic crisis. He criticizes both approach and ideology as being 'politically inappropriate as well as pedagogically inadequate curricular aims'.

Youth Unemployment in the United States: Problems and Programmes

Stephen F. Hamilton and John F. Claus

Perhaps the most difficult question to answer with respect to youth unemployment in the United States is also the most basic: What is the problem? It is easy to present frightening statistics, but to disaggregate these statistics sufficiently to inform a careful response to the problem is a complicated task. We attempt such analysis at the beginning of this chapter. Then we describe the most recent federal legislation aimed at high rates of domestic youth unemployment. The Youth Employment and Demonstration Projects Act of 1977 (YEDPA) was a broadly funded piece of legislation designed to test and gather information about different programs and approaches to the youth unemployment problem. We assess YEDPA and its associated programs in terms of their match with the problem as we define it and then we offer recommendations and a brief statement about the legislation that replaces YEDPA in September 1983.

Youth Unemployment Statistics

To the extent that youth unemployment is a serious problem in the United States, it is a problem not only of youthfulness but of race and class. The most extensive and damaging unemployment is experienced by low-income and minority youth. In order to substantiate this interpretation we must examine youth unemployment statistics carefully.

Even more than most social and economic indicators, youth unemployment statistics can very easily mislead. First of all, it is important to note that for a young person to be counted as unemployed in the United States, he or she must have no work and be 'in the labor force.' Being in the labor force requires that a person be either working or actively seeking work. Thus, a person who would like to work but has given up looking because they cannot find employment is officially not unemployed, because they are out of the labor force.

A second note of caution involves the fallacy of considering youth a homogeneous population. Age, educational status, gender, class, and race all play critical roles in young people's employment experiences. It is, thus, regrettable that youth employment statistics in the United States are primarily

Stephen F. Hamilton and John F. Claus

and rather imprecisely reported in terms of age. They generally refer either to teenagers (16–19) or to 'youth', but define youth as 16–21, 16–24, or sometimes 14–21. Even the smallest category, 16–19, includes high school students, dropouts, graduates and college students. The larger categories include these four groups and the graduates of both two-year and four-year colleges and training institutions. When the variables of gender, class, and race are added, the aggregate youth employment and unemployment statistics seem even less useful.

Wachter[1] has recalculated 1978 youth unemployment statistics for 16–19 year-olds in an attempt to minimize their all inclusive nature. His procedure is transparently designed, however, to lessen the severity of youth unemployment statistics. He treats youths in school and the military as part of the labor force but excludes from the ranks of the unemployed those students who are unsuccessfully looking for work. This has the effect of decreasing the proportion of the youthful labor force counted as unemployed. Nevertheless, Wachter's manipulations establish a very important point: the same procedures that reduce the 1978 unemployment rate for white males aged 18–19 from 10.9 to 6.1 reduce the unemployment rate for black males of the same age from 30.9 to 14.2. While it is plausible to argue that an unemployment rate of 6.1 per cent is not necessarily serious, an adjusted rate of 14.2 per cent demands attention. Wachter's adjusted unemployment rate for black females is even higher at 18.4 per cent.

Wachter's adjustments to standard youth unemployment statistics highlight the concentration of the problem among black youth. In addition, there are two bases for challenging the assumptions he used to reduce the magnitude of the problem. One is that some low-income, in-school youth need the earnings provided by part-time jobs for subsistence. While Wachter is right to claim that time in school returns greater long-term earnings than employment for many youth, there are some youth who do not have a choice. Although it is difficult to identify this group precisely, youth in female-headed households surely constitute a large part of it.

The second challenge to adjustments that reduce the magnitude of youth unemployment is the readiness of youth who are out of the labor force to enter the labor force when they have reason to believe they can find a job. The most dramatic demonstration of this readiness followed the implementation of the Youth Incentive Entitlement Pilot Projects (YIEPP) in Baltimore, Maryland. In an area of the city where Bureau of Labor Statistics reports and census data predicted a pool of 2,500 16–19 year olds seeking employment, 13,000 youth were actually enrolled after 18 months of operation. This was despite the imposition of extremely tight eligibility requirements, including continued enrollment or re-enrollment in school and a complex registration procedure.[2]

From one perspective, then, youth unemployment statistics overstate the magnitude of the phenomenon, because they include youth who are in school and in the military. From another, however, they understate the problem, because they exclude youth who would enter the labor force if they thought they could get a job. Most importantly, though, it is apparent that the youth unemployment problem is statistically most severe for low-income minority youth.

Race and the Youth Unemployment Problem

The importance of race has already been mentioned, but it is perhaps even better demonstrated by looking at youth unemployment and labor force participation rates over time. A review of the trend data from 1955 to 1978 indicates that the unemployment rate of young white males has remained between 10 per cent and 15 per cent while the non-white male unemployment rate has jumped from 16 per cent to 31 per cent (unadjusted rates).[3] In addition, the labor force participation rates of black and white youth were nearly equal in the 1950s. Since then white youth have participated in the labor force at an increasing rate while black youth participation has significantly declined.[4]

The negative impact of race on youth employment prospects is considerable; nevertheless, it is important to note that the majority of unemployed youth in the United States are white simply because the size of the white youth population is so much larger. According to Feldstein and Ellwood,[5] 'Approximately half of the difference between the unemployment rates of whites and blacks can be accounted for by other demographic and economic differences.' In other words, about half of the disadvantage of race in the youth labor market can be attributed to race itself while the other half is attributable to other factors, such as limited income and fewer years of schooling. Poor white youth, though less disadvantaged than poor black youth, *are* less likely than middle class white youth to find employment.

The Youth Labour Market

Youth in the US have been described as having a 'weak attachment' to the labor market because of the ease with which they move into and out of the labor force. This movement reflects the condition of most young people's lives. For youth there generally are the options of school enrollment as an alternative to work and the possibility of living with parents, which decreases the need for a steady income.

This movement in and out of the labor force also reflects the nature of the labor market that is open to youth. The youth labor market in the US is part of the 'secondary labor market,' which is characterized by low pay, low skill requirements, poor working conditions, little responsibility, and few opportunities for advancement. 'Youth jobs' are typically in such areas as food service, retail trade, and cleaning, and are usually found in small establishments. They involve little training and, as a result, tolerate high turnover.[6]

The combination of young people not necessarily needing steady employment and employers not expecting young workers to be long-term employees, creates a 'floundering period' that is typical for young men who are not in school. This period, which usually lasts only several years, is made up of frequent job changes punctuated by spells of unemployment.[7] The jobs are generally in the secondary labor market and with small firms. And for most young men they have no obvious connection to one another, either in terms of the skills they require or their occupational field. They are merely the best jobs that can be found at the time. Nevertheless, many of the young men who do not go on to college do eventually establish a career of some sort, typically about the same time their high school classmates who went to college are establishing theirs.[8]

There are, however, some exceptions to this pattern. Fewer low-income minority youth make the transition from the floundering period to a 'career.' For them the pattern of frequent periods of youth unemployment has a greater tendency to extend into adulthood and become chronic.[9] On the other hand, youths with access to jobs in certain unionized industries find higher quality entry level positions and exit the floundering period early. Marriage also tends to be associated with early departure from the secondary labor market. The responsibilities of wife and home apparently place a limit upon the amount of unemployment one may assume by choice.[10] It is also interesting to note that young women are not as likely as young men to experience the floundering period, an advantage that is offset by the fact that many of the lifetime careers young women enter soon after leaving high school have the same characteristics as the secondary labor market jobs that most young men eventually leave behind.

Some Consequences of Youth Unemployment

If there are important distinctions to be made concerning who the youth are who experience unemployment, then the consequences of youth unemployment are also likely to vary depending upon the characteristics of the youth sub-population examined. The consequences generally of greatest interest, in part because they are most easily measured, are employment and earnings effects as measured by economists. The most obvious and immediate consequence of unemployment is loss of earnings, and this loss is clearly most serious for older youth, poor youth, and young parents. The single, poor, unemployed 22-year-old mother of two is cause for greater concern than the unemployed 16-year-old high school student who lives with his or her parents.

Taking a longer view, there is evidence from the National Longitudinal Surveys (NLS), which followed the same young people from their late teens to their early twenties, that youth unemployment is associated with reduced subsequent employment and earnings. Stephenson[11] concluded that both black and white young men who are employed while in school experienced less unemployment and higher earnings in later years than those who were unemployed as students. This reduction in unemployment included both fewer and shorter periods of looking for work.

Focusing on a different NLS subsample, Stevenson[12] found that young men and women who were both out of school and unemployed as adolescents were most likely to be unemployed as young adults ages (23–26). Ellwood[13] disagrees with Stevenson's attribution of greater adult unemployment to unemployment experienced while a student, but agrees that earnings are depressed during the four years following unemployment as a student.[14] In general, earnings rise and the incidence of unemployment falls as a function of increasing age, but it appears that a serious consequence of unemployment among certain school age youth is the increased likelihood of unemployment persisting into adulthood.

Another potential consequence of youth unemployment is reduced attachment to the labor market and to society in general. This is a less easily measured phenomenon and has generally been addressed by sociologists, educational researchers, and blue ribbon panels making policy recommendations. Perhaps the best known of these panels was the Panel on Youth of the President's Science Advisory Committee (1974), chaired by James Coleman. The concerns of the Panel on Youth were not so much with disadvantaged youth and unemployment as with the perceived weakening of youth's commitment to the social order as reflected in violent political activism opposing the Vietnam war, increasing drug use, and riots by black urban youth. The Panel's diagnosis of the origins of these ills was that they were caused by the segregation of youth from adult society and its responsibilities. As a result, the Panel's prescription was to increase the community involvement of youth through employment and unpaid activities outside of schools.

A more recent panel, Carnegie Council on Policy Studies in Higher Education, has produced a related but more focused report.[15] The Carnegie Council was primarily concerned with the unemployment of disadvantaged youth and, although it explicitly linked its analysis and recommendations to those of the Panel on Youth, its report pays scant attention to the white middle class youth who were the principal target of the Panel on Youth's concerns. Indeed, one of the strongest points of the Carnegie Council's report is its careful attention to differences among the youth population. Adapting a typology of youth proposed by Martin Trow, the Council distinguished four large categories of youth depending upon family income and high school performance. The family income categories were: top two-thirds and bottom one-third. The high school performance categories were: completed high school and dropped out. Youth with family incomes in the top two-thirds who completed high school were described as 'advantaged' and estimated to constitute just over half of the population. Youth with identical family incomes who dropped out of high school were described as either 'personally deprived' or 'opt-outs.' Poor youth, those with family income in the bottom one-third, who, nevertheless, graduated from high school, were classified as 'financially disadvantaged' and estimated at 20 per cent of the population. The most disadvantaged group in this classification scheme was made up of those who had failed to complete high school and whose family incomes fell in the bottom one-third.

It is the low income group, the 'financially disadvantaged' and 'socially deprived', to which the Carnegie Council directed its attention. The Council estimated that this group constituted 38 per cent of the total youth population, and 60 per cent of the black and Hispanic youth populations.[16] In addition to its other benefits, this typology makes the often overlooked point that disadvantaged youth are very different from one another. While all disadvantaged youth suffer from economic constraints and many suffer from racial discrimination, some do succeed in obtaining educational credentials despite the barriers. Some also receive considerable non-material support from their families. Both groups of disadvantaged youth deserve policies and programs to help them overcome their disadvantages, but the needs of those who are both financially and socially deprived are much greater than of those who are only financially deprived.

Another way the Carnegie Council placed youth into categories was by 'activity status.' Most youth were classified as either in school or at work. Smaller proportions fell into the activity statuses of unemployed, homemaker, in the armed forces, institutionalized, or disabled. This schema also calls attention to a residual category, 'none of the above,' that, in 1977, included almost as many youth as the unemployed. The Council suggests that this group, 5.7 per cent of the total, along with the long-term unemployed (1.3 per cent), is subject to the most serious problems and should be targeted for the most intense attention.[17]

The Cause of Youth Unemployment

When the teenage (16–19) unemployment rate in the United States set a new record of 21.5 per cent in December, 1981[18] there were numerous explanations available:

(i) Overall weakness in the economy was felt most dramatically among low-skill workers whose services employers could do without.
(ii) The entry into the workforce of increasing numbers of women created competition with youth for part-time jobs in retail trade, food service, and similar occupations.
(iii) The long-term trend toward mechanized manufacturing eliminated large numbers of low-skill jobs once held by young people.
(iv) The movement of manufacturing and commerce from center cities to suburbs left low-income city dwellers without access to an adequate number of potential youth jobs.
(v) The minimum wage was too high for many employers to spend it on unskilled or unreliable youth.
(vi) Youth move in and out of the labor force and from job to job with great frequency, creating high 'frictional' unemployment.
(vii) Youth are unfamiliar with the labor market and search for employment inefficiently, thus prolonging their unemployment.
(viii) Poor schools result in youth who have few skills, including specific job skills and basic academic skills.

The preceding emphasis on identifying the specific sub-groups of the youth population experiencing unemployment helps to sort through these proposed causes. First, it must be acknowledged that all are plausible and that all can and probably do operate simultaneously. Next, the relation between various potential causes and the groups most affected by youth unemployment must be examined. Black youth unemployment was increasing while white youth unemployment remained stable, and there was a concentration of unemployment among those youths who were out of school and had been unemployed for long periods of time[19] (70–80 per cent last 15 weeks or more). Thus, two critical sources of the problem appear to be the limited educational opportunities and attainments of low-income minority youth and the lack of sufficient youth jobs in cities where there are high concentrations of these youth.

The choice of emphasis on these two, potentially complementary, explanations of youth unemployment is a momentous one. It represents the dual concerns of most recent federal youth employment legislation. As Ginzberg[20] has pointed out, one can try to explain youth unemployment primarily in terms of either the nature of the labor market — i.e. the lack of jobs — or deficits of the unemployed youth — i.e. their educational or attitudinal failings. The first explanation suggests that public policy be aimed at job creation through efforts such as public service job programs, tax credits to employers hiring the disadvantaged, or even the reduction of the minimum wage. In contrast, the second explanation suggests that policy be aimed at changing youth by doing such things as improving urban schools or providing alternative education or employment training programs.

We have argued previously[21] that it is possible and desirable to accept Ginzberg's contention that both perspectives have some truth. We have also argued that structural inequality is an additional factor underlying the distribution of youth unemployment. The US labor market is hierarchical and has large differences in status, income, and working conditions separating jobs at different levels. At the very bottom of the hierarchy are the unskilled and unemployed. Age, education, and previous work experience are central criteria distinguishing applicants for jobs at each different level and youth are, by definition, deficient in all three criteria. But the real problem is that while some youth will, in time, acquire the characteristics required to make them credible applicants for desirable jobs, others, primarily those who are low-income and minority, will not. Despite the promises of democracy, the strongest determinant of a young person's chances to achieve this transformation is family background.[22] There is convincing evidence that economic opportunity in the United States is structured unequally such that people adapt developmentally to their 'probable futures.' Many workers at the lower end of the job market assume beliefs and behaviors functional to their place in the hierarchy and transmit these to their children. In combination with race- and class-discriminating practices in the schools, workplaces, and other major institutions of the society, this leads to a tendency for class inequalities to be reproduced.[23] Structural inequality, then, seems another important cause of high rates of unemployment among low-income minority youth. These youth are subject to the same limited job market and employment problems their parents have experienced.

The Youth Employment and Demonstration Projects Act

We turn now to a review of recent youth employment programs in the United States. It is our intention to examine how they have translated various explanations of youth unemployment into program practice and whether they have been effective with regard to their immediate goals and the broad objective of reducing youth unemployment. Extensive funding and a diversity of programs in recent years have contributed to the development of a revealing knowledge base.

In 1977 the United States Congress legislated a large-scale attack on the problem of youth unemployment. At that time Congress amended and expanded the Comprehensive Employment and Training Act of 1973 (CETA) by passing into law the Youth Employment and Demonstration Projects Act (YEDPA). The CETA legislation, like much before it, had encompassed a wide variety of employment and training programs, only some of which were concerned with unemployed youth. With the introduction of YEDPA, Congress established a well-funded focus on the problems of those youth with especially high rates of unemployment.

The YEDPA program represents one of the largest single-issue social experiments in the history of American domestic social programing.[24] Funded at annual levels exceeding one billion dollars, YEDPA legislation served 750,000 youth through the creation of four major new programs: the Young Adult Conservation Corps (YACC) the Youth Community Conservation and Involvement Projects (YCCIP), the Youth Incentive Entitlement Projects (YIEPP), and the Youth Employment and Training Programs (YETP). It also authorized the expansion of allocations to two existing programs, the Job Corps and the Summer Youth Employment Program (SYEP), totaling another one billion dollars, and set aside considerable funds (up to 20 per cent of the total YEDPA budget) for 'knowledge development projects,' which included academic research, innovative demonstration programs and program evaluations. Despite the rather large number of employment programs implemented in previous years, only limited information was available to Congress in 1977 concerning the youth unemployment problem and the relative effectiveness of various program designs.[25] As a result, YEDPA legislation carried with it an explicit objective to innovate, experiment, and research for the purpose of testing different approaches to and developing a better understanding of the problems of unemployed youth.

YEDPA legislation was aimed primarily at the perceived employment and school-to-work transition problems of low-income, minority youth. Unemployment statistics made it clear that this group experienced the most difficulty in obtaining work and was the most severely affected in later years by a lack of early employment. Basically, YEDPA programs either attempted to remedy assumed deficiencies in these youth by offering them training and education or tried to expand their presumably limited job market by giving them jobs. Some programs tried to do both. As such the YEDPA programs were something of a large scale reflection and test of the dichotomy raised by Ginzberg[26] in his discussion of prevailing explanations for high rates of youth unemployment. There were YEDPA programs based on the argument that certain youth have difficulty getting jobs because they lack the skills and habits necessary for employment, and there were programs rooted in the view that the problem begins with a lack of demand for these young workers. There were also programs which reflected the belief that such explanations are not mutually exclusive.

Thus, even though neither the knowledge development nor the program components of YEDPA experienced very long life (a new presidential administration came to power in 1980, leading to drastic budget reductions and significant changes in policy), existing YEDPA research and evaluation materials constitute a rich resource for those concerned with finding solutions for high rates of unemployment among disadvantaged youth. The attention given to evaluating YEDPA programs and analyzing the youth unemployment problem during the YEDPA years has left us with a knowledge base useful both in assessing the value of various policy approaches and in improving our understanding of the causes of the problem.

Judgments concerning the relative effectiveness of these programs are not often easy or fair to make. The goals and target populations of YEDPA programs varied to such a degree that they are often incomparable. Nevertheless, if each major program is reviewed in light of certain basic questions, such as what services did it provide, what did it cost, who did it reach and what short and long-term employment effects did it achieve, some important program recommendations do come to light and at least a few theoretical conclusions can be drawn.

Youth Employment and Training Programs (YETP)

The YETP component of YEDPA was designed to improve the career preparation of both in-school and out-of-school youth, ages 16–21, who were economically disadvantaged and experiencing serious difficulty finding work. A major assumption underlying YETP was that many low-income youth suffer employment problems because they lack educational credentials and knowledge about how to break into the job market. Consistent with this assumption YETP offered a wide variety of primarily educational services including job training, remedial instruction in academic and vocational subjects, and career and academic counseling. There were school-based apprenticeship and community work programs, career-oriented alternative schools, classes to help participants obtain a high school diploma, academic credit options for work experience, and courses which taught job-getting skills. Above all else, YETP attempted to foster collaborations between employment programs and educational agencies in the interest of smoothing the school-to-work transition for low income youth.

The YETP record is mixed. Consisting largely of classroom and short-term work experience programs, YETP was able to reach large numbers of disadvantaged youth never before included in employment-oriented social programs. YETP enrollments were twice those of the YCCIP, Job Corps, YIEPP and YACC programs combined, and more than 80 per cent of these participants were youth living in families with incomes below the poverty line[27]. YETP also achieved a relatively low negative-termination-rate. While only 25 per cent of all YETP enrollees actually completed their programs, another 40 per cent left for positive reasons such as entering the military, entering another YEDPA program, or continuing in school. This means that only about 35 per cent of YETP enrollees left their programs for negative reasons before finishing[28]. Relative to many pre-YEDPA work programs this is successfully low. In addition, YETP appears to have had a positive, although modest, impact regarding two key objectives. The immediate post-program wages of YETP participants who found jobs showed a $.32 per hour gain over the pre-program wage or earning power of all YETP program participants[29]. And YETP was generally able to improve communication and understanding between work programs and public schools[30].

At least on one level then, YETP was successful. It reached a population in need, increased somewhat their chances for further education or a better wage, and improved the institutional network within which the school-to-work transition occurs. Nevertheless, these achievements appear modest to inconsequential when considered in light of additional evidence and of the grand scale of the problem. For example, YETP was designed to serve out-of-school as well as in-school youth. The main out-of-school target group, disadvantaged high school dropouts, is the one identified by the Carnegie Council as the neediest and hardest to serve. Sadly, YETP was unable to attract many youth in this category; fewer than 20 per cent of all YETP enrollees were low income high school dropouts.[31] These youth were apparently not interested in work programs with a school or classroom orientation[32]. Furthermore, the wage increases associated with YETP completion can be discounted almost entirely by wage inflation during the period[33], and the use of 'positive termination rates' obscures the fact that only 25 per cent of all YETP participants found work at the end of their programs[34]. It is also important to note that reports of collaborations between YETP programs and the public schools are countered by other studies which suggest that such collaboration had little real impact on program participants' educational attainment. Only 17 per cent of all YETP youth, for example, received academic credit for their YETP participation in the year 1979[35].

Thus, despite YETP's extensive funding and specific targeting it seems to have fallen short of expectations. Many youth in need were involved, but when the total program is considered in terms of identifiable participant outcomes it is apparent that YETP was able to achieve only modest gains.

Youth Incentive Entitlement Pilot Projects (YIEPP)

The pattern described above with regard to the effectiveness of YETP is a familiar one in the review of YEDPA programs. The YIEPP component of YEDPA, for example, produced similarly limited effects. YIEPP programs were designed around the goal of providing low income unemployed youth between the ages of 16 and 19 with a work incentive to complete high school. As with YETP, the primary purpose of YIEPP programs was to raise the educational levels of these youth. Eligible youths in targeted poverty areas were guaranteed year-round jobs (twenty hours a week during the school year and up to forty hours a week in the summer) if they would agree to continue in high school, return to school, or enroll in a high school equivalency course. The intention was to draw these youth back to and through high school with entitlement to a job.

YIEPP did achieve some success. Nearly 50,000 youth were placed in public or private sector jobs annually. Seventy-five per cent of these youth were black and almost all were poor, came from areas of extreme poverty, and had been unemployed for over a year. Eighty-five per cent of the YIEPP jobs these youths filled represented employment that would not have occurred without the program[36]. If nothing else, then, YIEPP meant work at the minimum wage or better, where little had previously existed, for a sizeable number of severely disadvantaged youth. YIEPP also meant work of good quality. A well-documented problem with previous work programs was that the work often seemed to be 'makework' or meaningless in terms of workers' development and workplace or societal contributions[37]. In an evaluation of 520 YIEPP work sites, the jobs in six out of seven were deemed worthwhile in terms of supervision and training[38]. This represents a considerable improvement over previous efforts. Additionally, YIEPP was able to increase somewhat the school enrollment and retention rates of participating youth. About 10 per cent of the high school dropouts eligible for YIEPP programs were attracted back to school as a result of the work entitlement incentive, and about seven per cent of the eligible in-school youth could be said to have remained in school because of YIEPP[39]. These are modest improvements but improvements nonetheless.

Despite these achievements, however, YIEPP had a number of problems. As with YETP, few school dropouts were attracted to the program. Only 13 per cent of YIEPP participants were out-of-school youth[40]. This group did not find the prospect of returning to school appealing, even with the enticement of part-time paid work. Collaborations between YIEPP and private sector employers were also limited and problematic. Part of the YIEPP plan was to find work in the private sector of the economy for as many participants as possible. Research shows that private sector work experience has the most positive effect on employability[41]. But, even offering private sector employers a 100 per cent wage subsidy for all program participants hired, YIEPP could never place more than 20 per cent of its participants in private sector jobs[42]. Finally, post program employment rates for YIEPP participants were not very good. Even though these rates had not been fully determined for YIEPP when funding for YEDPA was eliminated in 1980, early data had suggested that net employment effects were modest[43].

Thus, YIEPP programs were moderately effective as a vehicle for increasing the school participation rates of some poor unemployed youth. They also provided participating youth income producing jobs. But, as with YETP, the main clients of the program were in-school youth, the least needy of all eligible youth. And participants' work experiences were generally restricted to the public sector. Furthermore, post-program employment experiences did not reveal significant program effects.

This, then, raises questions concerning the cost effectiveness of programs like YETP and YIEPP. It also calls into question the assumptions underlying these programs regarding the courses of and possible solutions to the youth unemployment problem. It may be, for example, that educational credentials and knowledge about the job market have little to do, at least for these youth, with success in the world of work.

Youth Community Conservation and Improvement Projects (YCCIP)

In contrast to the educational orientation of YETP and YIEPP, the YCCIP component of YEDPA was aimed primarily toward the creation of jobs. Participants were to receive academic credit wherever possible, but the fundamental goal of YCCIP was to 'develop the vocational potential of jobless youth through well-supervised work of tangible community benefit'[44]. Aimed at unemployed 16–19 year olds, with no income restrictions and a preference

for out-of-school youth with severe employment problems, YCCIP established housing rehabilitation projects, railroad repair groups, a hydroelectric
dam repair project, and various other community development ventures in the
interest of employing eligible youth in jobs of both personal and community
value.

YCCIP was not particularly large in scope (20,000 jobs annually), but it
was successful in a number of ways. For one, YCCIP was able to attract
significant numbers of seriously disadvantaged out-of-school youth. Over 80
per cent of the YCCIP enrollees were high school dropouts, 84 per cent were
living below the poverty line, and more than 50 per cent were from
disadvantaged minority groups[45]. YCCIP also complemented its work experiences with good support services. YCCIP work projects often operated with a
supervisor-to-youth ratio as low as 1:6[46] and was able to augment the work
experience focus with job training that kept participants' interest[47]. In addition, and possibly of most interest, YCCIP participants who found work in
the private sector following the program often got jobs in the generally more
lucrative construction trades, leading to a gain of $.64 over their assumed or
actual pre-program wage[48].

These findings speak well for YCCIP and its focus on work experience.
But, as with many other youth work programs, indications of YCCIP's
successes were tempered by a number of less positive findings. YCCIP, like
YIEPP, was unable to open up many jobs in the private sector. It also had
difficulty attracting young women. Fewer than 30 per cent of the YCCIP
participants were females while in YETP and YIEPP the proportion was
about 50 per cent[49]. Certainly much of this difference resulted from YCCIP's
preference for out-of-school youth. Young women who are out of school are
more likely than their in-school counterparts to have childcare responsibilities which could keep them out of a work program. Nevertheless, unemployed out-of-school young women represent a significant population in
need, and YCCIP was unable to reach as many of them as its planners would
have liked[50].

YCCIP also cost a great deal. The annual estimated cost of serving a
participant in YCCIP was almost twice that of the average of other YEDPA
programs (U.S. Department of Labor, 1980b). And this expense was reflected
in the estimated dollar value of the product of YCCIP participants' work,
which was about half that of the average for other YEDPA programs[51].
Furthermore, the YCCIP post-program employment rate was disappointing.
Only one in every five YCCIP participants found work when they left the
program[52]. Thus, while YCCIP indicates that disadvantaged out-of-school
youth can be enrolled in work programs if the emphasis is on jobs rather than
schooling, it also supports the view that program completers continue to face
barriers in the job market.

Young Adult Conservation Corps (YACC)

Like YCCIP, YACC was a fairly straightforward work program; however, it
included enrichment or counseling far less frequently. Directly descended

from the Civilian Conservation Corps (CCC), a program run from 1933 to 1942, and the Youth Conservation Corps (YCC) of the early 1970s, YACC created conservation work and other jobs with the federal and state park services for young people, ages 16–23, who were out of school and unemployed. The work was part-time during the school year and full-time during the summer and generally involved manual labor for the purpose of developing and maintaining public lands and recreational facilities. In addition to its conservation emphasis, YACC was different from other YEDPA programs in two interesting ways. It served youth of all socio-economic backgrounds, making it the least targeted of all YEDPA endeavors, and, it had very little money set aside for education, research, or evaluation.

The virtues of the YACC design rest primarily with the kind of work YACC youth produced and the somewhat heterogeneous grouping of participants. The estimated dollar value of the output of the YACC workers was far and away the highest of all YEDPA programs, being higher by half than the output of YETP participants, YACC's nearest competitor on this criterion[53]. In addition, YACC had a more positive image among eligible youth than did other YEDPA programs. It was less frequently associated with welfare in their eyes, due to its inclusion of youth from a variety of socio-economic backgrounds[54]. Thus, the net wage expenditure for YACC work seemed a good investment and, consistent with findings for the YCC, YACC was generally a well-liked program.

Regrettably, though, these virtues did not seem to translate into significant developmental outcomes for YACC youth. Very little evaluative research exists with regard to YACC, but it is clear that much YACC work was not very meaningful in terms of developing marketable job skills. While the work did mean employment, income, and a social contribution, it was often simple and boringly repetitious. It also tended to lack the kind of supervision which might have made even simple work a useful social experience[55].

In the absence of information about the socialization or employment effects of YACC, reviews of YACC indicate that it did provide jobs but with little apparent developmental potential. One must not underestimate the value, in and of itself, of in-program employment here — it did in many cases mean income where there was a serious need — but, without attention to the quality of the work, from the perspective of the workers' development, it seems there was little to improve participants' chances for development and post-program employment.

The Jobs Corps

The Job Corps is a unique and successful work program which YEDPA legislation doubled in size. Under YEDPA it was able to serve about 40,000 youths annually. Created in 1964 under the Economic Opportunity Act, the Job Corps was designed as and remains an intensive residential training program for out-of-school, unemployed, low income youth, between the ages of 16–21. Although it began with something of a conservation work orientation, the Job Corps today emphasizes job training and education in connection with work and specific work opportunities in the private sector of the economy.

The Job Corps' residential training centers are often held up by the Department of Labor as model youth work programs. After considerable evaluation, criticism, and refinement in the early years, these centers have become the cornerstone to what has been called a 'social experiment that works'[56]. Indeed, the Job Corps' record far surpasses that of other YEDPA programs.

Of all youth employment programs in the USA, the Job Corps generally enrolls those youth with the poorest educational background and employment prospects[57]. Many are poor, unemployed minority youth who have dropped out of high school and have a record of juvenile arrests[58]. Job Corps centers provide these youth with training, work experience, basic education, counseling, and health care in a setting away from home, and there is evidence that they do this effectively.

In a 1977 evaluation it was found that of the Job Corps participants for that year, 64 per cent obtained jobs, 23 per cent returned to school, and 6 per cent entered the military. This means that 93 per cent of all Job Corps participants in 1977, including program dropouts, were effectively removed from the out-of-school, unemployed category[59]. In addition, those who were employed were greater in number and were earning a slightly higher wage seven months after they left or completed the program than were employed youth in a control group[60]. Not surprisingly, then, Job Corps participants also experienced reduced welfare participation and arrest rates, contributing to greater employability and a reduction in public costs for welfare, legal, and correctional services[61]. It is also noteworthy that in the post-program period studied Job Corps youth were 40 per cent more likely to obtain a high school diploma and 60 per cent more likely to enroll in college or post-secondary training programs than were control group youth[62].

These successes have generally been attributed to three key features of the Job Corps design. First, the residential nature of the training centers gives the program more control over participating youth and their development. There is less opportunity for the home environment and its various requirements and distractions to compete or interfere with the job training intervention[63]. Second, the training and education offered through the centers is primarily on-the-job in format and focused on the requirements of a particular job. This provides participants with directly applicable job skills and credentials which often lead to employment. And third, the Job Corps centers have often been able to establish and subsidize specific links to, and collaborations with, private sector employers. Cooperative training and placement arrangements between the Job Corps and various labor unions, for example, have led to some Job Corps programs which train to fit union needs and jobs. These efforts have, in turn, led to favorable placement rates.[64]

There are a number of positive lessons to be learned from the Job Corps program. However, it is important to note that some of the Job Corps' present successes followed fourteen years of experience and corrected mistakes. This is a luxury few other youth work programs have had. In addition, the Job Corps model is not easily transferred to more localized programs, and it is not without its problems. One of the virtues of the centralized residential format, for example, is that youth can be moved away from areas where employment opportunities are meagre and placed in regions of greater growth. This allows for stronger links to the private sector, and it encourages greater optimism on the part of participating youth regarding their opportunity. These virtues are generally lost amid the limiting conditions extant in the home locales of targeted youth[65].

Furthermore, some of the virtues of the Job Corps design are also its vices. The residential program, for example, is apparently not well suited to all targeted youth, especially those between 16–18. There is a high dropout rate in the Job Corps in general (over 50 per cent) and many of the dropouts are younger enrollees[66]. Much of this results from the requirement of living away from home and the conditions at the centers. There are many complaints of homesickness, poor food, and sub-standard living arrangements. There are also complaints about low pay (on the average, $100 per month). The high dropout rate is a particularly important problem, because the longer participants spend in the Job Corps the more likely they are to complete the program, and for those who finish there do tend to be benefits[67].

A final problem associated with the residential format is its expense. Compared to other YEDPA programs the Job Corps' annual per capita cost is very high. At $13,000 in 1979 it was about a third again as high as the next most expensive program and about twice the average program's per capita cost[65]. But because the Job Corps is effective in many respects, for many observers the return justifies the large investment. The Job Corps is the most successful of U.S. youth employment programs.

The Summer Youth Employment Program (SYEP)

SYEP, formerly called the Summer Program for Economically Disadvantaged Youth (SPEDY), has existed as long as the Job Corps. Its image and documented effectiveness, though, have been much less positive. Even though SYEP has annually reached more disadvantaged youth between the ages of 14 and 21 than all other youth work programs combined, it has had a reputation, especially during the pre-YEDPA years, of providing public 'makework' for inner city youth in an attempt to keep them off the streets and limit their potential for violent expressions of discontent.[69] A number of critics have called SYEP 'federally legislated fire insurance' for the inner city.[70]

Under YEDPA, the quality of the work experiences provided by SYEP did improve somewhat. Intensive monitoring and enrichment efforts led to the finding in 1980 that only 10–15 per cent (as opposed to 40–50 per cent in prior years) of SYEP worksites were inadequate in their supervision and training.[71] Nevertheless, the impact of SYEP has never gone much beyond the wages earned by its youthful (primarily 14–17) and often inner city minority participants. In a 1980 evaluation, for example, SYEP registered no significant impact with regard to post-program wages, full-time employment, arrest rates, or attitudes. SYEP participation *was* associated with gains in school enrollment and part-time work, both of which are consistent with school age youth, but even these effects were quite modest.[72] SYEP, then, stands as negative testimony regarding the value of short-term work experiences in which the primary goal is income transfer. Without question, income transfer can be an important outcome of youth work programs, but where increasing participants' employability is concerned it is clearly insufficient.

Explanations for the Limited Effects of Youth Employment Programs

The most common conclusion to YEDPA program evaluations is one of modest accomplishment. Consistent with findings concerning earlier work programs[73], many YEDPA programs have no measurable impact, or if they do they only affect targeted youth for short periods of time or in small numbers.[74] Four types of explanations tend to be offered for this general program failure: implementation flaws, the magnitude of the resocialization task, resistance on the part of other institutions, and program design problems.

There is often considerable difference between a program's design and its practice. By the time policy and design features are translated at various levels of bureaucracy and are funded across widely divergent regions and administrative personnel, they can become far removed from their original form. Rist reports such problems in the way certain YEDPA programs established collaborative efforts with other agencies,[75] and the General Accounting Office similarly criticized many SYEP programs for failing to carry out clearly stated work supervision goals.[76] Poor implementation can be a serious problem and avoiding it requires close project monitoring.

Another reason given for limited program impact is that employment-dysfunctional attitudes and habits are too well ingrained and functional in the home environments of many poor, unemployed youth to be replaced by attitudes and behaviors associated with success in the primary labor market. Walther[77] calls this a problem of 'competing competencies,' arguing that employment and training programs cannot expect to compete with the amount of time targeted youth spend in settings which encourage 'street' rather than 'work' skills. A.L. Nellum Associates[78] have discussed the poor records of a number of inner city SYEP programs in these terms, and Goodwin, in reviewing the attitudinal effects of a variety of YEDPA programs, uses this argument to explain the absence of long-term effects where short-term effects had previously been documented. This is a controversial interpretation in that there is substantial research to suggest that most of the youths in question want to work and are capable of appropriate behaviors if the work exists and carries with it a promise of opportunity for growth and reward.[79] Nevertheless, the success of the Job Corps residential centers and the failures of many localized inner city projects lend credence to the argument in the eyes of some observers, even though the respective success and failure of these programs can also be explained in terms of whether they did or did not offer work and training with perceptible opportunity and rewards attached.

A third common explanation for work program failures is that their activities often meet with resistance from important institutions. Public schools, for instance, often resisted giving YEDPA youth credit for their work or training, despite its educational content and goals.[80] And private sector employers were reluctant to hire YIEPP participants, even when offered a 100 per cent wage subsidy.[81] In the former situation the problem was one of conflicting criteria, professional boundary staking, and miscommunication. In the latter, it was often an issue of their employer misperceptions concerning the characteristics of YIEPP participants,[82] insufficient time and money to take on the responsibility of job training, or a simple lack of jobs. Problems with the schools could possibly be solved by giving them more control over work programs' educational components; with private sector employers, work programs might be more effective if they promised to train youth first for the specific jobs in question. Nevertheless, breaking into the private sector on a significant scale seems a critical problem not as easily solved as the problems with public schools.[83]

A final explanation for the modest effects of youth work programs involves additional design problems. Work programs are often criticized, for example, for offering nothing but handouts in the form of wages for meaningless work.[84] Program evaluators have also observed that the homogeneous targeting of many youth work programs may stigmatize participants in the eyes of employers and create peer situations within the programs which tend to reinforce rather than alter participants' employment-dysfunctional behaviors.[85] These problems could be addressed by ensuring that work experiences provide relevant job skill development and by opening up program enrollments to create groups with a wider variety of socio-economic backgrounds. But, of course, the latter of these solutions has problems itself, in that it may direct some valuable funding away from the youth who need it most.

We find merit in many of these arguments and accept as valuable many of the recommendations flowing from them. Nevertheless, it is sometimes difficult to sustain optimism regarding the potential of programs that basically have a short-term resocialization and income transfer focus. Regardless of program designs and expenditures there remain for low income, unemployed minority youth the problems of insufficient jobs and inequality in the structure of economic opportunity. Research conducted as part of the YEDPA knowledge development effort reveals that aggregate demand factors in the job market are an important source of the current youth employment problem. Freeman,[86] for example, shows that local job conditions are a key determinant of youth employment rates. Not suprisingly, geographic areas with high overall labor demand have relatively low rates of youth unemployment. In addition, Smith and Vanski[87] and Clark and Summers[88] provide convincing national evidence that high rates of youth unemployment are the result of a generally limited demand for workers. They show that youth unemployment rates decline, even among the most seriously disadvantaged eventually, as the demand for workers increases. This suggests that the youth unemployment problem is less one of training than it is of a limited demand for labor. It also explains the recent program evaluation finding that immediate post-program employment and wage gains are often unrelated to longer term gains.[89] There simply are not enough private sector jobs.

Unemployed, economically disadvantaged minority youth suffer the additional problem of unequal opportunity. For these youth there appears to be discrimination in hiring practices as well as long term difficulty breaking into the primary labor market. A national evaluation of various YEDPA programs found that white youths were significantly more successful at obtaining post-program, full-time employment than were blacks, regardless of type of program, local labor market conditions, reading ability, career knowledge, attitude scores, and educational level.[90] This is consistent with other studies concerning minority opportunity,[91] and it suggests that even as some work programs contribute to the employability of their participants, they fail to alter the disparity between minority and white employment rates. It has also been found that through a pattern of discrimination and adaptation, minority workers are much less likely than whites to be promoted from entry level jobs into the primary labor market.[92] Given that much of the work for which employment programs train participants is of an entry level and secondary labor market nature it would appear that current work programs can do little to alter the inequality extant in the duality of our labor market.

Thus, we are persuaded by the radical view of U.S. youth employment programs which suggests that they can have no more than marginal effects because of a structurally unequal distribution of unemployment and underemployment in the economy.[93] Recent youth employment programs fail to overcome this inequality, because they tend to address a symptom of the problem, not its cause. They attempt to intervene at the non-determining point of individual behavior. We believe, based on the evidence, that a desirable level of employment opportunity can only be achieved through a broad restructuring of the economy and its workplaces.

The implications of such a conclusion are broad and complex. Space does not allow their full discussion here, but, as we have written elsewhere[94] the abstract and distant goal of restructuring the economy must not discourage us from developing program and policy options which may address both current problems and ultimate goals. Thus, in conclusion we offer a set of program recommendations which, if satisfied, could help programs simultaneously respond to the immediate problems associated with high rates of youth unemployment and contribute to structural change in the economy.

Recommendations

The YEDPA knowledge development material does offer some useful insights into what may constitute effective employment programing for unemployed disadvantaged youth. Despite the limited impact of YEDPA and many of its associated programs, there were successes worthy of optimism and attention. It appears that recent work programs have been most effective when they offered long-term (at least a year) paid work experiences within a framework of job-relevant training, educational credit, and links to the private sector. Income producing jobs are almost universally attractive to unemployed disadvantaged youth, and training, educational credit, and private sector connections are the enrichments required to give these work experiences the promise of opportunity and the power to increase participants' employability.[95]

We would add to this list the recommendation that youth work programs provide disadvantaged unemployed youth with experiences and skills functional to participation in the primary labor market. They can do this by offering the widest possible range of job experiences as far up the occupational hierarchy as is feasible and by promoting the development of entrepreneurial and democratic-participation skills. This might improve the chances of disadvantaged unemployed youth as they seek work in the primary job market, and it might also give them the skills and motivation necessary to work toward the development of more democratic, i.e., less hierarchical, workplaces. In this way work programs could improve the job competitiveness of targeted youth and at the same time increase their potential to affect some of the structural inequality underlying the youth unemployment problem.[96]

Work programs should also be designed and targeted to recognize the differences among disadvantaged youth. There are numerous sub-populations of youth in need and many require special services if they are to be attracted to employment and training programs. Young unemployed single mothers are a poignant case in point. In addition, we stress that youth work programs must attempt to create new long term jobs in the private sector. This might be done through a combination of tax incentives, wage and machine-purchase subsidies, specific pre-work job training, and close support for employers as they first engage targeted youth. Only when it is genuinely profitable to private sector employers will they get involved and have reason to employ work program participants after wage subsidies are withdrawn.

Finally, given the larger view, we recommend that federal policy be designed to foster the development of more democratically structured workplaces. Worker owned and managed businesses currently face problems obtaining financing, and conventional, hierarchical companies have little incentive to change. Tax breaks, low-interest financing, and federal knowledge development and dissemination might all be employed to encourage democratic experiments in the workplace. Such change would contribute significantly to a reduction in the socio-economic and developmental inequality so prevalent in the U.S. economy today, and this, in turn, would give greater promise to youth employment programs and the disadvantaged youth they serve.

A Postscript: The Job Training Partnership Act

The Job Training Partnership Act (JTPA) replaced the Comprehensive Employment and Training Act (CETA) and YEDPA at the end of September 1983. The new legislation bears the conservative stamp of the Reagan administration. First, it substantially reduces the amount of funding for employment and training programs. The reduction is accomplished in large part by eliminating CETA's principal job-creation component: public service employment. Adult and youth programs alike, including YETP, YIEPP and YACC, are gone. The emphasis of the programs now authorized under JTPA is on training, not on job creation. Wherever employment is part of a program, it is limited in scope and takes the form of on-the-job training. This emphasis is made concrete by strict limits on the proportion of funds that may be used to pay participants' wages. Seventy per cent of the money must be spent on training.

The administration of JTPA also reflects the present administration's conservatism, stressing state and local control and the involvement of the private sector, in contrast to CETA's administration, which was more firmly in the hands of the U.S. Department of Labor. Specifically, control over a major portion of the funds and authorized programs goes to the state governors. Local Private Industry Councils (PIC's), in turn, have major responsibility for selecting and overseeing the particular programs they decide are needed. (One criteria is that at least 40 per cent of these funds go to youth 14–21). The PICs must have a majority of private sector representatives on their membership, and only a private sector representative may serve as chair of a PIC.

JTPA, in short, chooses employment training as the appropriate response to youth unemployment and nearly ignores all the other criteria we have proposed. Indeed, the only point of agreement between JTPA and our analysis is the retention of the Job Corps among the seven federally administered programs and authorized services.

Perhaps this decision was based upon the strong evidence summarized above of the Job Corps' effectiveness with the neediest youth. If so, it represents one small but worthwhile achievement of recent research and demonstration efforts on youth unemployment. The other lessons available from these efforts await a more favorable political climate for application.

Acknowledgement

The authors would like to thank Judith Hyman for her thoughtful assistance in the preparation of this chapter.

Notes

1 Cited in SULLIVAN, S. (1982) 'Youth unemployment' in MEYER, J.A. (Ed) *Meeting Human Needs: Towards a New Public Philosophy*, Washington, D.C., American Enterprise Institute for Public Policy Research.
2 PINES, M.W., IVRY, R. and LEE, J. (1980) 'The universe of need for youth employment: the reality behind the statistics' in LINDER, B. and TAGGART R. (Eds) *A Review of Youth Employment Problems, Programs and Policies, Vol. 1, The Youth Employment Problem: Causes and Dimensions*, Washington D.C., U.S. Department of Labor, Employment and Training Administration.
3 GINZBERG, E. (1980) 'Youth unemployment', *Scientific American*, 242, pp. 43–9.
4 SULLIVAN, S. (1982) *op cit.*
5 FELDSTEIN, M.D. and ELLWOOD, D. (1982) 'Teenage unemployment: what is the problem?' in FREEMAN, R.B. and WISE, D.A. (Eds) *The Youth Labor Market Problem: Its Nature, Causes and Consequences*, Chicago, University of Chicago Press.
6 OSTERMAN, P. (1980) *Getting Started: The Youth Labor Market*, Cambridge, Mass., MIT Press; GREENBERGER, E., STEINBERG, L.D. and RUGGIERO, M. (1982) 'A job is a

job is a job … or is it? Behavioural observations in the adolescent workplace? *Work and Occupations*, 9, p. 7996.

7 BARTON, P.E. (1976) 'Youth transition to work: the problem and federal policy setting' in National Commission for Manpower Policy, *From School to Work: Improving the Transition*, Washington D.C., U.S. Government Printing Office.

8 OSTERMAN, P. (1980) *op cit*.

9 STEPHENSON, S.P. JNR. (1979) 'From school to work: a transition with job search implications', *Youth and Society*, 11, pp. 114–32.

10 BACHMAN, J.G., O'MALLEY, P.M. and JOHNSTON, J. (1978) *Adolescence to Adulthood: Change and Stability in the Lives of Young Men*, Ann Arbor, Institute for Social Research.

11 STEPHENSON, S.P. JNR. (1979) *op cit*.

12 STEVENSON, W. (1978) 'The transition from school to work' and 'The relationship between early work experience and future employability' in ADAMS, A.V. and MANGUM, G.L., *The Lingering Crisis of Youth Unemployment*, chapters 5 and 6, Kalamazoo, WE Upjohn Institute for Employment Research.

13 ELLWOOD, D.T. (1982) 'Teenage unemployment: permanent scars or temporary blemishes?' in FREEMAN, R.B. and WISE, D.A. (Eds) *op cit*.

14 See also MEYER, R. H. and WISE D.A. (1982) 'High school preparation and early labor force experience' in FREEMAN, R.B. and WISE, D.A. (Eds) *op cit*.

15 Carnegie Council on Policy Studies in Higher Education (1979) *Giving Youth a Better Chance: Options for Education, Work and Service*, San Francisco, Jossey Bass.

16 *Ibid*, p. 19.

17 *Ibid*, pp. 8–11.

18 U.S. Department of Labor (1982) *Employment and Training Report of the President*, Washington D.C., U.S. Government Printing Office.

19 HAHN, A. and LERMAN, R. (1980) *Representative Findings from YEDPA Discretionary Projects*, Waltham, Mass, Center for Employment and Income Studies, Brandeis University.

20 GINZBERG, E. (1979) *Good Jobs, Bad Jobs, No Jobs*, Cambridge, Mass, Harvard University Press.

21 HAMILTON, S. and CLAUS, J. (1981) 'Inequality and youth unemployment: can work programs work?', *Education and Urban Society*, 14 (1), pp. 103–26.

22 BRITTAIN, J. (1977) *The Inheritance of Economic Status*, Washington, D.C., Brookings Institute; BOWLES, S. and GINTIS, H. (1976) *Schooling in Capitalist America*, New York, Basic Books.

23 See de LORE, R. (1979) *Small Futures: Children, Inequality and the Limits of Liberal Reform*, New York, Harcourt Brace Jovanovich; BOWLES, S. and GINTIS, H. (1976) *op cit*; BOURDIEU, P. and PASSERON, J.C. (1977) *Reproduction in Education, Society and Culture*, Beverly Hills, Sage; OGBU, J. (1978) *Minority Education and Caste: The American System in Cross-Cultural Perspective*, New York, Academic Press; OGBU, J. (1979) 'Social stratification and the socialization of competence', *Anthropology and Education Quarterly*, 10 (1), pp. 3–20; APPLE, M. (1979) *Ideology and Curriculum*, London, Routledge and Kegan Paul.

24 HAHN, A. (1979) 'Taking stock of YEDPA: the federal youth employment initiatives — part 1, *Youth and Society*, 11 (2), pp. 237–61.

25 COLE, L. (1983) 'The Youth Employment and Demonstration Projects Act (YEDPA) study: an overview', paper presented at Annual Meeting of American Educational Research Association, Montreal.

26 GINZBERG, E. (1979) *op cit*.

27 U.S. Department of Labor (1980a) *A Report on Monitoring and Corrective Action Efforts for the 1979 SYEP*, Washington, D.C., U.S. Government Printing Office.

28 HAHN, A. (1980) 'Early themes from YEDPA: the federal youth employment

Stephen F. Hamilton and John F. Claus

initiatives — part 2', *Youth and Society*, 12 (2), pp. 221–46.
29 U.S. Department of Labor (1980b) *Quarterly Summary of Participant Characteristics and Quarterly Progress Report — the Regional Automated System* (RAS), Washington, D.C., U.S. Government Printing Office.
30 U.S. Department of Labor (1978a) *Impacts of YEDPA on Education/CETA Relationships at the Local Level: Five Case Studies*, Washington, D.C., U.S. Government Printing Office.
31 U.S. Department of Labor (1980b) *op cit.*
32 HAHN, A. (1980) *op cit.*
33 *Ibid.*
34 U.S. Department of Labor (1980b) *op cit.*
35 HAHN, A. (1980) *op cit*; BANKER, N. (1980) *Current State of Knowledge Regarding the Awarding of Academic Credit for Work Experience*, Washington, D.C., Youthwork.
36 HAHN, A. and LERMAN, R. (1980) *op cit.*
37 General Accounting Office (1979) *More Effective Management is Needed to Improve the Quality of SYEP*, Washington, D.C., U.S. Government Printing Office.
38 BALL, J., GEROULD, D. and BURSTEIN, P. (1980) *The Quality of Work in the Youth Entitlement Demonstration*, New York, Manpower Demonstration Research Corporation.
39 Manpower Demonstration Research Corporation (1980a) *Early Impacts from the Youth Entitlement Demonstration: Participation, Work and Schooling*, New York, Manpower Demonstration Research Corporation; (1980b) *Preliminary Findings on the Quality of Work and Impacts on School Attendance Under Entitlement*, Youth Knowledge Development Report 11.3, New York, Manpower Demonstration Research Corporation.
40 HAHN, A. (1980) *op cit.*
41 GILSINAN, J. and TOMEY, E. (1980) *Public versus Private Sector Jobs Demonstration Project: An Analysis of In-program Effects and Outcomes*, St Louis, University of St Louis.
42 DIAZ, W., BULL, J., JACOBS, N., SOLNICK, L. and WIDMAN, A. (1980) *Entitlement Implementation — Two Years Experience*, Youth Knowledge Development Report 11.2, New York, Manpower Demonstration Research Croporation.
43 HAHN, A. (1980) *op cit;* Congressional Budget Office (1980) *Policy Options for Youth Employment and Education*, Washington, D.C., Congressional Budget Office.
44 HAHN, A. (1979) *op cit.*
45 U.S. Department of Labor (1980b) *op cit.*
46 Corporation for Public/Private Ventures (1979) *Ventures in Community Improvement*, Interim Report, Philadelphia, Corporation for Public/Private Ventures.
47 WURZBURG, G. (1978) *Improving Job Opportunities for Youth: A Review of Prime Sponsor Experience in Implementing thte Youth Employment and Demonstration Projects Act*, Washington, D.C., U.S. Department of Labor.
48 U.S. Department of Labor (1980b) *op cit.*
49 *Ibid.*
50 HAHN, A. (1980) *op cit.*
51 ZIMMERMAN, D. and MASTERS, S. (1979) 'A pilot study of the value of output of youth employment programs' in U.S. Department of Labor, *Compilation of Reports in the 1978 Summar Youth Employment Programs*, Washington, D.C., U.S. Government Printing Office.
52 U.S. Department of Labor (1980b) *op cit.*
53 ZIMMERMAN, D. and MASTERS, S. (1979) *op cit.*
54 U.S. Department of Labor (1978b) *Implementation of the Young Adult Conservation Corps*, Office of Program Evaluation Report 48, Washington, D.C., U.S. Department of Labor.

55 *Ibid.*
56 LEVITAN, S. and JOHNSTON, B. (1975) *The Job Corps: A Social Experiment that Works, Policy Studies in Employment and Welfare No 22*, Baltimore, The John Hopkins University Press.
57 HAHN, A. and LERMAN, R. (1980) *op cit.*
58 U.S. Department of Labor (1979) *Job Corps Expression and Enrichment: A Report on Progress, Problems and Prospects*, Washington, D.C., U.S. Government Printing Office.
59 *Ibid.*
60 *Ibid.*
61 MALLAR, C. (1978) *A Comparative Evaluation of the Benefits and Costs of the Job Corps after Seven Months of Post-program Follow-up*, Princeton, Mathematical Policy Research.
62 *Ibid.* HAHN, A. (1980) *op cit.*
63 WALTER, R. (1976) *Analysis and Synthesis of DOL Experience in Youth Transition to Work Programs*, Springfield, National Technical Information Service.
64 SHERRADEN, M. (1980) 'Youth employment and education: federal programs from the New Deal through the 1970s', *Children and Youth Services Review*, 2 (1 and 2) pp. 17–40.
65 BUTLER, E. and DARR, J. (1980) *Lessons from Experience: An Interim Review of the Youth Employment and Demonstration Project Act*, Waltham, Mass, Center for Public Service, Brandeis University.
66 U.S. Department of Labor (1979) *op cit.*
67 HAHN, A. (1980) *op cit.*
68 U.S. Department of Labor (1980b) *op cit; ibid.*
69 General Accounting Office (1979) *op cit.*
70 BUTLER, E. and DARR, J. (1980) *op cit.*
71 U.S. Department of Labor (1980a) *op cit.*
72 NELLUM, A.L. and ASSOCIATES (1980) *Impacts of SYEP participation on Work-related Behaviour and Attitudes of Disadvantaged Youth*, Washington, D.C., U.S. Department of Labor.
73 TAGGART, R. (1980) 'Lessons from programme experience' in LINDER, B. and TAGGART, R. (Eds) *A Review of Youth Employment Problems, Programs and Policies Vol. 3: Program Experience*, Washington, D.C., U.S. Department of Labor; GINZBERG, E. (Ed) (1976) *From School to Work: Improving the Transition*, Washington, D.C., U.S. Government Printing Office.
74 ROCK, D. (1983) 'The effectiveness of YEDPA programs on youth', paper presented at the Annual Meeting of the American Educational Research Association, Montreal; HAHN, A. (1980) *op cit.*
75 RIST, R. (1981) *Earning and Learning: Youth Employment Policies and Programs*, Beverly Hills, Sage Publications.
76 General Accounting Office (1979) *op cit.*
77 WALTHER, R. (1976) *op cit.*
78 Nellum, A.L. and Associates (1980) *op cit.*
79 Center for Human Resources Research (1980) *Findings of the National Longitudinal Survey of Young Americans*, Washington, D.C., U.S. Department of Labor.
80 BANKER, N. (1980) *op cit*; HAHN, A. (1980) *op cit.*
81 DIAZ, W. *et al* (1980) *op cit.*
82 GOTTLEIB, D. (1983) 'Employers perception of YEDPA Youth', paper presented at Annual Meeting of American Educational Research Association, Montreal; HAHN A. and LERMAN, R. (1980) *op cit.*
83 GILSINAN, J. and TOMEY, E. (1980) *op cit.*
84 General Accounting Office (1979) *op cit*; BUTLER, E. and DARR, J. (1980) *op cit.*

85 General Accounting Office (1979) *op cit.*

86 FREEMAN, R. (1980) *Economic Determinants of Geographic and Individual Variation in the Labor Market position of Young Persons,* Youth Knowledge Development Report 2.9, Washington, D.C., U.S. Department of Labor, pp. 259–97.

87 SMITH, R. and VANSKI, J. (1980) *The Volatility of the Teenage Labor Market: Labor Force Entry, Exit and Unemployment Flows,* Youth Knowledge Development Report 2.1 Washington, D.C., U.S. Department of Labor, pp. 20–49.

88 CLARK, K. and SUMMERS, L. (1980) *The Dynamics of Youth Unemployment,* Youth Knowledge Development Report 2.9 Washington, D.C., U.S. Department of Labor, pp. 298–342.

89 GAY, R. and BORUS, M. (1980) 'Validating performance indicators for employment and training programs', *Journal of Human Resources,* 15 (2), pp. 29–48.

90 ROCK, D. (1983) *op cit.*

91 OGBU, J. (1978) *op cit.*

92 *Ibid;* BULLOCK, P. (1973) *Aspiration vs Opportunity: 'Careers' in the Inner City,* Ann Arbor, Institute of Labor and Industrial Relations.

93 BOWLES, S. and GINTIS, H. (1976) *op cit;* O'TOOLE, J. (1977) *Work, Learning and the American Future,* San Francisco, Jossey Bass.

94 HAMILTON, S. and CLAUS, J. (1981) *op cit.*

95 See ZIMMERMANN, D. (1980) 'Public sector job creation for youth: some observations on its role and effectiveness' in *Vice President's Task Force on Youth Employment, Vol. 3,* Washington, D.C., U.S. Government Printing Office; WURZBURG, G. (1978) *op cit.*

96 For a full discussion of this point see HAMILTON, S. and CLAUS, J. (1981) *op cit.*

Reference

Panel on Youth of the President's Science Advisory Committee (1974) *Youth: Transition to Adulthood,* Chicago, University of Chicago Press.

Career Development and the Commodification of Student Labour in Canadian Approaches to Youth· Unemployment

Don Dippo

In Canada, as in most countries of the industrialized west, the problem of youth unemployment has reached crisis proportions. With the national unemployment rate of youth aged 15–24 expected to remain at the current high levels of between 18–22 per cent, what had been regarded as a 'frictional' problem explained in terms of a 'natural' tendency of young people to change jobs frequently is being increasingly understood as a 'structural' problem linked to more fundamental shifts in the dynamics of the Canadian labour market. In the language of labour economists, the problem is one of 'market imbalance' — a mismatch between the supply and demand for labour. Indeed it is the language and logic of labour economics which have provided the dominant rationality within which most Canadian policy options and program alternatives have been formulated to meet the 'youth unemployment crisis'.

Canadian youth unemployment rates over the last ten years have not been tied simply to the recessionary periods in both our local and the world economy. During the 1960s and early 1970s there was a rapid influx of young people in the labour force. This was the result of the maturation of the postwar baby boom, a massive increase in immigration to Canada after the Second World War, and an increase in the labour force participation rates of young people. Furthermore, the presence of large numbers of youth possessing higher levels of education has aggravated the mismatching of supply and demand. There have been two main reasons for this put forward in policy debates. First, youth often lack the preferred or required work skills or job experience to fill vacant positions. Second, some employers, accustomed to hiring from the primary labour force, choose to employ few or no young people (the mass media popularization of youth culture and the attack on the quality of public education has significantly added to the distrust of youth). Even further the enormous increase in the participation rate of women in the labour force has given employers an additional supply of labour. This has been especially true in the service sector which has been the fastest growing sector in Canada in terms of employment opportunities. These factors in addition to the growing importance of new technology in all sectors of the economy and the reassertion of the recurring argument that the size of Canadian markets is too small to support a full employment (creating the demand for higher levels of productivity so that Canadian goods and services can successfully compete in world markets) present the complex context in which government intervention has been attempted.

Understanding the policy of governments in Canada with respect to the relation between education and employment is not an easy task. The division of responsibilities between federal and provincial levels (and with departments of the state apparatus at each level) produces a picture of, at times, a bewildering inconsistency that makes it impossible to identify any one policy that may be said to be the operative one. The root of this problem is to be found in the origins of the Canadian State. In Canada's founding constitutional document, the British North America Act (1867), the historic tensions between French and English Canada as well as the competing economic interests of various geographic regions were encoded in a compromise which divided the legislative prerogatives of federal and provincial governments. As the provinces were relatively culturally homogeneous regions with strong feelings about remaining so, education was defined as a provincial responsibility. Thus for over one hundred years the provinces have resisted and quarreled and compromised over federal efforts to develop a manpower policy that has included the use of education to affect the quantity and quality of the supply of labour. Increasingly over the last thirty years the federal government has been allowed to contribute financially to secondary and post-secondary education but it has had no formal input to the contents of these programs. However federal government has long tried to justify its authority over programs to alter the labour supply by arguing for a distinction between education and training. This position is well illustrated by the following remarks of L.B. Pearson during his tenure as Prime Minister:

> The federal government recognizes that education is and must remain within provincial jurisdiction. Certain interpretations have been placed on the scope and meaning of the word 'education' which in our view are not valid. Specifically, the federal government believes that the training and retraining of adults for participation in the labour force are well within the scope of federal jurisdiction. They are manifestations of the federal government's responsibility for national economic development. Once the normal process of education for an individual has been completed and that individual is established in the labour force, measures of training thereafter to fit him to the constantly changing technological world are not 'education' in the constitutional sense[1]

Yet it is not only in attempting to distinguish between education and training that the federal government has intervened in preparing young people for work. The Ministry of Employment and Immigration has developed an extensive repertoire of career development programmes and materials. These programmes and materials are not only distributed to government employment counseling centres but have wide currency within counseling departments and work preparation programs in secondary schools. Such efforts can be understood as direct attempts to alter the attitudes and information young people bring to the marketplace so that their choice behavior will be in greater correspondence to the demands of the market. It is important to understand how this is so and what problems and limitations are inherent in the approach which provides the *foundation* for a large number of youth employment preparation programs found at all levels of educational responsibility (provincial curricular guidelines, local school board courses of study, non-profit counseling centres). The approach is based on the principle of commodification and is aimed at enhancing the saleability of labour by transforming people into more marketable goods. It is an approach which continues to affirm the basic assumptions that the marketplace metaphor is sufficient for understanding, and labour market mechanisms are capable of resolving, the problem of youth unemployment.

This process of labour commodification is particularly apparent in the materials used in vocational guidance and what is termed 'career development'. Such materials are designed to maximize exchange opportunities for students by, in effect, packaging them (or helping them package themselves) in such a way that their 'lists of ingredients' are what enable them to negotiate entry into the labour market and participate in the exchange relations which are the basis of a capitalist economy. Saleability then provides the rationale for a process of producing a version of self-understanding based on commodity forms and exchange relations.

The wide variety of career development programs and packaged materials developed by Employment and Immigration Canada have been designed to assist students in the process of 'choosing a suitable career'. Close inspection of these materials, however, reveals a striking uniformity of approach as to what constitutes good career guidance based on the principle of commodification worked into a procedure which can be characterized as 'talent-matching'.

Quoting from one of the counsellor's guides:

> The Index to Canadian Occupations and the Occupational Exploration Questionnaire are designed to help clients to explore the world of work and choose career goals. Users can find suitable careers by choosing characteristics that they feel describe them or the kind of work they want. Occupations that fit several (but not necessarily all) of a user's chosen characteristics probably best suit that person's career needs.[2]

Generally speaking the talent-matching procedure involves four steps:

1 *Discover your personal qualifications*
The basic assumption of the entire procedure is that if you can know yourself, you will be able to systematically and rationally explore what career options will be the most plausible and satisfying to you. Such self-knowledge, however, must be articulated in such a way that it is useful to career planning. The system therefore specifies how a self-assessment is to be organized and articulated. The typical procedure is to respond to a standardized instrument (sometimes administered by a counselor, sometimes self-administered) that allows one to develop a profile of ratings on each of the following dimensions: Interests, Temperaments, Abilities, Physical Activities Preferred, Environmental Conditions Preferred, Educational or Training Route Accomplished.

2 *Find the occupations that fit your personal qualifications*
In order for there to be a career planning system that allows the information

developed in Step 1 to be used rationally there must exist a directory of occupations which specifies the work characteristics required by different occupations in terms of the assessment of personal characteristics previously made. Given such a directory, the entire document can be searched either mechanically or electronically to find a set of occupations that creates matches between personal attributes and work requirements.

3   *Determine the best fit between you and sub-set of potential careers developed in step 2*
Now the list of possible careers must be narrowed by focusing on only those careers that maximize the number of matches between oneself and one's future work. This step also allows for differential weighting to be applied to each of the personal attributes previously assessed.

4   *Look up more information on the careers chosen as a result of step 3*
The procedure here often references a large number of support documents that provide information on specific occupations including required qualifications, job prospects, earnings, duties, etc.

The most widely celebrated 'tool' for career counseling developed by the federal government is the computerized system called CHOICES which provides users with information on a wide variety of occupations. It is a matching system and as such is aimed at helping individuals to identify those occupations which are likely to be 'satisfying' based on interests, abilities, educational and training requirements, desired income, working conditions and so on. Though the system is expensive to operate and maintain (information must be updated regularly) it is generally regarded as an efficient method of providing information for career planning and guidance.

CHOICES, however, is only the most recent manifestation of what continues to be the dominant approach to vocational and career guidance. Matching systems in the form of workbooks or mechanical search exercises have been used for years in employment centres and in guidance departments of secondary schools. While this chapter will focus on materials produced by the Department of Employment and Immigration, it should be emphasized that these materials are not unique. What they exemplify is a logic and a set of underlying assumptions that provide the foundation upon which the overwhelming majority of career development programs are built. Thus what is at issue here is not the federal government materials per se, but the rationality behind these materials that defines the dominant approach to helping youth enter the labour market.

This chapter is an assessment of the adequacy of career development discourse and the ideology which it articulates to deal with the problems faced by students in the current economic crisis. Of central concern here are the understandings (both of self and of the larger social formation) which students produce in working through these materials. As Richard Johnson notes, 'It is not so much a question that schools ... *are* ideology, more that they are the sites where ideologies are produced in the form of subjectivities.'[3] The commodification of student labour presupposes and hence 'requires' two related personal characteristics to which students must comform. They are encapsulated in the concept of 'possessive individualism'.[4] Through these materials students are encouraged to construct a commodified form of identity based upon the 'possession' of certain standardized (hence, by implication, socially recognized and valued) technical skills and personality traits. To enhance the saleability of themselves as commodities, students must either accumulate more 'skills' or find a way of repackaging those they already possess. The second feature of possessive individualism entered into the discourse through the construct of 'choosing a career' is that students are expected to accept the legitimacy of 'whatever material outcome emerges from their particular exchange relationships — particularly if this outcome is unfavorable to them. Such outcomes must, in other words, be attributed to either natural events or to the virtues and failure of the individual'.[5] Apple reinforces the concern when he states:

> The characteristics embodied in the modes of technical control built into the curricular form itself are ideally suited to reproduce the possessive individual, a vision of oneself that lies at the ideological heart of corporate economics.[6]

This chapter will argue that the commodification of student labour power and the reproduction of possessive individualism are politically inappropriate as well as pedagogically inadequate curricular aims. In order to make this argument clear, what we need to understand is how talent-matching in the guise of career development works to legitimize and reproduce labour in the commodity form. The methods employed here are derived in large measure from Dorothy Smith's analysis of what she terms 'documentary reality'; a socially produced form of knowledge which is essential to the work of administering society and in this case of managing the economy[7] (Smith, 1974, 1978, 1980).

> A documentary reality is fundamental to the practices of governing, managing, and administration of this form of society. The primary mode of action and decision in the superstructures of business, government, the professions, and other like agencies, is in symbols, whether words, mathematical symbols, or some other. It is a mode of action which depends upon a reality constituted in documentary form.[8]

What enquiry into the documentary form and its social construction permits is a critique of the ideological presuppositions which 'substruct' its categories and procedures. In this case the critique will focus particular attention on the interest, problematic, and form of rationality upon which the talent-matching apparatus is built.

Interest

The question of what constitutes an appropriate form of work education relative to the issue of whose interests are served has been discussed and debated by vocational and career educators since the turn of the century. Proponents of separate vocational schools argued that traditional 'common school' curriculum was inappropriate for the 'masses' of students who were destined for work in industry. David Snedden for example argued that:

> ... It is desirable that boys and girls shall be encouraged to remain in schools of general or liberal learning as long as their economic resources and position justify.... When the time comes to turn to the vocational school, concentration of effort shall be required for the latter purpose.... It is required that the pupil be able to give at least six or eight hours per day of undivided attention to the ends of vocational education.
> ... The controlling purpose in vocational education is to produce certain fairly definite forms of skill and power which shall enable the learner to become a successful producer of valuable service....[9]

One of the most articulate voices opposed to the idea of segregated vocational programs was that of John Dewey. In 'An Undemocratic Proposal' he suggested that such programs are inappropriate for any school system in that they take the interests of students and make them subservient to the interests of employers.

> Those who believe in the continued separate existence of what they are pleased to call the 'lower classes' or the 'labouring classes' would naturally rejoice to have schools in which these 'classes' would be segregated. And some employers of labour would doubtless rejoice to have schools supported by public taxation supply them with additional food for their mills.[10]

He argued instead for an integrated program of vocational education which took as its primary objective

> ... the development of such intelligent initiative, ingenuity and executive capacity as shall make workers as far as may be possible, the masters of their own industrial fate .... The kind of vocational education in which I am interested is not one which will 'adapt' workers to the existing regime; I am not sufficiently in love with the regime for that. It seems to me that the business of all who would not be educational time-servers is to resist every move in this direction, and to strive for a kind of vocational education which will alter the existing industrial system and ultimately transform it.[11]

In the 1980s the relationship between education and work is still a primary concern. The terms of reference have shifted however from specific vocational training to an emphasis on 'basic,' 'life,' and 'employability' skills. In 1980 the Ontario Ministry of Education announced its intention to completely review the secondary school system of the province. As part of its mandate the project would address:

> ... mounting public concerns about certain aspects of today's secondary school system. Foremost among these were discipline, the school's effectiveness in teaching basic literacy and number skills, and the apparent gap between the school and the world of work. Much of the criticism stemmed from the existence of high youth unemploy-

ment at a time when many employers complained that they could not find enough skilled labourers.... The view is frequently expressed, particularly by employers, that this unsatisfactory youth employment picture results partly from the schools concentrating too much on catering to students' individual interests or in preparing them for college and university, and too little on equipping students with the basic skills, personal attributes and technical training required for obtaining jobs and performing them satisfactorily.[12]

The report goes on to point out that '... employers make it clear that they value communication skills and attitudes such as reliability, acceptance of responsibility, and ability to work well with others, more highly than specific job related skills'[13]. The main thrust of this educational solution to the problem of youth unemployment is neither the integrated vocational education proposed by Dewey nor the specific skills training advocated by Snedden but a program of basic skills and attitude development. This comes as no surprise. Just as the movement for specific skills training in the early part of this century drew some of its strongest support from the business community, so too the push for basic skills and attitude development today receives equally strong support from the same sector of society.

In contrast to the industrial growth which characterized the economy at the time of Dewey and Snedden, a slow decline in manufacturing employment together with concomitant expansion in the service industries is what characterizes and shapes the occupational requirements in the current economic period. A popular interpretation of these labour market shifts emphasizes the expanding employment opportunities in professional and technical jobs. While it is true that such jobs, requiring high levels of education and training, are increasing, so too are the poorly paid and unstable occupations in the service sector. What are decreasing, however, are the employment opportunities in that sector of the economy that combined specific skill requirements with decent pay and job security, such as blue-collar production jobs in large scale manufacturing.[14] Specific skills training therefore is less suited to the needs of employers today than it was when first put forward. The new emphasis on basic skills and attitudes corresponds to contemporary labour market demands which have been strongest at the top and at the bottom of the skill hierarchy. Increasing technocratization of the means of production and the concomitant polarization of skill level requirements in the labour market has obfuscated the role of the secondary school in the production of a skilled work force. While the shift in emphasis from specific skills training to basic skills, life skills and career education has been justified by some as a positive move '... from a primary concern about developing competent persons as defined by the needs of specific occupations to a much broader perspective that emphasizes the development of personal competencies as defined by individual needs and the emerging perspectives provided by research and theory in career development',[15] there are others such as Alison Griffith who observe that in-school technical skills training is rarely sufficient for entry into a skilled occupation. What's more, she points out, in its final report on secondary education in Ontario the Ministry of Education ignores demands for the direct involvement of the schools in the development of a 'skilled' labour force.[16]

The important point in this discussion regarding the relationship between school and work is not the shift from technical education to basic or life skills training. Rather, it is the continuity of approach which allows employers to prescribe what will be regarded as the most appropriate kind of education for work. The dominant mode both then and now is devised in terms of talent-matching: helping individuals to meet the demands of employers.[17]

Part of this help is provided through curriculum materials designed to enable students to identify those use values (i.e. basic skills and attitudes) which will maximize their opportunities to enter into exchange relations. While employment must be a central concern for any program of work education, it is not the only aim, nor does it justify the degree to which schools, and the guidance counseling profession in particular, have taken up, albeit indirectly, the smooth and efficient functioning of the labour market as in their own interest by relying almost exclusively on the talent-matching model as a foundation for 'career development'. The educative thus gives way to the instrumental as the structures of self-understanding are determined by the pre-established categories of the talent-matching apparatus and knowledge of the work world is restricted to an examination of standardized job requirements profiles. Not only does such an approach ignore the social, political, and economic issues which students will confront and be required to deal with upon entering the labour force but as a process it contributes to the production of an alienating version of self and a reified version of the work world that in effect suppresses any sense of agency which would enable students to participate and to act effectively on their own behalf in the contestations and struggles which inevitably lie before them as they enter into the social relations of economic production. Dewey's plea for an integrated program of vocational education which had '... as its supreme regard the development of such intelligent initiative, ingenuity and executive capacity as shall make workers ... the masters of their own industrial fate' remains as a challenge to all those concerned with developing progressive modes of work education aimed at serving more directly not only immediate needs but also the long-term interests of students which extend beyond the problem of finding a job.

Rationality

An essential feature of all talent-matching schemes is the provision of an analytically compatible system of describing and classifying both people and jobs. The system used in most Canadian materials is derived from the Canadian Classification and Dictionary of Occupations (CCDO). This system of description and classification was initially developed in response to an administrative concern on the part of the State with organizing and managing the productive capacity (i.e., the labour power) of the work force. 'Occupationologists' as they were known in the 1930s set about gathering the 'scientific facts' about the work world 'as it exists' and developed strict methodological procedures for how jobs were to be identified and described. In his critique of occupational analysis, George Smith points out:

It is the ability of these procedures to standardize the production of job descriptions under different conditions which gives these descriptions the appearance of being factual and which provides for their 'public,' 'objective' and 'scientific' character. The facticity of a job description, in other words, is not grounded in the work setting itself, but in the *procedures* for describing the work.[18]

What's more, the descriptive categories and conceptual procedures used

... express, in a taken-for-granted fashion, a structure of relevance which reflects the raison d'etre of this kind of work. These categories by their very nature are administrative categories; and administrative conceptual practices ... (T)his way of knowing allows the facts of work to be read off as such by making the categories and procedures it uses appear naturally to reflect what is actual. Actuality worked up in this way, consequently, appears to intend its own description.[19]

These descriptions, however, only make sense within a particular mode of rationality that confers intelligibility on them. Their meaningfulness is structured by a set of basic assumptions which conform to what Habermas has termed technocratic rationality. In a discussion of the major constitutive interests that have guided educational theory, practice, and research in the United States, Henry Giroux states:

Technocratic rationality takes as its guiding interest the elements of control, prediction, and certainty ... (A)s a result of its strong support of the methodological procedures associated with the natural and physical sciences it upholds an epistemology in which 'knowledge starts from the concrete and is raised to general propositions through a process of abstraction/generalization' [Marcuse 1978:471]. Another feature of this perspective is its strong dependence on the assumption that theoretical categories are independent of observational categories. Not only does such a position reduce theory to the level of being the result of evidence gathering and 'fact' collecting, but it denies the very notion of a determinate theoretical problematic.[20]

In other words, it is claimed that the knowledge produced from within this set of assumptions and practices is value-neutral, dis-interested, and generalizable. Operating from within this mode of reasoning occupational analysts take for granted that the job descriptions they produce are objective and factual rather than implicated in the management and control of the labour force. The CCDO seeks to absolve itself from responsibility with the claim:

In the program of studies to determine the data for inclusion in this publication, many thousands of jobs were examined and analyzed to determine their content. No facts were collected, however, on such matters as hours of labour, wages or salaries, or other related employment practices.

It should be noted further that the content of a specific job varies with each individual establishment; therefore, most of the occupational definitions are described in broad terms. For these reasons, the data in this publication cannot be considered as standards for setting working conditions, pay scales or related employment conditions, and the Department of Manpower and Immigration has no responsibility for the settling of these or other jurisdictional matters.[21]

The structure of relevance which organizes the version of the work world contained in the pages of the CCDO is one which discounts such primary worker concerns as 'hours of labour, wages and salaries, (and) other related employment practices' in favour of taking up only those features which serve the underlying managerial interest as reflected in the overarching problematic — that of talent-matching or the 'fitting together' of people and jobs.

Problematic

The problem of fitting applicants to jobs is largely alleviated of course if the applicant's 'training, experience or knowledge' has been worked up into the same classification schema used to analyze and describe occupations — if what were formulated in the first instance as 'job characteristics' can now be reformulated as 'personal characteristics'. This is indeed the primary function of the guidance materials under consideration: to help students come to 'know themselves' in terms which are intended to facilitate their movement through the talent-matching apparatus resulting in a better fit between themselves and the 'careers' they 'choose'. This problematic is clearly articulated in a counseling package produced by Employment and Immigration Canada entitled *Access a Career by Traits* (ACT).

> Numerous studies have indicated that there is a significant correlation between job satisfaction and a positive interest in the work. For our purpose 'INTEREST' is defined as a tendency to become absorbed in an experience through concern in or attraction for certain types of work activities or experiences ...[22]

> It has been demonstrated that certain aptitudes are important for job success, so eleven aptitude factors have been used in estimating what is required of an individual for average, satisfactory work performance ....[23]

This way of thinking about job satisfaction and labour market entry is drawn from the perhaps most clearly and unabashedly straightforward version of this logic as put forward by John Holland.

> According to Holland's theory, people can be divided into six different categories according to the kinds of things and activities they are interested in. Occupations can also be divided into the same categories according to the types of people in them and the types of activities that are involved in doing the job. These categories include: Realistic, Investigative, Artistic, Social, Enterprising and Conventional....[24]

> This theory is ideal for career exploration purposes in that individuals can determine which of the six types best describes them, and can then

locate occupations which are of the same type. Individuals can discover their personality type by using Holland's Self-Directed Search or by merely going through an informed exercise to determine words and phrases which best describe them. Using the three-letter code, occupations can be located which match the code....[25]

In so far as these materials provide a quasi-theoretical framework for thinking about entry into the labour market, they can be said to express a particular problematic which

> ... represents a conceptual structure whose meaning is to be found not only in the questions that command the range of answers provided, but also in the questions that are *not* asked. Thus, the problematic defines both the field of the visible as well as the boundary of the invisible ... (I)t also serves as a mode of theorizing that articulates a particular relationship between individuals and classes, and the social, political, and economic interests that govern the dominant society.[26]

Within the conceptual framework set out in these materials, the not so implicit messages are: (a) that people choose the work that they do; and (b) that satisfaction is related to the 'wisdom' of their choices. So that when, for example, we are presented with statements like: 'An expert has said that 80 per cent of the working people are in the wrong jobs,';[27] or 'In a recent survey in the U.S., 47 per cent of the people interviewed said their jobs were uninteresting, and 31 per cent said they would quit if they could afford it',[28] the problematic of the text structures the questions we ask and the conclusions to be drawn are obvious. The 80 per cent in ill-fitting jobs '... didn't make horrible occupational choices. They simply could have made better ones'.[29] Forty-seven per cent of people uninterested and 31 per cent ready to quit prompts the question, 'Why do we have so many poor matches?' And the answer, 'It is because many people are choosing occupations with too little information about (1) themselves; (2) occupations; (3) both'.[30]

What is seldom, if ever, addressed in the career development literature based on this problematic is the relationship between the versions of self-knowledge and job knowledge proposed. In fact it is *not* two types of knowledge but one type of knowledge and one method of knowing organized in the relevance of labour force administration. What guidance materials based on such a rationality and problematic provide is an interpretive frame through which students come to know themselves as a composite of characteristics which somehow qualify them for certain kinds of jobs. The same set of categories and conceptual practices which determined the production and organization of 'knowledge of work' are now employed in guidance materials to produce and organize 'knowledge of self' in terms which are relevant to the procedure of allocating people to jobs. The knowledge produced in both instances shares the same fragmented, compartmentalized, and abstract character as a result of being rooted in a form of rationality where the superiority of generalized principles and de-contextualized 'facts' is taken for granted.

The irony here is that the conceptual schema that typically organizes self-knowledge (Interests, Aptitudes, Temperaments and so on) within such guidance material 'stands between' the student and the object which is him or her self. The actuality of the student's life is assigned a set of descriptive categories and organized through a conceptual structure which obliterates the relationship between experience and its concrete context. In *Moving On*, another career development package produced by Employment and Immigration Canada, students are told, 'Everybody has interests. People talk about "I'm really interested in deep-sea fishing, I'm really interested in money, I'm really interested in Garry", and everybody knows what they mean.' Such taken-for-granted and context dependent formulations of interests however are dismissed by this package as being not very helpful when it comes to choosing a career. The ideological operation of an interest inventory (be it 'I'm Interested In . . .' from *Moving On*, the Canadian Occupational Interest Inventory [COII], the Occupational Exploration Questionnaire from the Index to Canadian Occupations [ICO] etc.) serves to sever the relation of what are understood as interests from 'the particular local and biographical settings in which they arise'.[31] The meaning of an expressed interest is linked with a specific context and is therefore to be understood only in relation to the circumstances, events or settings upon which it depends for its meaningfulness on the part of the 'interested' person. An interest in deep-sea fishing, in money, or in Garry, may have serious implications for work-related decisions depending on the context within which the decisions must be made. The intention of an interest inventory however is not the production of knowledge of self, situated within social, historical, or economic conditions, but rather it is the production of an essentialist and abstracted version of self as a personality type suited to certain equally essentialist and abstracted characterizations of kinds of jobs.

As a second example consider the social construction of 'Temperament Factors' which appears in many of the guidance materials which claim to help students choose their work in the world. Here we see the same ideological structure of concepts and procedures which produce the notion of Interests. Students are required to 'choose' from a list of temperament factors those which indicate or best describe 'those personality qualities which remain fairly constant and reveal that person's characteristic response in terms of a preference, inclination, or disposition'.[32] The selection of descriptors here is based on a series of 'Do you like . . .?' 'Do you feel . . .,' 'Are you happy . . .' type questions which call for contextualization on the part of the student.

Let us suppose that there is a student who works part-time at a fast-food restaurant. Many of her friends also work at the restaurant and generally they agree that it's a pretty good job. On any given shift a student may spend time 'working in the back' unpacking buns, slicing tomatoes, refilling condiments, 'working at the grill' frying burgers, making french fries, microwaving hot apple pies; 'working the counter' by taking and filling orders, getting drinks, or 'working the cash,' or working 'up front' clearing and wiping tables, changing trash bags, etc. To be stuck at any one of these jobs for an entire shift would be boring. Moving around to where help is needed provides the opportunity to interact with different people as well as the chance to have a cigarette when assigned a less visible job (like clearing the tables outside or picking up trash in the parking lot).

While filling out the Occupational Exploration Questionnaire this student uses her work experience to make sense of the following questions:

'Can you keep track of several different things at once?'
'Are you happy to drop what you are doing in the middle of it and start something new and different?'
'Do you like situations in which things are never settled and new things are always popping up?'
'Do you like situations in which you don't know for sure what you will be doing the next day or the next week?'
'Do you like to be kept moving from place to place?'

By answering 'yes' to each of these questions, this student has identified herself 'for CCDO purposes' as the kind of person who has a 'preference, inclination, or disposition' for work with 'variety and change'. In other words her Temperament is coded 'T.1-Versatility'. As with the career guidance concept of 'Interests', these questions are the initial steps in the process of ideological transformation 'through which a fact can be represented as an expression of a principle originating in that same fact'[33]. What the questions do in this case is separate the student's 'preferences' from the actual settings in which they arise. Moving from buns to burgers or from burgers to outside tables becomes 'moving from place to place' in general. The next step in this process involves 'the interpolation of a redundant principle, i.e., one which merely describes again at the level of 'reflection' a relation which has already been described at the factual level. The *particular* character of the relation disappears in the process'.[34] Both student and restaurant disappear in the naming and formulation of the temperament category.

T.1-Versatility; Many duties which change often, including shifting to a second activity before completing the first, and unexpected pressures and situations. Tendency to seek out variety and situations that permit attention to be shifted from one thing to another rather than being focussed on the same thing for long periods.[35]

That this student likes her work at the restaurant is taken as evidence by the student herself that she does indeed possess a personality quality or temperament which is suited to variety and change. But the ideological transformation is not yet complete. The final step is an inversion of the original relation between the actuality of working in the restaurant and the general description of a temperament factor where the category T.1-Versatility is understood as an abstraction from the facts. Transformed, the facts become understood as expressions or illustrations of the abstraction. She likes her work *because she has* a temperament suited to variety and change. The procedure is complete when 'causal efficacy or agency is attributed to the principles. The empirical process, the 'facts,' are treated as caused, determined or motivated by the principles or extrapolations of principles'.[36]

For talent-matching purposes one further transformation is required. Explanations of preferences are not sufficient for allocating people to jobs. The abstraction must not only explain the facts but must be capable of generating a whole new set of facts — of projecting the context for a new, as yet unrealized actuality. She *will have* a preference for work with variety and change because that kind of work suits her temperament.

Educational Consequences

As an interrelated set of reified concepts and ideological practices Interests, Aptitudes and Temperaments do more than organize students' lives in a way that facilitates the talent-matching process. They structure the way students come to know themselves and the world in a way that may actually disorganize their own lived experience. For example, as a way of understanding the satisfaction which might be associated with working in a fast-food restaurant, terms like sociability or camaraderie which suggest a structure of social relations existing within the workplace are useful for reasons not the least of which is that they reference what for students might be a recognizable quality of their own experience. The categories and terms these materials employ however have been developed in accordance with market criteria and are not particularly interested in the constitution of experience. If saleability is the objective, the self-understanding must be formulated in terms of identifying characteristics which are marketable, that is, characteristics which improve the opportunity for students to engage in exchange relations. Versatility (Temp. 1) is therefore a more useful term than either sociability or camaraderie because it can be posited as an individual possession which may have some use value for a potential employer. These materials encourage students to build their identities into such commodified forms. They serve to reproduce a version of possessive individualism which suggests that, because the self is defined in terms of sets of commodifiable use values, to improve their exchange positions individuals must accumulate more and better qualifications. Exchange opportunities are enhanced for those who are able to make themselves more saleable.

In addition to proposing a fragmented version of self unrelated to a social or material context, there are several implicit messages contained in these materials which are expressions of the technocratic mode of rationality they share. The first of these messages is that for every person there is a 'right' job and for every job there is a 'right' person. Talent-matching is based on this assumption and promises to be a useful method of getting the two together. The implication being that dissatisfying work is attributable to a poor match. This has two related effects; first, it diverts attention away from the material conditions or employment practices which may be at the source of dissatisfaction; while tacitly suggesting changing jobs in hopes of a better fit, and second, for those unwilling or unable to simply pack up and quit their jobs there is an implied fatalism — that a mistake was made or something didn't work out but it's too late now, there's nothing that can be done.

The relationship between problematic and economic interest is clear. Social, historical and economic conditions which might account for such high levels of alienation go unaddressed. Questions regarding the organization of work and technological change remain unposed. Powerlessness in control of the work process, meaninglessness with regard to the product of one's labour, isolation, all are beyond the ken of this particular mode of theorizing. Dissatisfaction is explained in terms of poor job choice. The solution to these problems lies not with improved working conditions or reorganized processes of production, but rather with adjustments and modifications to the mechanism for matching people and jobs — providing students with ever more 'information' that would enable them to 'choose suitable careers'.

With extensive youth unemployment many students are unable to find jobs, let alone 'choose suitable careers'. Even among those who are working, it is not so much a question of choosing a career as it is taking whatever jobs they can find. At a time when even the archetypical youth labour market job at the fast-food counter is at a premium, when entry level jobs with prospects for skill acquisition and promotion are either disappearing in the wake of major technological changes or are being filled by experienced workers whose jobs have been declared redundant, at a time when most job vacancies are filled by people already known to employers or known by people who already hold jobs in that particular field; in times such as these, reducing the problem of becoming established in the labour market to a question of 'choosing' an occupation that 'fits' an interests, aptitudes, and temperaments profile actually *increases* the probability that students will leave school ill-prepared to deal with the harsh realities of the social and economic conditions that will confront them. As a way of thinking about the working world, talent-matching is profoundly irrelevant. Its structuring problematic completely ignores the social relations implicated in particular modes of production and the power relations implicated in certain technological and organizational 'advances'. Instead it focuses almost exclusive attention on personal responsibility for finding satisfying work. Such an orientation is of limited value when trying to understand the social forces which influence and shape people's working lives. When simple 'fitting in' simply doesn't work, students who lack such an understanding are disadvantaged when it comes to effectively participating in the contestations and struggles that mark the changing terrain of the work-place. In so far as major social, historical, and economic issues remain unaddressed within the problematic set out in these materials, they contribute nothing to students' understanding of what they can do to gain some measure of control over their own lives as they enter into and participate in the social relations of the economic order. What they, in effect, encourage is drifting from job to job in search of the 'better match', the 'perfect fit'. Students so ill prepared to enter the work force are most likely to end up alienated, exploited, and chronically unemployed.

Quite clearly there is a need for some form of critical intervention on the part of the school. We would agree with those who recommend that education for working not be confined to the senior levels of secondary school but rather should begin in the elementary grades with a general exploration of the world of work and be continued into the middle school with more complex economic concepts being introduced.[37] What we would argue against however is the continuation of talent-matching as the predominant ideological form and its modification for use in classrooms with younger and younger students. Contrary to what many people believe, relevant work education does *not* begin with the question, 'What do you want to be when you grow up?' Rather, it begins with the proposition that 'knowing about' precedes 'wanting to be' and should therefore constitute the primary focus of early work education programs. Just as 'fitting in' as a structuring problematic is an extension of 'wanting to be,' so too 'effective participation' is an extension of

Don Dippo

'knowing about' the social, political, and economic context that structures relations of production.

Acknowledgement

I wish to acknowledge Roger Simon, Jeff Piker and the members of the *Project Learning Work* at the Ontario Institute for Studies in Education for their comments, criticisms and suggestions.

Notes

1 PEARSON, L.B. (1968) opening remarks at a Conference of Financing Higher Education, 24 October 1966 in Federal Provincial Conference, 24–28 October, Ottawa, Queen's Printer.
2 GOVERNMENT OF CANADA (1978) *Index to Canadian Occupations: Counselors Guide, Department of Employment and Immigration*, Occupational and Career Analysis and Development Branch, Ottawa, Ministry of Supply and Services.
3 JOHNSON, R. (1979) 'Three problematics: elements of a theory of working class culture' in CLARKE, CRITCHEN and JOHNSON, R. (Eds) *Working Class Culture — Studies in History and Theory*, London, Hutchinson, p. 232.
4 APPLE, M. (1982) 'Curricular form and the logic of technical control: building the possessive individual' in APPLE, M. (Ed) *Cultural and Economic Reproduction in Education Essays on Class, Ideology and the State*, Boston, Routledge and Kegan Paul.
5 OFFE, C. and RONGE, V. (1981) 'Theses on the theory of the state' in DALE, R., ESLAND, G., FERGUSSON, R. and MACDONALD, M. (Eds) *Schooling and the National Interest, Volume 1*, Lewes/Milton Keynes, Falmer Press/Open University Press, p. 84.
6 APPLE, M. (1982) *op cit.*, p. 261.
7 SMITH, D. (1974) 'The social construction of documentary reality' *Sociological Inquiry*, 44, pp. 257–68; SMITH, D. (1978) 'On sociological description: a method from Marx', *Human Studies*, 4, pp. 313–37; SMITH, D. (1980) 'No one commits suicide: textual analysis of ideological practices', unpublished manuscript, Department of Sociology in Education, Ontario Institute for Studies in Education, Toronto.
8 SMITH, D. (1974) *op cit.*, p. 257.
9 SNEDDEN, D. (1977) 'Fundamental distinctions between liberal and vocational education', *Curriculum Inquiry*, v. 7 1, spring.
10 DEWEY, J. (1974) 'An undemocratic proposal' in LAZERSON, M. and GRUBB, W.N. (Eds) *American Education and Vocationalism: A Documentary History 1870–1970*, New York, Teachers College Press, pp. 143–7.
11 *Ibid.*
12 Government of Ontario (1981) *Secondary Education Review Project Report*, Toronto, Ministry of Education, p. 1.
13 *Ibid.*
14 See FREEMAN, M. (1982) 'The structure of the labor market and associated training patterns' in SILBERMAN, H.F. (Ed) *Education and Work*, Chicago, National Society for the Study of Education
15 HERR, E. L. (1982) 'Career development and vocational guidance' in SILBERMAN, H.F. (Ed) *op cit.*, p. 2.
16 GRIFFITH, A. (1983) 'Stalling for life/living for skill: the social construction of life

skills in Ontario schools', unpublished manuscript, Department of History and Philosophy, Ontario Institute for Studies in Education, Toronto.
17 See BECKER, R.J. (1982) 'Education and work: a historical perspective' in Silberman, H.F. (Ed) *op cit.*
18 SMITH, G. (1978) 'Occupational analysis', unpublished manuscript, Department of Sociology in Education, Ontario Institute for Studies in Education, Toronto, summer, p. 41.
19 *Ibid*, pp. 31–2.
20 GIROUX, H. (1981) *Ideology Culture and the Process of Schooling* Lewes, Falmer Press, pp. 9–10.
21 GOVERNMENT OF CANADA (1971) *Canadian Classification and Dictionary of Occupations,* Ottawa, Department of Manpower and Occupations, vii.
22 GOVERNMENT OF CANADA (nd) *Access a Career by Traits (ACT)* Department of Employment and Immigration, Occupational and Career Development Branch, Ottawa, Ministry of Supply and Services, Interests, p. 1
23 *Ibid.,* Aptitudes, p. 1.
24 *Ibid.,* Holland Codes, p. 1.
25 *Ibid.,* p. 7.
26 GIROUX, H. (1981) *op cit.,* p. 9.
27 YORK COUNTY BOARD OF EDUCATION (1980) *Inventory of Needs for Life Planning,* prepared by the Task Force, Senior Guideline, York County Board of Education, Division of Planning and Development, Toronto, University and College Placement Association, 1–1
28 *Ibid.,* 13–3.
29 *Ibid.,* 1–1.
30 *Ibid.,* 13–3.
31 SMITH, G. (1978) *op cit.*
32 Government of Canada (1971) *op cit.,* VII: xv.
33 SMITH, G. (1978), *op cit.,* p. 34.
34 *Ibid.*
35 Government of Canada (1979) *Aid in Using the Occupational Exploration Questionnaire,* Department of Employment and Immigration, Occupational and Career Analysis and Development Branch, Ottawa, Ministry of Supply and Services, p. 5
36 SMITH, G. (1978) *op cit.,* p. 35.
37 HERR, E.L. (1982) *op cit.*

References

DEWEY, J. (1977) 'Education vs trade training: Dr Dewey's reply' *Curriculum Inquiry,* v. 7 1, spring.
GOVERNMENT OF CANADA (nd) *Moving on! A Career,* Department of Employment and Immigration, Occupational and Career Analysis and Development Branch, Advanced Development Division, Ottawa, Ministry of Supply and Services.
GOVERNMENT OF CANADA (nd) *Moving on! To a Job,* Department of Employment and Immigration, Occupational and Career Analysis and Development Branch, Advanced Development Division, Ottawa, Ministry of Supply and Services.
GOVERNMENT OF CANADA (nd) *Moving on! By Staying On,* Department of Employment and Immigration, Occupational and Career Analysis and Development Branch, Advanced Development Division, Ottawa, Ministry of Supply and Services.
GOVERNMENT OF CANADA (nd) *CHOICES,* Department of Employment and Immigration, Occupational and Career Analysis and Development Branch, Ottawa, Ministry of Supply and Services.

Don Dippo

GOVERNMENT OF CANADA (nd) *A Handbook of CHOICES*, Department of Employment and Immigration, Occupational and Career Analysis and Development Branch, Ottawa, Ministry of Supply and Services.

GOVERNMENT OF CANADA (1978) *Index to Canadian Occupations: A New Way to Help Clients to Identify Career Goals*, Department of Employment and Immigration, Occupational and Career Analysis and Development Branch, Ottawa, Ministry of Supply and Services.

GOVERNMENT OF CANADA (1979) *Occupational Exploration Questionnaire*, Department of Employment and Immigration, Occupational and Career Analysis and Development Branch, Ottawa, Ministry of Supply and Services.

GOVERNMENT OF CANADA (1981) *Your Personal Occupational Selector: To Confirm or Discover New Occupational Goals*, Department of Employment and Immigration, Advanced Development Division, Occupational and Career Analysis and Development Branch, Ottawa, Ministry of Supply and Services.

GOVERNMENT OF ONTARIO (1982) *The Renewal of Secondary Education in Ontario: Response to the Report of the Secondary Education Review Project*, Toronto, Ministry of Education.

LAZERSON, M. and GRUBB, W.N. (1974) (Eds) *American Education and Vocationalism: A Documentary History, 1870–1970*, New York, Teachers College Press.

MARCUSE, H. (1978) 'On science and phenomenology' in ARATO, A. and GEBHARDT, E. (Eds) *The Essential Frankfurt School Reader*, New York, Urizen Books.

CHINA

The author of this chapter on the People's Republic of China is Dr Henry J. Sredl and the chapter is based on Sredl's five visits to the People's Republic of China and on related research.

Almost any aspect of the People's Republic of China is affected by its enormous population, and unemployment and vocational training are no exceptions. If the People's Republic of China experiences only a 3 per cent unemployment rate, then around twelve million people are officially out of work. Each year sees an estimated twenty-three million youngsters leave school, of whom around 5 per cent receive some form of vocational training. Plans for the future of vocational training and employment prospects for China's school-leavers depends, then, upon the success of current measures to restrict overall population size by rigidly enforcing birth control policies. But the vast majority of the Chinese population lives off the land, with urban access restricted, and it is in the rural areas where the majority of young 'workers waiting for jobs' are also to be found. The majority of jobs, however, are in the towns. The highest priority for China is, according to Sredl, 'modernization' — in effect quadrupling its industrial and agricultural output by the year 2000 — and involving investment in modern technological advances the appropriate education and training of the workforce. The task which confronts China is how to provide for vocational training for a burgeoning population without experiencing the shanty-town sprawl familiar to cities of the Third World and whilst continuing the drive for modernization.

The People's Republic of China

Dr. Henry J. Sredl

Introduction

Officially, the People's Republic of China (PRC) has no unemployment, only people 'waiting for jobs.' The number presently waiting for jobs is uncertain; gathering and verifying demographic data in a country of one billion people is difficult, especially when 80 per cent live in the countryside. China's work-force numbers over 400 million people. Of these, approximately 115 million are employed as workers in urban areas; approximately 320 million are peasants (farmers).

China's Economic Research Centre under the State Council claimed the percentage of city dwellers waiting for jobs to be 2.6 per cent as of the end of 1982, 80 per cent of whom were youths. This was a decrease from the 1979 job-waiting rate of 5.5 per cent (Ren and Bing, 1983). An aspect of the unemployment problem not evidenced by official statistics is the number of rural youths living illegally with relatives and friends in cities. The peasant workforce of 320 million is growing by more than 20 million new workers each year, more than half of whom are unskilled youth leaving or graduating from school.

In an effort to prevent urban sprawl and the accompanying decay of cities, such as is afflicting Third World countries, China is enforcing what is perhaps the most rigid urban policy in the world. To live in a city, you need a city registration. Without such registration you cannot rent an apartment, send children to school, obtain medical treatment, or get a job. To get a job, you need city registration. Thus, only individuals with desperately needed skills or political position are given permission and the necessary credentials to move into and within urban areas. So rigid are the regulations on moving that special credentials to move are usually valid for the individual worker only and not for his or her family. This policy has isolated China's surplus labor supply in the countryside and has precipitated the illegal movement of rural unemployed youth into the cities.

A conservative national unemployment estimate of 3 per cent creates an unemployed number of over 12 million; some estimates are as high as 20 million and more. Most of those waiting for jobs are youths and consequently

China is increasingly concerned about the large number of unskilled youths and their assimilation into the existing, basically unskilled, workforce. The concern has received a high national priority and extends to China's young adults.

At the pinnacle of China's list of current priorities is the achievement of the goal of modernization. In its most recent form this goal calls for the quadrupling of China's gross industrial and agricultural output value by the year 2000. The drive toward modernization is confronted with two major social problems: population and employment. Both have a profound impact on China's youth employment strategies.

Additional factors are affecting employment strategies: a history of political unrest resulting in profound changes in employment and unemployment and vacillation in national policy; a student body of 200 million and an educational system struggling to provide technical and job-related skills needed for employment; an attempt to replace an existing system of state controlled job placement and guaranteed life-long employment with a new system of 'responsibility;' and finally, thirty years of a comparative increase in living standards and the escalating expectations of China's populace for an even greater rate of increase.

Population

China's population has almost doubled in slightly more than three decades, from 580 million people in 1949 to slightly more than 1 billion people as of the 1982 census. Throughout this time China's population has become progressively younger. According to the 1982 census and the State Family Planning Commission[1], as of 1982 half of the total population was under 21; 65 per cent of the population was under 30. And in a land where the respected elder was a traditional symbol, only 6 per cent of the people were older than 65.

Projections based on current birth rates are phenomenal. In the next 18 years, an average of 20 million young people will annually reach the marriageable age. At the 1981 birth rate of 14.5 per thousand, China's population will reach 1.3 billion by the year 2000. One hundred years from now it will be an overwhelming 2.5 billion.

Chinese officials are greatly concerned about the economic consequences of an uncontrolled birth rate. Severe measures have recently been put into effect to develop a nation where one child per family will be the standard for the next 25 years. But traditions in China compete fiercely with changing ideologies and perhaps nowhere is this conflict more apparent than in the present government policy on birth control and the limitation of family size to one child. For centuries, the Chinese fostered large, extended families. Tradition favored sons whose labor in the field was a necessity for survival. For the 80 per cent of the Chinese (800 million strong) who live in rural areas and are supported by or derive their livelihood from farming and farm-related work, this tradition has not been forgotten.

Chinese tradition mandated that children, specifically sons, care for parents throughout old age. Consequently, a necessary form of old age insurance was a large number of children, especially sons. The latest Chinese doctrine attempts to allay the fears of poverty and abandonment at old age by promoting pensions. But pensions are presently given only to employees of state-owned factories and collectives which account for only a small percentage of China's workforce. Policies governing the large proportion of the population living in rural communes promote care of the aged by the commune. But with China's everchanging emphases, present policy is little comfort to elders living in regions where Beijing (the capital city) is but a name of some far-off land.

Employment

Full employment of China's masses has been a major goal since the founding of the People's Republic in 1949. Throughout the PRC's thirty-four-year history unemployment has fluctuated as a product of various political and economic reforms. But despite official claims, unemployment in China has never been totally abolished.

Periods of serious unemployment existed in the early 1950s, as China struggled with the problems of political and economic transition. Dixon attributes early unemployment to the rise in per capita production due to industrial reform, the elimination of many 'decadent and extravagant industries set up by the past bourgeois regime,' the increasing number of housewives seeking work, and the influx into the cities of surplus rural labor.[2]

Determined to improve living standards and the national economy, China turned to Russia in the 1950s for economic and technical assistance under the Sino-Soviet Treaty of Friendship, Alliance and Mutual Assistance. The Soviet economic development model was adopted, emphasizing capital-intensive projects in basic industries and the use of worker incentives such as piece rates and bonuses. Under the Sino-Soviet Treaty China was promised loans, industrial materials and technical expertise. Using teachers trained in the USSR, a Soviet-style education system, with an emphasis on science and engineering in the technical institutes and universities, was implemented to support the industrial changes.

The 'Great Leap Forward,' announced by Mao Zedong in 1958 created employment for virtually all. It was heralded as an 'intellectual and psychological bounding into the twentieth century[3] emphasizing boldness and experimentation. The Great Leap was designed to achieve maximum mobilization of China's labor force by harnessing the revolutionary enthusiasm of the masses. Peasants were encouraged to produce iron and steel in backyard smelters. '"To dare" was the motto impressed upon youth when once it was "to obey"'.[4]

Unemployment again increased in the early 1960s with a major setback to the Great Leap as the Soviets abandoned the Sino-Soviet Treaty in July 1960 and abruptly withdrew their 12,000 technicians and advisers. Many Chinese factories and other major construction projects were left partially completed; other projects were abandoned on the drawing boards. Vital building materials were withheld, new orders cancelled. This withdrawal of Soviet aid accentuated the technological arrest already being felt as a result of the three years of natural disasters (1959–61) that caused the poorest harvest in China since the turn of the century.

Although severely damaged, China's drive toward technological development continued and with it employment again increased. In the early 1960s Mao Zedong and Zhou Enlai (Chou En-lai) outlined the Four Modernizations, a staggeringly ambitious plan designed to move China, by the year 2000, to the high levels of technology found in the advanced nations of the world. The modernizations covered four major areas: science and technology, industry, agriculture and national defense. Technology, and the education essential to it, was considered central to the success of the other three modernizations.

But China's development was destined for another dramatic interruption with the Great Proletarian Cultural Revolution; with it came chaos in workforce and employment patterns. The revolution began in 1966 and, coupled with the reign of the Gang of Four, lasted through a tumultuous decade.

The revolution had a profound effect on youth employment. Previous authority and social structure were disregarded as cadres (administrators, supervisors, officials) and leading workers were 'sent down' to the countryside for 're-education.' Untrained peasants and the youthful Red Guards were sent to the factories as replacements in an effort to purge 'revisionists' from education, industry, medicine, and the military. Their major qualification was loyalty to Mao's new revolutionary doctrines. Industrial planning and organizing were the responsibility of the three-in-one alliance of workers and peasants, the People's Liberation Army, and teachers and students.

Because of China's policy of life-long employment, commonly known as the 'iron rice bowl,' the cadres and workers promoted during the Cultural Revolution are still holding their positions. In many instances, workers whom they replaced have been reinstated in parallel positions causing internal conflict. Workers who were formerly Red Guards during their teens and early twenties are now ostracized for their revolutionary roles; many conceal their part in a movement which once idolized them.

The Cultural Revolution and its impact on education and subsequent youth employment strategies will be discussed in the following section.

Education

Traditionally, education in Imperial China was solely the right of the sons of the learned gentry. Education emphasized the academics and was based on the Confucian Classics; manual work and education for it were despised. Coveted appointments to government posts were made strictly on the basis of academic examination scores, although undoubtedly some appointments were made through the 'back door.' The respect and power held by the educated few was disproportionate to their numbers. Revered by the illiterate masses and often heeded by the rulers, the educated were looked upon as superior beings.

By the beginning of the twentieth century, however, the Confucian-style educational system began to disintegrate, especially as the western nations exerted increasing military and political influence over China. In 1905 the classical Chinese examination process was abolished as Chinese policy makers realized that a new approach to education was needed to meet the challenge of industrialized nations. But despite the establishment of Western-style schools and colleges and the need for technicians, engineers and scientists, most education in these new schools emphasized the humanities and was in reality still available to only the privileged descendents of families of wealth and power, whose major career goal was more wealth and power.

The problem of keeping a balance between China's intellectual and practical education was addressed by Mao Zedong during the formidable 1930s. In his philosophical essay, 'On Practice,' Mao argued that knowledge cannot be based solely on theoretical understanding. He contended that knowledge begins with direct experience (work) and that the perception acquired through this experience is then raised to the level of rational knowledge. This knowledge must then be tested and modified through practice. Dialectically, moving between theory and practice, knowledge is developed and refined. Mao concluded

> Discover the truth through practice, and again through practice verify and develop the truth. Start from perceptual knowledge and actively develop it into rational knowledge; then start from rational knowledge and actively guide revolutionary practice to change both the subjective and the objective world. Practice, knowledge, again practice, and again knowledge. This form repeats itself in endless cycles, and with each cycle the content of practice and knowledge rises to a higher level.[5]

Mao's theories on education and work were applied early in the PRC's history. Faced with a population of 580 million, 80 per cent of which was illiterate, new China's early educational policies focused on providing education concurrently for the young generations and for the adults. For assistance in this China turned to the USSR and during the decade of the Sino-Soviet Treaty of Friendship, Alliance and Mutual Assistance the Russian influence over Chinese education was almost total. The Russian style educational system was modelled, consisting of five years of primary school, two years of junior middle and three years of senior middle school. In reality, however, most peasant children's education ended with primary school, usually because of the dearth of schools and teachers. The completion of a middle school education was usually a luxury of the more fortunate urban children.

The question of correct balance between educational theory and practice was again addressed in the educational reforms resulting from the Great Leap Forward in 1958. 'Half-work, half-study' schools (referred to by some as 'half-work, half-politics' schools) were advocated to increase access to education while minimizing the cost of such schooling. These schools combined education with productive labor on the theory that if teachers and students labored with workers and peasants the notion of educational superiority would dissolve. During the Great Leap, schools established their own factories and farms while factories and farms established their own schools. The Chinese axiom of 'walking on two legs' (the combining of theory and practice, general education with vocational education) was basic to Mao's educational policy prevalent at the time. This theme is visible in China's current educational and employment strategies.

During the early 1960s, there was increased emphasis on secondary level vocational and technical education programs. In many areas, more than half of the middle school (equivalent to American secondary school) students participated in some form of skill training before graduation. Post-secondary schools, often operated by industry in industrial settings, supplemented the secondary programs.

But all such programs were abolished during the Cultural Revolution as student revolutionaries violently disrupted, and often curtailed, both education and production. Mao saw China's youth as the key to the success of the revolution and consequently he and his followers started working through the schools to mobilize support. This led to the formation of the infamous Red Guards of the Cultural Revolution, the first unit of which was formed in the spring of 1966 in a Beijing (Peking) secondary school.[6] Using the youth, Mao sought to rid China of what was labeled as revisionism, the emphasis of professionalism over ideology, in such areas as industry, education, medicine, and the military.

The future employability of China's youth was severely hampered as the revolution's activities closed vocational and technical schools, colleges and universities. As colleges and universities opened, admission was granted not on the basis of entrance examinations or academic potential but upon political allegiance and peer nomination. All students had to work for at least two years in the army, factories or communes before being eligible for university application. University curricula were reduced from five to three years.

Workforce development programs were redesigned to equalize the masses ideologically as opposed to producing a stratified work force based on individual potential and reflecting investments in human capital. The Cultural Revolution was a decade of academic and intellectual famine which will affect the development and employment of China's youth for decades to come.

The devasting effects of the Cultural Revolution are reflected in current statistics. There are slightly over 200 million students in China, roughly the equivalent of the total population of the United States. According to China's Ministry of Education, each year 23 million youths leave school or complete their schooling. But because of the dearth of higher education facilities and faculty, a result of the Cultural Revolution, only 4 to 6 per cent of the graduates pursue further study at colleges and universities. With the destruction of secondary-level vocational and technical schools and programmes, until recently only 2 per cent of the 23 million students had some vocational or technical training. Thus, an overwhelmingly large percentage of China's young people are untrained for any kind of skilled work and must be absorbed annually by a labour force already overburdened with unskilled workers. Consequently, vocational and technical education is one of China's highest priotics. A present goal of China's leaders is to increase partipication in secondary vocational and technical education to the pre-Cultural Revolution level of 50 per cent.

Vocational schools prepare skilled workers through programmes offered in cooperation with large enterprises such as factories and railroads. Technical schools work with bureaux, commercial departments, and other organizations to prepare semi-professional or technical workers. Graduates of such programs are often placed in the workforce as cadres. The major differences between vocational and technical schools are the nature of entrance requirements and the emphasis placed on theory and practice. Vocational schools have less stringent entrance requirements than technical schools and devote more time to practice than theory. Vocational programmes generally last from two to three years, while technical school programmes last from three to four years.

Work Study

Work study programmes are being revived on both the primary and middle school levels. There are two major reasons for this: (1) to spur the development of vocational and technical skills prior to graduation from middle school; and (2) to provide much needed revenue to upgrade both primary and middle school facilities. Usually found in rural areas where state subsidies for locally operated schools are minimal, work-study programmes provide funds for the operation of the school as well as introduction to the socialist work ethic.

Primary students engage in farm and industrial production while developing elementary work skills. The actual labor equivalent is one-half month per school year, a requirement consistent with the national work standard for all primary students. On the middle school level, work-study programmes develop students' skills in agriculture and technical areas such as machine operation and mechanical maintenance and provide them with technical knowledge needed for advanced study. The manual labour requirement at the middle school level may increase to two weeks per semester in the lower middle and three weeks in the upper middle school.

Work-study programs are getting assistance from various groups including trade unions and professional groups. The national forum on education sponsored by the Ministry of Education in December 1980, urged the restructuring of middle school education with the development of vocational and technical education with work-study components.[7] School-run industry-education consortiums are being established to ascertain that workshop and farm activities do not dominate an educational program at the expense of the students' education. Supporters of work-study programs claim that students have exceeded the average scores on examinations for higher education and have been prepared for technical jobs in the work force.

As of 1982, China had one million primary and middle schools, including 431,000 which have work-study programmes; 40,360 school-run factories; 240,000 hectares (approximately 600,000 acres) of school-run farms and tree nurseries.[5]

On-the-Job Training/Apprenticeship

On-the-job training (OJT) continues to prepare the masses of China's youth for their first job, usually an unskilled or semi-skilled position. Such programmes are generally operated by the employing organization on a formal or informal basis. OJT programmes may last for a period of a few weeks to several years, depending on the complexity of the job. The training is provided in various forms and may be full-time, part-time or 'spare-time.' (For further discussion of part-time and spare-time programs, see section under 'Post-Secondary Programmes.') Workers in OJT programs are paid basic wages during the period of training; an incentive bonus may be earned on jobs where such bonuses are given regular workers.

Apprenticeship is the primary method used to prepare China's skilled workers. Although the system existed in China for centuries, it was given formal recognition after the founding of the People's Republic in 1949. More than one million workers annually have been enrolled in apprentice programs in recent years.[9]

An apprentice is usually a graduate of a junior middle school (8th grade). Typically, the apprentice receives no wages, only an allowance for food, clothing and living expenses. In addition, the apprentice receives free medical care and has access to welfare facilities and the equivalent of disability insurance. A typical apprenticeship lasts three years but may vary from two to four years depending on the job.

On-the-job training and apprenticeship will continue to be an integral part of China's youth employment program for many years to come.

Post-Secondary Programmes

'Part-Time' Education

The greatest growth by far in vocational and technical education has taken place on the post-secondary level through 'part-time' programmes. While it is difficult to obtain an exact enrolment in part-time education, it is estimated that many millions of workers, peasants, and cadres (including youths waiting for jobs) are involved in some form of part-time study. (Part-time programmes were previously referred to as spare-time programmes. The terms 'part-time' and 'spare-time' are often used interchangeably.)

The Shanghai Workers Part-time University with ten branch colleges is an example of a flourishing programme. From a total enrolment of approximately 17,000 students, 6000 come to class at the colleges; the remaining 11,000 attend university classes through television facilities. Both day and night courses are offered.

Competition for credit enrolment in part-time programmes is strong. Admission requires a recommendation from the student's work unit, successful completion of an entrance examination, completion of senior middle school or its equivalent, and three years of work experience.

Part-time programmes may last anywhere from several months to several years. In a typical programme, students attend classes three half-days and two evenings every week while receiving full pay. Tuition is covered by the work units of each student. Both general and technical education is provided. Popular courses include the study of technology, engineering, mathematics, foreign language and environmental protection, a new field in China particularly promoted in large urban areas where pollution is a major problem.

Part-time education may be offered through many agencies including city trade unions, technical schools, colleges and universities.

Instructional Television

The largest university in China is the Central Broadcasting and Television University (CBTU). Headquartered in Beijing, it is referred to as Television University. A growing number of colleges and universities supplement the work of the CBTU with their own television studios and programs.

CBTU was founded in 1979 and presently has over 400,000 regular students scattered throughout almost all parts of China. In addition, approximately 200,000 students are auditing courses while countless more benefit from informal viewing. Regular students are enrolled for credit after having been recommended for study by their work unit and after passing entrance examinations. Those who successfully complete a prescribed program are awarded a certificate or appropriate academic degree.

A most attractive feature of televised education (considered a form of part-time education) is the opportunity to provide education and training throughout China to millions of workers without disrupting those workers from their jobs. Both basic and specialized courses are offered by CBTU. The courses can be divided into two categories: (i) technical courses such as mechanics, electronics, and agricultural science; and (ii) general education including mathematics, physics, chemistry and foreign language. The study of foreign language is an important component of post-secondary technical training. Competency in a foreign language is essential for reading original technical materials. English is the most common foreign language offered.

Televised education is under the joint sponsorship of the Ministry of Education and the Broadcasting Administrative Bureau.

Job Placement and Responsibility

Job placement of China's youth was until recently the responsibility of the State. Upon leaving school or graduation, youths were assigned to jobs through a bureaucratic process on the basis of a master plan for labour determined at the State, commune, or city level. Once assigned, a cadre's or worker's job was considered guaranteed for life regardless of the quality or quantity of work performed. The system was known as 'the iron rice bowl.' Related to the iron rice bowl was 'the big pot,' the Chinese interpretation of Karl Marx which guaranteed every worker a share of the communal and national bounty based on need, regardless of quality and quantity of work.

Concepts of career development and job mobility were unheard of. Since over 90 per cent of China's youth had no marketable skills upon leaving school, random job placement and on-the-job training served the economic growth of China as well as any other system could. Theoretically, under the system everyone was employed.

Basic to the concept of the iron rice bowl was the nature of China's money supply and the financing of factories, communes and other enterprises. Operating revenues were distributed at the state's recommendation by financial institutions such as the People's Bank of China. The money was appropriated by the Ministry of Finance according to central planning with no plan for repayment and no charge for interest. The state merely took all profits made by the organization receiving the grant. If an operating loss was sustained, it was covered by the state. This obviously did little to promote productivity and the development and efficient utilization of the workforce.

By 1979, it was evident that China's drive towards modernization was again in danger and that the existing system of job placement and financial distribution needed revision. The new remedy, presently in effect, was a series of progressive reforms originally called economic readjustment; it is now referred to as the responsibility system.

Major results of the responsibility system include: (i) a changed nature of the money supply; (ii) the introduction of a profit motive in the operation of factories, agricultural communes, and other enterprises; and (iii) new training and employment opportunities for job-waiting youth. The responsibility system is based on an ideological shift in socialist principle: from 'to each according to his needs,' to 'to each according to his work.' Under the responsibility system, all enterprises are expected to make a profit, part of which is to be kept by the enterprise for further reinvestment and distribution to workers in the form of various bonuses. Losses must be covered by the enterprise.

The responsibility system is spawning new youth employment policies which the government hopes will be more effective than their predecessors. Under emerging policies, the government labor departments have a decreasing role in job placement, encouraging job-waiting youths to organize in collective undertakings or engage in self-employed jobs. The biggest growth areas include light industry, commerce, food servicing and the service trades, many of which were neglected under previous policies. An integral part of the responsibility system is the reform of the secondary educational system which includes converting a number of general middle schools into secondary vocational schools where students will learn the skills required in future work.

The responsibility system is rapidly transforming work roles and practices in the countryside. Under a form of the responsibility system called the household contract system, distribution of farm wages and profits is also based on production levels. The household contract system is based on three-party contracts signed by the state, the collective (production team) and the peasant household. The state determines a plan for rural production which designates certain crops and products for a particular area. Based on this plan the production team contracts out the tracts of land to peasant households who agree to grow given quantities of a designated crop.

New reforms have shifted the employment of approximately 100 million peasants from grain production to other lines of work including fish and poultry breeding, processing industries, transportation, commerce and service trades. China hopes that the responsibility system will encourage millions more of its peasants to develop the potential of the abundant natural resources in China's vast mountainous regions. These areas account for 69 per cent of the national territories and are six times as large as the total acreage of farmland. Activities suited to these areas include forestry, animal husbandry and possibly small industry.

The responsibility system is also spurring the industrialization of the countryside and with it new employment opportunities for youth. This move is prompted by the limited amount of available farmland in proportion to the number of peasants: 100 million hectares (250 million acres) of farmland, averaging 0.3 hectare (approximately 0.8 acre) per peasant.

The Future

According to the Sixth Five Year Plan (1981–1985), 29 million new workers will be added to the urban labor force. Of these, 11 million will be employed in state organizations and enterprises, another 11 million in collective enterprises in cities and towns. One-and-a-half million will find self-employment while another 5.5 million will enter state and collective units to replace those who retire. By the end of 1985, 'nearly all those entering the urban labor force for the first time will be placed'.[10] Projecting beyond 1985, the Economic Research Centre predicts that all those who enter the urban labor force can be productively absorbed *providing* that the population growth reflects present population control policies and that the scale of economic growth keeps expanding.

But the two provisions cannot be taken for granted. The long-term success of China's birth control policy are difficult to determine at this time. Young urban people who view as more important the material amenities and who have never experienced extensive toiling on the land, tend to accept the party line that national good should take precedence over individual desires and that one-child families are in the 'national good.' But 80 per cent of China's population lives in the countryside where the current responsibility system awards contracts and subsequent payments to families, not individuals. There are increasing reports in the Chinese press related to female infanticide, an indication that the enforcement of the present birth control policy of one child per family may present severe problems.

Basic to China's continued economic growth is the rate at which it can prepare its workforce for the increasingly skilled jobs which are an integral part of such growth. National strategies for the employment of China's youth will continue to emphasize work-study, on-the-job training, apprenticeship and vocational education for the millions of school-age youths about to enter the workforce. It will also increase its programs of part-time education to reach the millions of youths and young adults who are currently employed, underemployed or waiting for jobs.

China is placing considerable hope for economic and technological growth on its recently established Special Economic Zones (SEZs). There are presently four SEZs, the largest and most successful of which is located in Shenzhen encompassing 327 square kilometres (126 square miles) and sharing the northern boundary of Hong Kong. Within these zones, China expects to lure foreign investors into joint ventures. Through such ventures China expects to not only improve its economy but its technology as well and to transfer the effects of both to other parts of China.

Presently, there is an apparent euphoria about the opportunities available under the responsibility system and its ability to provide jobs for millions of China's out-of-school youth. But this feeling of well-being may be superficial as millions of Chinese vividly remember the violence and purges of an ideological movement just a decade or so ago which ostracized those fellow countrymen who were successful in applying the principles of another responsibility system.

National strategies for minimizing the number of China's job-waiting youth will have a profound effect on China's ability to achieve its goal of modernization: the quadrupling of its gross industrial and agricultural output value by the year 2000. With one quarter of the world's population involved, the extent to which China achieves this goal will impact significantly on the remaining three quarters.

Notes

1 OIAN, X. (1983) 'Controlling population growth', *Beijing Review*, 26 (7), 14 February, pp. 21–6.
2 DIXON, J. (1981) *The Chinese Welfare System 1949–1979*, New York, Praeger Publications, p. 337.
3 HERDAN, I. (1976) *Introduction to China*, London, Anglo-Chinese Educational Institute, p. 21.
4 *Ibid.*, p. 31 quoting HAN, S. in *China in the Year 2001*.
5 MAO, T. (1983) On practice, *The selected works of Mao Tse-Tung*, Vol. 1, Peking, the Foreign Language Press, p 308.
6 Keesing's research report (1967) *The Cultural Revolution in China*, New York, Charles Scribner's Sons.
7 Forum on Educational Work (1981) *Beijing Review*, 24 (1), 5 January, pp. 8–9.
8 LI, Y. (1982) 'Work study programmes in primary and middle schools', *Beijing Review*, 25 (45), 8 November, pp. 21–4.
9 ZHENG, J. (1982) 'Employment, wages, workers' welfare and labour protection in China' in MUGIAO, X. (Ed) *Almanac of China's Economy 1981*, Hong Kong, Modern Cultural Company Ltd..
10 REN, T. and BING, Y. (1983) 'Population and employment', *Beijing Review*, 23 (13), 28 March, p. 22.

FIJI

In the late 1970s and early 1980s employment prospects for Fiji's school-leavers became increasingly adversely affected by declining emigration opportunities and the inability of the supply of jobs to keep abreast of population growth and an upturn in female participation in job-seeking. Although Fiji had enjoyed a developing system of education in the preceding decade, employers were demanding more and higher qualifications as a method of sifting job applications. It was becoming more and more difficult for young people in Fiji to be 'meaningfully active' after leaving school. The developing situation was a cause for concern amongst Fijian young people and the wider society as a whole. Part of the government response was to establish the Fiji Employment and Development Mission with funds from the EEC. In 1982 the author of this chapter, John Cameron, was invited to join the Mission as a Core Consultant, a post he held for a year, and a time when the material for this paper was gathered.

Cameron describes the situation in Fiji which led up to the present economic recession after the initial 'honeymoon' expansion period post-Independence in 1970. He analyzes the policy responses to a growing criticism from parents, educationalists and the media of the increasing vulnerability and exposure of the young to adverse market forces, and categorizes these responses under the headings of 'reactionary', 'reformist' and 'innovatory' — all of which could be found in Fiji in 1983.

The Nature of and Responses to Growing Unemployment among Young People in Fiji[1]

John Cameron

The Socio-economic Background: Shared Affluence, Divided Culture and Political Vulnerability

Fiji is an archipelago in the South Pacific with a population of around 600,000 people. The natural resource base is strong in terms of cultivatable land, hydropower energy possibilities, commercial timber, and subsistence and commercial fishing. Access to land is relatively widespread through a complex set of communal land-holding and tenancy arrangements. Thus only a minority of families have no claim to land, and the vast majority of households have sufficient income to give a standard of living well above physiological subsistence with little risk.[2] The creation of this unusually egalitarian situation in terms of access to the means of production and, to a lesser degree, incomes, is the outcome of a historical process during the period 1874 to 1970, when Fiji was part of the British Empire. The British not only confirmed communal ownership of 83 per cent of the land area by the indigenous people on a clan basis in the early part of this period, but also presided over the breaking down of sugar plantations on the remaining, generally easily cultivatable, land into small tenant sugar cane farms for former landless labourers in the 1930s. Increasingly secure rights of tenure were granted over time on this 'freehold' and 'crown' land and also tenancy agreements were extended to 'native-land' giving a good basis for wages and salary claims outside agriculture.[3]

These tenants are almost entirely of South Asian origin and mainly descendants of people who came as indentured labourers on five year contracts in the period 1879 to 1916, to work on the plantations and in the sugar mills. Thus two very different ethnic groups now dominate the population of Fiji. In the national population census of 1976, 51 per cent of the population was recorded as 'Indian' (though many are now second-generation Fiji-born and will be called Fiji-Indian hereafter in this chapter), and 44 per cent were recorded as 'Fijian' (claiming residence from before the cession in 1874 of Fiji to the British Empire). These two ethnic groups have different first languages and different religions. Interaction between members of the two groups appears very limited and no cross-marriages are known to me, though I knew several cross-marriages between people of European or Chinese origin and Fijians. Neither major ethnic group is simply homogeneous in itself, but the relationship between the two groups is notably tense with cultural difference threatening to become a chasm through which any frustration may vent itself violently.

Nevertheless, the political experience up to 1983 since Independence in 1970 has included four strongly contested general elections with little or no violence. Though the same political party has formed the government for the whole period, there is a large opposition in the legislature. Also trades unions and an uncensored press operate freely in Fiji giving the impression of a society with very similar basic political values to those of the United Kingdom. Unfortunately, there are two significant qualifications to this appearance of tolerance and stability. Firstly, the political parties mobilize their votes at election times strongly along ethnic lines, a tendency encouraged by a Constitution which formally uses ethnicity as a criteria for allocating votes to legislative constituencies. Secondly, whilst ethnic balance is maintained informally in the civilian public sector in recruitment and promotion procedures, the military is dominated by men of Fijian ethnicity.

Fiji's rich natural resource base has been utilized by the people of Fiji to produce an average standard of living, including social welfare provision, which places her in the upper middle income class of the 1981 per capita income league table and in the top fifty of the world's economies with an estimated life expectancy at birth close to seventy years.[4] If the term 'economically 'underdeveloped' has any relevance to Fiji, it could only be used to bring out the continuing dependency for foreign exchange on exports of sugar. But even in this industry, Fiji is estimated to be a relatively low cost producer by world standards and one of the countries better adapted to weathering the difficult market conditions of the mid-1980s (though, by no means, costlessly). Whilst all the macroeconomic indicators for Fiji (inflation, GDP growth, international indebtedness, and unemployment) have moved adversely in the 1980s compared with the 1970s, they still stand at relative levels which would be considered utopian in many countries.[5] For instance, formally defined unemployment (with respect to a reference week and being willing to and unable to find work), probably stood at less than 5 per cent in the late 1970s, though it has risen substantially since 1979. But even so, it was still estimated in 1983 at less than 9 per cent on the basis of two separate estimates.[6] In a paper for the OECD which examined the general conditions of life in Fiji, compared with Malaysia and Hong Kong, using a technique called 'active life profiles', this author arrived at the conclusion: 'Fiji looks like a nice place to live but not capable of going anywhere very fast'.[7]

That conclusion may hold as a general proposition but the rest of this chapter is concerned with the question about what specifically Fiji was offering her young people in 1983. A question to which the answer is much less comfortable than that given by the overall assessment and does seem to demand significant, urgent movement.

Development in Schooling in Fiji Since 1970 and Some Growing Questions

A leading commentator on education in the South Pacific described the Fiji schooling situation at political independence in the following terms.

Educational development intensified in Fiji in the second half of the 1960s as primary and secondary enrolments continued to rise steadily in the wake of rising economic prosperity and social demand. Regrettably, however, there was little or no lessening in the disparity between the quantity and quality of education, principally because of the acute shortage of trained teachers that prevailed throughout the period.[5]

Schools also had problems both through wide variations in equipment provision due to being run by local committees and also being of single group ethnic composition in a multi-ethnic society. The school system had grown unevenly with the most notable change being the tremendous advances by Fiji-Indians after 1950 from a position of inferiority in average length of schooling to Fijians to superiority in 1970. At Independence, all Fiji children could enrol in a neighbourhood school at the age of six, and reportedly well over ninety per cent did. However, only fifty six per cent of all 15 to 16 year olds were in school in 1970. Thus ten years of schooling and associated passes in public examinations were an assured passport to wage or salaried employment virtually as a matter of course in the expanding non-agricultural economy.

The central objectives of the education policy of the Fiji government after Independence in 1970[9] were to make ten years of schooling availabe to every child and to reduce school fees, with fees for children in primary schools being abolished over a period of a few years. However, it was decided to continue with local school management committees, with central government controlling teacher certification and the curriculum. Whilst schooling was not made compulsory for children of any age, the combination of increased places, growing population, and possible improved quality of teaching (partially due to higher teacher qualifications, partially due to reduced-class sizes) resulted in a doubling in numbers of people passing the Fiji Junior Certificate of Education (the national public examination generally taken at age 16) in 1979 compared with 1970. This result was achieved without the proportions of national resources allocated to education being significantly increased until 1976, when an upward shift of a percentage point occurred in both the proportions that education took out of Government expenditure and National Income. In conventional human capital terms, it appears reasonable to conclude that Fiji's school system achieved a great deal, given development objectives at a relatively low resource cost. Some education development indicators for Fiji in the 1970s are shown in Table 1.

However, even in orthodox schooling terms, certain problems did remain at the end of the 1970s. The average length of schooling and formal qualifications on leaving school had increased but a considerable tail in the distribution of length of schooling remained. Significant numbers of children were leaving school well before the age of 16, some as early as 12 or 13 years of age at the normal time of moving from primary to secondary school. In 1970, early school-leaving could be treated as representing the dominant social attitudes towards gender as female school enrolment was significantly lower than male (at this time 47 per cent of all people enrolled in school were female and estimates suggest well under 45 per cent of secondary school enrolments).

Table 1:   Education development indicators for Fiji, 1971–1978

Year	Percentage increase in secondary school rolls	Fiji Government educational expenditure on percentage of GDP at factor cost	Full time students over 15 as percentage of total population 15 to 64
1971	13.3	3.7	6.2
1972	17.0	4.2	6.7
1973	12.3	3.4	7.1
1974	10.2	3.0	7.4
1975	7.1	3.4	n.a.
1976	9.6	4.2	7.9
1977	7.3	5.0	8.1
1978	4.5	4.9	8.2

Sources: Departmental Reports of Ministries of Education and Finance and Bureau of Statistics and Fiji Registrar General

By 1979, the gender ratio in schools at all ages was much closer to those in the overall age group and less politically acceptable demographic characteristics of early school-leaving were becoming prominent. Early school-leaving was now seen by politicians as being related to being rural, Fijian and male and thus indicating deepening imbalances in society along the most vulnerable fault lines in Fiji society.

These were experiments in the 1970s in specific institutional provision for rural Fijian children (so-called junior secondary schools) amounting to a form of positive discrimination. But these experiments qualitatively seemed to reinforce a sense of peer group academic inferiority in single race boarding schools remote from family and village life and thus did not discourage early school leaving. Also quantitatively, an ideology of equality of educational opportunity did not permit any schemes involving positive discrimination to be generously financed or a radically new curriculum to be designed and introduced. Thus whilst political Independence proved a turning point in the quantitative expansion of schooling with conventional academic goals, it failed to come to terms with some qualitative structural problems with a worrying ethnic dimension. These problems could be tolerated in a period of overall economic growth and salaried job creation, but left vulnerabilities once economic growth and job creation slowed, as they did in the 1980s.

Options on Leaving School and Their Tendencies to Narrow

Access to cultivatable land in Fiji is notably widely distributed. The option of working on and or subsisting off family controlled land for several years after leaving school was still real in 1983 for the majority of young people. For Fijian young men the prospect of possessing land in their own right on marriage was virtually certain. Fiji-Indian young men faced more diverse situations and the pressure to find other employment was generally greater. For young women of both ethnic groups there still appeared to be little family pressure to find wage or salaried employment between school and marriage though, on the other hand, obstacles to such employment from families did not appear to be widespread. For those young people whose families' urban commitment was longer than one generation, an economic base in a family business often existed with a possibility of some expansion or substitution of family labour for wage labour to provide economic activity and income for younger members of the family. Nevertheless, a significant group of households existed without access to means of producing a comfortable income. Calculations by the author on the nature of poverty in Fiji suggest that in 1977 around ten per cent of young people were in households whose level of economic deprivation would force them to seek additional income immediately on leaving school and, indeed, possibly force them to leave school without sitting for the public examinations they wished to attempt and were assessed as capable of passing.[10]

Further education, as a post-school option (including vocational training) for those young people passing the New Zealand School Certificate or the New Zealand University Entrance examinations was frequently sought abroad. There are Fiji migrants in the UK, New Zealand, Australia, Canada, the USA and India who provide a possibility of supported temporary or permanent emigration for many Fiji young people especially those with internationally recognized school-leaving qualifications. This is reflected in the numbers studying at universities at the end of the 1970s. The University of the South Pacific, which was established in 1968, had 974 Fiji Residents enrolled in 1978. By comparison High Commissions reported 610 students in tertiary education in New Zealand, 380 in Australia, 101 in the UK and 600 in India. Non-University post-school technical and vocational training in Fiji expanded rapidly overall in the post-Independence period in parallel with increasing numbers of people staying on in secondary school, with a stress on stenography and teacher training. In 1970 it was reported that 1302 people (of whom 235 were women primarily in stenography and teacher training) were enrolled in such courses. By 1976, this number was reported to have risen to 2304 (of whom 1390 were women). Between 1976 and 1979, the number of people in full-time technical/vocational training increased by another seven hundred (all statistics in this paragraph from Fiji Bureau of Statistics, 1979). During the 1970s, post-school full-time education opportunities in Fiji increased faster than the client population whilst opportunities for emigration by young people for further education remained buoyant, but nevertheless still only involved approximately 10,000 people in total at any one point in time out of a minimum of 100,000 young people in the most relevant age group, 18 to 25.

Thus, pressure on wage and salaried jobs for Fiji's young people was kept manageable in the 1970s by the widespread availability of family work, aided by emigration opportunities and growth of post-school education places in Fiji. But though the supply of wage and salaried jobs rose strongly in the 1970s, overall this was still not much faster than the growth rate of the labour force, due to population growth and increased female participation. Getting a wage or salaried job for school leavers was increasingly difficult and, through the 1970s, public examination qualifications of applicants for identical jobs tended to rise, a tendency dramatically illustrated in Table 2. Use of increasingly higher qualifications to filter numerous applicants down to manageable short lists by employers was widespread. Within a decade after political

Independence, clerical jobs which had been filled in 1970 by people with no public examination qualifications were attracting applicants with the New Zealand School Certificate. By 1983 applicants for such jobs could be found offering passes in the New Zealand University Examinations. Formally defined unemployment (the proportion of self-defined economically active population with no work in a reference week) of people aged 15 to 24 was measured at the 1976 census as 17.1 per cent. But 1976 was a bad year for new job creation and it may be that formal employment in this age-group at the end of the 1970s was around 12 per cent, compared with an overall formal unemployment rate of around 5 per cent.

Table 2   Number of students passing Fiji Junior Certificate of Education compared to numbers of new salaried jobs available

Year	Number of people passing FJCE*	Year	Estimate increase in number of salaried jobs	Number of new salaried jobs per FJCE pass in preceeding year
1970	3042	1971	1583	0.52
1971	3646	1972	1019	0.28
1972	3717	1973	1239	0.33
1973	4181	1974	2800	0.67
1974	4798	1975	750	0.16
1975	5056	1976	1746	0.35
1976	5196	1977	1993	0.38
1977	5791	1978	1796	0.31
1978	5885	1979	343	0.06
1979	6056	1980	100	0.02

* Fiji Junior Certificate of Education, generally taken at age 16
Sources: Ministry of Education Reports and Censuses of Employment

The 1970s became increasingly uncomfortable for young people seeking to be meaningfully active as the decade went on. In the early 1980s, this discomfort was being widely acknowledged in Fiji as becoming acutely painful for young people and worrying for the wider society. The existence of the Fiji Employment Mission at this time was indicative of that concern, as is this chapter! Work-sharing arrangements in agriculture, especially in the vital area of cane-harvesting, were stretched to the extent that many people involved were working less than four hours a day, five days a week, for seven months of the year. The Fiji Government had decided in the Eighth Development Plan for the early 1980s (Fiji Government 1980) not to set new goals for education and thus young people were being offered few new opportunities as students at school or post-school. Also, the Government drastically reduced teacher training places as well as virtually freezing new recruitment to the civil service in 1983. Finally, private sector employers were making employees redundant on a significant scale and across a wide range of activities for the first time since political Independence. Economic recession in Fiji and the end of the Independence 'honeymoon' expansion period of the public sector, especially in education, left young people very exposed. This exposure was generally recognized as complaints from parents and critical reports from educationalists were received in all parts of the political system and the media.

However, though policy suggestions were numerous, they were often contradictory in terms of assumptions about causes and half-hearted in implementation, when implemented at all. To try and interpret these conflicting directions of response to the generally acknowledged problem of young people's situation, the remainder of this paper is divided into three sections labelled 'reactionary', 'reformist' and 'innovatory'.[11] All three types of response could be found in Fiji in 1983 and the struggle over which will dominate continues, thus inhibiting determined action and appropriate resource allocation. The 'reactionary' strategy has strong support in the Fiji government, in areas of the trades union leadership and from international capital; 'reformism' finds spokespeople in the bureaucracy, especially the educationalist bureaucracy; 'innovation' is confined to some radical experiments close to universities, churches and aid agencies and has great problems of credibility in terms of political constituency and replicability. In Fiji, the policy outcomes of current debates are still uncertain and the purpose of this chapter is not to predict or rank, rather the intention is to expose the arguments in a systematic framework.

The 'Reactionary' Response

At the basis of this form of response is the belief that increased schooling has changed values in young people for the worse. Aspirations towards salaried work and complex consumption patterns have replaced contentment with manual work on the family land and a simpler subsistence life-style. Such a model for a 'traditional' life-style exists in the living memory of Fijian people of chiefly status, as the British ruled very indirectly in Fiji and incorporated chiefly juridicial authority at the village level into the colonial administration up until the mid-1960s. A clash between values inculcated by rural life (especially Fijian village life) and values inculcated by school is seen to be crucial to explaining the restlessness of young people — a restlessness to be eased by diminishing the independent influence at school in terms of time and curriculum. School should reinforce, not challenge, the 'traditional' values of village life in formal and hidden curricula including gender roles and attitudes. As the two major racial groups have very different cultures this would also suggest support for the principle of single race schools. However, the problem of Fijian advancement in the professions would remain; suggesting a requirement for increasing positive discrimination in higher education employment and in favour of any Fijians who are 'creamed off' at an early stage.

But young people for whom rural life, conventional marriage, or family employment is not an option do need urban wage work. In the 'reactionary' scenario this work (mainly for Fiji-Indians) would be provided by international capital, though this would need hourly wage rates to be drastically reduced in Fiji. For instance, an Export Processing Zone (EPZ) was being actively proposed in Fiji as part of a new development strategy in 1982 despite the fact that average hourly wage rates in Fiji were several times higher than those prevailing in the Philippines, the most obvious regional competitor. In this zone, tax collection, trades unions rights and much worker protection legislation would be suspended in an effort to encourage transnational corporations to establish enclave plants. It is notable that some trades union leaders appear ready to accept an EPZ, apparently seeing them as isolatable and thus capable of reducing excess labour supply to the non-enclave sector and improving the overall negotiating position for established workers. Also those international institutions which advocate free market economics, notably the International Monetary Fund, tend to see EPZs as a progressive step in diminishing 'inefficient' government interference in resource allocation.[12]

For the remainder of young people outside the rural areas and not in the EPZs, the reactionary response is to offer spells of disciplined activity in national service, youth camps or prison depending on the degree of social nuisance caused. National service might be civilian or military. For instance, in recent years the participation of Fiji in UN peace-keeping forces has involved a regular flow of Fijian young men through the armed forces. A national youth camp exists for voluntary short residential courses for young people but it had been little used up to 1983 as recruitment and administration had proved difficult. By contrast, the number of people in prison, especially Fijian young men, was disproportionately high by world standards. Thus attitudes and to some extent facilities for an authoritarian approach to young people's problems already exist in Fiji and support for relatively coercive policies appears to be widespread.

The 'Reformist' Response

The 'reformist' position also sees curriculum change away from 'academic' subjects as an appropriate response to young people's problems. Academic learning has undoubtedly dominated technical training in the Fiji school system. Therefore, a different curriculum which prepared young people for self-employment using tools and machinery in non-agricultural activities is needed. However, equipping schools with suitable staff and resources is costly and needs large, and arguably multi-racial, units to justify the investment. Thus reactionary and reformist positions disagree on important policy issues. At the attitudinal level, experience of 'multicraft' courses financed by New Zealand aid in Fiji, suggests that systematic technical training in schools is regarded by parents as an option for academic 'failures'. This parental conservatism is influential through free choice of secondary schools, which leads to those schools with good academic records being heavily favoured, and parental domination of school management committees, which are crucial in deciding on and financing capital projects. Reformists are therefore faced with not only the economic problems of justifying extra resources for schools at the centre, but also politically overriding or changing parents' views at the school management committee level.

In the face of this local parental conservatism, which is also a problem for the 'reactionary' response as it too is concerned about the curriculum being too academic, one 'reformist' response has been to press for improved 'careers guidance' at an earlier age. In 1983, official careers guidance was split between volunteer teachers in secondary schools and a small section in the Ministry of

Education. The work of the Ministry office, and therefore probably most teachers involved in careers guidance given their dependence on the central office for information, was almost entirely concerned with the transition from school to further education and the associated allocation of Government controlled scholarships. No information was being collected centrally on the aspirations and experiences of people leaving school before the age of 17. Putting resources into careers guidance for younger people, including increased contact with employers, is seen as a method by reformists of improving the match between people and jobs in the labour market and, perhaps more importantly, helping attitudes of young people and their parents to adapt to a more 'realistic' view of access to 'white-collar' salaried job opportunities whilst still at school.

But if such 'realism' could be avoided whilst at school, the experience of the world after school produces swift, painful realization of the facts for most young people seeking wage or salaried employment. In 1983, when virtually no new salaried jobs were created there was no help available to young people who had left school and were facing indefinite unemployment other than an ineffective Government employment exchange system with no requirements of vacancies' registration by employers. Also most public sector technical and vocational training courses had been established on a basis of employer sponsorship for trainees or in-house training programmes for employees with limited government subsidies. Thus unemployed young people faced double access problems of place availability and financing. Non-governmental organizations like the Salvation Army, two Roman Catholic orders of monks, the YMCA and the Muslim League had set up vocational courses for especially vulnerable, specific groups of young people with varying degrees of professionalism and amounts of resources. But the total number of young people involved was small and the programmes were vulnerable to resource loss in financial and/or leadership terms. A reformist position would undoubtedly want to see public sector and non-governmental organizations' activity extended to permit more young people to develop skills and gain job experience after leaving school in a more flexible system not dependent on existing employment, prison experience, or religion. But the resource implications of effective action are unclear and the prospect of more trained young people chasing the same number of jobs for the rest of the 1980s is real and unattractive to economic fiscal conservatives or educationally radical innovators.

The 'Innovatory' Response

Faced with the prospect of a relatively fixed demand for labour and increasing supply of people seeking work, one obvious innovatory response is to increase the number of jobs by increasing the amount of work and sharing it as widely as possible. Increasing the amount of work in this response in current depressed economic circumstances rests firmly with government and its own employment policy. But, whilst this response may accept a substantial government budgetary deficit, some complementary economic response to potential deterioration in the international balance of payments in a small, open economy is also needed, i.e. suggesting protectionism.

Similarly work-sharing has obvious political attractions but the uncomfortable economic corollary of income sharing must also be faced. In Fiji, work-sharing and income sharing in sugar cane harvesting has been a notable feature of limiting the growth of formal unemployment but a parallel change in non-agricultural employment would face resistance from employers, including government, and employees, voiced through a strong trades union movement. Both sides are very suspicious that they would end up disadvantaged as the work-sharing/income-sharing trade-off unrolled.

When work is difficult to find, then another innovatory response is to establish that a non-work life has value and worth. Personal development is then seen as an alternative, albeit a difficult one, to an identity secured through work. The easiest access to personal development for many young people appears to be through physical development and the medium of sport. Team games are popular in Fiji and community projects for young people frequently involve improved provision of sports facilities. However, peer group solidarity in the face of widespread unemployment appears as likely to lead to self-destructive or socially disruptive activity as personal or group self-development. In the face of this reality, innovative projects for young people tend to be fire-brigade activities — attempting to reach out with limited resources to groups showing signs of deep alienation, for whom the prison yard has become a more relevant space for gaining status than the football field.

Finally, it seems logical after all the previous discussion to suggest that the most innovatory response to the situation of young people in Fiji must be based on the recognition that they are disproportionately suffering the pains of changes over which they have had no consultation. The gerontocratic aspects of power in Fiji society have ensured that young people of both sexes and both major races will take a disproportionate share of the strains of any recession in the economy. Certainly the vast majority of these young people will not go hungry and most will have a reasonable pattern of consumption by current world standards. But around twenty per cent are being left formally un-employed by a society which has only given them employment as a measure of worth, and many more are living dependently in family situations when they would prefer the independent status of a wage or salaried job. Here and there in Fiji, projects exist which are attempting to give young people (usually Fijian young men) access to land in their own right as individuals, or groups, at an earlier age than customary. Thus these projects tend to require the participants to integrate themselves into village life with its gerontocratic hierarchies but nevertheless do give young people some control over the means of production. As first small steps, such projects do give an innovative challenge to Fiji society about the exclusion of young people from control over the means of production and the links of this exclusion to their frustrations.

Notes

1 This paper owes much to the people whom the author met whilst working for a year as a core team consultant to the Fiji Employment and Development Mission. The Mission was funded by the EEC Development Fund and administered by the Institute of Development Studies at the University of Sussex. The views expressed in this chapter are those of the author and are not necessarily those of the Mission.

2 CAMERON, J. (1983a) 'Development dilemmas in Fiji', *Discussion paper 137*, Norwich, School of Development Studies, University of East Anglia; (1983b) 'The extent and structure of poverty in Fiji' *Discussion paper 145*, Norwich, School of Development Studies, University of East Anglia.
3 Neither of these historical processes was simple or uncontested. France (1969) describes the curious manner in which clan (or *matagali*) land was allocated and recorded; Gillion (1977) captures the political tensions at the time of the breaking up of the sugar plantations.
4 See WORLD BANK (1983) *World Development Report*, Ontario.
5 CAMERON, J. (1983a) *op cit.*
6 The first estimate constructed flows into and out of the labour force since the population census in 1976 as a base. The second estimate came from a national sample survey of employment and unemployment in 1982. The unemployment rate of young people between 15 and 24 years of age in the 1982 survey was more than twice the overall average.
7 CAMERON, J. (1983b) *op cit*, p10.
8 WHITEHEAD, C. (1981) *Education in Fiji*, Canberra.
9 Fiji Government (1970) *Fiji Development Plan 1970–1974 (DP VI)*, Suva, Fiji.
10 CAMERON, J. (1983b) *op cit.*
11 This organization of material is intended to organize the complex debates which are going on in Fiji into a framework for the purposes of this chapter. Two problems result. Firstly, there is a problem of reading coherence and rationality into the many, piecemeal contributions to the debates on young people's problems. Secondly, the debate continues at the time of writing and expression of positions is still largely oral and often in informal and unofficial form. The best methodology for scientifically investigating such 'smoke-filled rooms' is unclear, and that for rooms with official 'grog bowls' is even more hazy. The final criteria for assessing what follows in the text are left to the reader but this author suggests comparison with the reader's own knowledge as the appropriate starting point. The organizing framework is meant to be transferable to situations outside Fiji after making limited allowances for local circumstances and, if it does, then it has cleared one important hurdle.
12 See WORLD BANK (1983) *op cit*, on this general issue.

References

CAMERON, J. (1983c) *Expectancy as an Integrating Concept for Social and Demographic Data: the Fiji Country Study*, Paris, Organization for Economic Cooperation and Development (OECD).
Fiji Bureau of Statistics (1979) *Social Indicators for Fiji*, Suva, Fiji
Fiji Government (1980) *Fiji Development Plan 1980–1984 (DPVIII)*, Suva, Fiji.
FISK, E.K. (1970) *The Political Economy of Independent Fiji*, Canberra.
FRANCE, P. (1969) *The Charter of the Land*, Melbourne.
GILLION, K.L. (1977) *The Fiji Indians*, Canberra.

THE THIRD WORLD

In industrialized countries the notion of unemployment carries with it the baggage of assumptions and expectations which come with work for pay as a way of life. In situations where a majority of the population live a peasant existence, unemployment must be placed in a different context, as in many of the less developed countries. Similarly, where a good number of a population receive, at best, a rudimentary education, then the concept of vocational training is subject to an alternative interpretation. However, many less developed countries aspire to modernization and industrialization and see the development of their education system — often along Western lines — as a necessary step in order to achieve this end. When the number of available jobs does not correspond to the increased output of qualified personnel, then the educated unemployed may be inserted into the equation. If the majority of the educated unemployed are under the age of 24, then the result is a problem of unemployed school-leavers for the less developed countries. A paradox, as Rafael Irizarry describes in this chapter, of those with the greatest educational attainment — 'the strategic human resources for economic development' — being those with the highest rates of unemployment.

Educational Policies and the Educated
Unemployed in the Less Developed Countries

Rafael L. Irizarry

Third World countries (or less developed countries as they are more commonly designated) are confronting a very serious paradox regarding their educational policies in the context of their developing strategies to promote
industrialization and modernization. Since the initial phases of development
efforts in the post war period, when most of them attained political independence from their respective metropolies, the ideology of rapid industrialization
and social modernization assigned education a crucial role.[1] For development
to take hold, these countries needed to increase manpower resources to
manage government and economic institutions, to adopt and operate modern
production technology in factories, mines and farms, and to provide the basic
services in the fields of health, education and social welfare. Therefore,
education, which was allotted as much as one-third of the public budget in
some countries, was to be developed and expanded, particularly the higher
levels; that is, secondary and post-secondary educational institutions.[2] This
was even done at the cost of extending basic education to the population of
primary school age. However, this model of accelerated industrialization,
which has been developed within the structural configuration of dependency
has proven to be highly limited in its dynamics of attaining high levels of
production and spreading the benefits of more human living conditions for the
mass of the population of developing countries.[3] So, in addition to the
persistence of mass poverty, malnutrition, squalid housing, disease and
illiteracy, LDCs are also facing a more acute problem of unemployment due to
the displacement of labor generated by the distorted patterns of dependent
industrialization.[4]

In this context, the problem of the educated unemployed persons with
secondary and university levels of education who are out of work has turned to
be a paradox for these persons, who are a minority of the labor force, were
seen as the strategic human resources for economic development, and now
they have the highest rates of unemployment among groups with different
levels of educational attainment.

A cursory look at the data shows that unemployment among university
graduates in Latin America is 25 to 30 per cent; in Africa it is around 12 per
cent; in the Philippines one-third of the college graduates are without jobs. In
Sri Lanka, 72 per cent of the unemployed are those with high school and

university qualifications and in India the absolute number of unemployed higher education personnel is now more than 3 million.[5]

Now, for the most part the statistics available on this matter in the different LDCs do not illustrate other social characteristics of this educated unemployed youth. But studies in India and Sri Lanka show that the major part of this group are persons under the age of 24. Older age groups with the same high levels of education tend to have lower unemployment rates. It can be generalized then that a similar pattern occurs in other LDCs, and that unemployment of the highly educated is mostly a phenomenom of unemployed youth.[6]

However, there is a structural imbalance between educational output and the capacity of absorption of the labor market that affects the duration and magnitude of the educated unemployed. Adiseshiah again points out the low proportion of the number of secondary and university graduates in relation to the number of non-manual jobs (rate of absorption of the labor market)[7]

Asia	22 per cent
India	26 per cent
Republic of Korea	27 per cent
Latin America	21 per cent
Africa	20 per cent

This gap between school leavers and graduates is reinforced by the higher rates of population growth in relation to the increase in the number of opportunities in the labor market.

In Latin America for example, it is projected that within the present economic and technological structures, employment will grow at a yearly rate of 2.2 per cent while the economically active population will grow at more than twice that rate: 5 per cent.[8] Another disturbing factor is that the patterns of population growth of LDCs (increasing survival rates of newborns, and a relatively high adult mortality rate) have the effect of concentrating population growth among the young. In general, 50 per cent of the population is below 15 years of age, 60 per cent is below 25 years.[9] In addition, this growing population is increasingly concentrated in urban centers. In Latin America, it is now 64 per cent. This change from the rural to the urban social world has a significant impact in their lifestyles and aspirations; particularly the types of jobs they want to obtain.[10] Closely tied to this change is the perception of the need to attain higher levels of education to accede to the desired jobs in the urban sector.

In fact, school enrollments in LDCs particularly those of the higher levels have been increasing rapidly for the past two decades, more so than in developed countries.

There are variations in the enrollment ratios among developing countries, but on the average, from 1960 to 1980, there has been a substantial increase in the proportion of the young enrolled in secondary and university education: 12.6 per cent to 31.8 per cent of the corresponding age group in secondary level, and from 2.1 per cent to 7.2 per cent in the university level. In Latin America, the enrollment ratio of the tertiary level is 14.9 per cent, which is nearly as high as in some developed Western European countries. Some countries in Latin America even have much higher ratios, for example,

Table 1: Enrollments in Schools, by levels. Developed and Developing Countries. Years: 1965 and 1978

Number of Pupils Enrolled in Schools (in Thousands)				
	Year	First Level	Second Level	Third Level
Developed	1965	135,325	61,880	14,937
Countries	1978	126,890	81,366	28,868
Developing	1965	164,104	36,777	4,569
Countries	1978	277,700	86,227	13,790

Source: UNESCO, STATISTICAL YEARBOOK 1981, table 2.2
The percentage increase during this period has been the following for both groups of countries.

Table 2: Percentage increase of enrollments in all levels of schools.
Developed and Developing Countries 1965–1970 and 1970–1978.

Percentage increase (+ %)				
Period	First Level	Second Level	Third Level	Total
Developed	1965–1970	0.6	2.3	7.2	1.6
Countries	1970–1978	−1.2	2.0	4.0	0.4
Developing	1965–1970	4.2	8.0	11.6	5.2
Countries	1970–1978	4.1	6.0	7.1	4.6

Source: UNESCO, STATISTICAL YEARBOOK 1981, table 2.2

Table 3 Gross Enrollment Ratios by levels.
Developed and Developing Countries. 1960–1980.

	Year	First Level	Second Level	Third Level
Developed	1960	105.8	55.1	13.1
Countries	1980	106.2	78.9	31.0
Developing	1960	60.8	12.6	2.1
Countries	1980	85.5	31.8	7.2

Source: UNESCO, STATISTICAL YEARBOOK 1981, table 2.10

Venezuela (18.96 per cent); Argentina (28 per cent) and Puerto Rico (35 per cent).[11]

Since 1970, the rate of expansion of enrollments of secondary and higher education has been three to four times higher than the rate of growth of the labor force in Latin America so the growth of population groups with higher levels of education is higher than the number of jobs in occupations whose rank is equivalent to these educational levels.

This unemployment and underutilization of educated young entails a tremendous cost for these developing societies:

- the wastage of this educated manpower;
- the loss of the financial and social resources invested in their preparation; and
- the high opportunity costs in terms of the sacrifice of other more basic human needs — which are not attended because of the diversion of public financial and social resources into the higher level educational institutions.

The problem is compounded on the other hand, by the frustrations of educated youth in not finding employment or a job whose skills, prestige and remuneration are in harmony with their expectations and deeply rooted aspirations. This generates unconformism or apathy among the young, who cannot envision what is to be their future role in economic production and in social creativity.[12]

Current and Proposed Policies to Remedy Educated Youth Unemployment

It is evident that the problem of unemployed educated youth has a structural dimension that surpasses the institutional parameters of education and of labor market policies. There are demographical, cultural and political angles to this matter, so that any single institutional approach will be of extremely limited effect.

However, the fact is that the majority of LDCs whose governments have become aware of this problem as well as those international agencies concerned with economic and social development of LDCs, have taken the approach that this is a question of 'matching job aspirations with employment opportunities.' Taking the existing structure of employment opportunities as given, the policy variables are directed to temper the heightened aspirations of the young which are seen as induced to a great extent by formal schooling. In LDCs, schools and universities are critically viewed as excessively academicist and oriented to credentialism, with general traditional humanistic curricula inherited from the colonial era, oriented to a great extent to traditional independent professions (law, medicine, architecture, etc.) and clerical type, non-technical and non-manual occupations, and patterned along the urban type of living, and work styles. Therefore, policy remedies to address these factors are, by way of a summary, the following:

- educated unemployment can be dealt with by restricting the expansion of education through the imposition of ceilings on the number of places in the three educational cycles: primary, secondary, and tertiary, or by assigning quotas within each district.
- raise the tuition fees to cover the full costs of higher education, thus reducing the private rate of return to higher education. At the same time, alter the structure of monetary incentives in the labor market, by having the state pay differentials between the more and the less educated people in the public sector.
- ruralize the curricula, emphasizing both theoretical and practical courses in farming.

- vocationalize the curricula of urban schools, providing technical and other occupational skills, and opportunities for complementary work experience.
- provide training and attitude formation for self-employment and entrepreneurship; and giving more emphasis to achievement motivation; that is, a desire to excel for its own sake.
- diversify educational offerings with the varieties of informal and recurrent education.
- incease the educational institutions' capabilities to match their output with the occupational skill requirements by selecting the correspondingly able students through aptitude tests which would replace the achievement examinations.[13]

In this chapter we shall examine in more detail the following policy proposals: limits to enrollments in higher educational levels, vocationalization of schools, the expansion of out-of-school technical training programs, and education for self-employment. These policies have been more common in LDCs, and are generally voiced by government and international agencies. To some extent these policies also include or take into account aspects of other policies.

Limit Enrollments in the Higher Levels of Educational Institutions

An obvious remedy that comes to the mind of anyone concerned with this problem, particularly if he is familiar with the selective and restrictive policies of admission to secondary and university educational institutions that are common in Europe and Japan, is to impose strict limitations to enrollments in these educational levels. Very few LDCs have been able to adopt and put into practice this rule, and also, very few have even advanced the idea. Others whose government or relevant public agencies have either brought it up for public discussion or have made attempts to implement it have encountered political obstacles, or the same rules have been circumvented by other institutional means. For example, as in the story told by Blaug, Thailand had a tightly rationed admissions policy to the university but political pressure contributed to maintain a part-time open door admissions. In India most colleges, which are administered by the local states,' ... automatically admit anyone who is a matriculate. In these circumstances it is suicidal for a political party to demand quantitative restriction of higher education ...'[14] Laska attests to the same phenomenon in secondary education. He cites from the Ministry of Education Working Group on Education which admits that it was politically impossible to halt the expansion of its enrollments, in direct contradiction to the principles and priorities set in the Draft of the Five-Year Plan for Education for the period 1961–66.[15] Another illustrative and eloquent case is Brazil, where a military governed bureaucratic authoritarian regime imposed ceilings to admissions to universities in the 1960s. This resulted in having only half of the applicants admitted to the universities. As observed by Heimer, those rejected applicants belonged to the middle-class, which was the main social base of support of the regime. The state then reversed this policy of admissions and thereafter enrollments increased by 487 per cent during the period from 1969 to 1975.[16]

Another mechanism by which demands for higher education are satisfied is the private sector of education. These have grown in the past decade to the point that they comprise at least 40 per cent of university enrollments. In the Philippines, of the 2,700 institutions of higher education, only twenty-three are state operated and 92 per cent of the funds devoted to higher education are private funds.[17] At one moment the government of South Korea decreed limits to the number of enrollments in higher education. However, college enrollments increased by 90 per cent due to the growth of the private sector, which increased its percentage of total enrollments in secondary and higher education from 26 per cent in 1953 to 55 per cent in 1970.[18]

Many students of this phenomenon attribute this excessive demand for higher education to persistent traditional preferences for non-manual, desk-type jobs of the people in LDCs, and their distaste for technical or manual type of work. However, these observers do not take into account the structural configuration of dependency of LDCs. Among other structural aspects, the distorted pattern of development of these countries has brought on the premature concentration of employment in the services (tertiary) sector of the economy, where the public bureaucracy accounts for a large share of the best type of jobs. The fact is that manufacturing or agricultural technical type of jobs are very few. Now, to gain access to these jobs in the services sector, one needs credentials of higher level educational institutions. For example in 1961 71 per cent of all matriculates and 82.8 per cent of all graduates in India, were employed in trade, commerce, transportation and communication, and services (including government) sectors, though these sectors only accounted for 52 per cent of non-agricultural employment.[19] The competition for these relatively few, and most desired jobs is channelled through the acquisition of higher levels of educational credentials. The consequent devaluation of credentials only reinforces the pursuit of even higher level credentials. In the context of scarcity of good jobs, the attainment of higher levels of education becomes not only a mechanism for upward social and occupational mobility, but a matter of survival and preservation of the present social status. Hence, the political pressures and social demands for expanding the higher tiers of educational institutions.

Vocationalization of School Curricula

One of the more commonly advocated policies to remedy the unemployment and underutilization of educated youth is to emphasize vocational technical and terminal programs in secondary schools and to orient university curricula to professional technical careers. As mentioned before, secondary education in LDCs is viewed as being oriented for the most part to prepare students for higher education studies, or for bureaucratic and clerical type of jobs. As attested by the World Bank, '... high percentages of the graduates were in low priority fields from a developmental point of view and had no readily employable skills. Thus, in countries in which the bank has supported

Rafael L. Irizarry

education projects, the median percentage of students in vocational education has been only around 10 per cent compared with close to 30 per cent in the most developed countries.'[20]

But efforts taken in this direction by LDCs have been rather ineffective. Formal technical vocational programs are costly and LDC educational systems do not have the resources or the expertise to develop a diversified program of courses that will correspond to some degree to the diversity and levels of complexity of the occupational skills in the economy. It is often the case that the perceptions of the demand for technical skills are ill-founded or exaggerated and many graduates of these programs do not find jobs in which they can employ their learned skills. Philip Foster's classic work about the case of Ghana's agricultural vocational programs is an eloquent testimony of this phenomenon. Paradoxically, graduates of this program did not find appropriate jobs, and they ended up as clerical or administrative employees of the civil service. Foster underscored the point that the humanistic type of educational programs are in fact vocational in as far as they provided the type of skills that corresponded to a higher degree to the employment opportunities in the economy.[21]

The available reports on vocational technical programs in different LDCs present a similar picture of obsolete facilities and curricula which result in poor preparation for the occupational tasks in the modern firms. Employers all over coincide in asserting the poor performance of the graduates of these courses.[22]

India's repeated plans to increase the number of vocational programs in the formal educational system have fallen short of the goals that have been set. In 1966 the Education Commission set the target of increasing the enrollments in these programs to 20 per cent in the lower secondary level, and to 50 per cent in the upper secondary level. By 1975 only 6.4 per cent of total secondary enrollments corresponded to vocational programs[23] (Ghandi 1977).

Out of School Technical Training Programs

In view of these handicaps of the educational institutions to develop an array of adequate vocational technical programs to provide employable occupational skills, many LDCs have developed these training programs outside of the formal educational system. In Latin America, there is an entrenched tradition of out of school (or non-formal) training programs which were developed mostly by the private industrial and commerce business sector. This initiative of the private sector did not arise by a concern for unemployment, but as a mechanism to provide the manpower training needs. But in time these out-of-school training programs were seen by government and international agencies as a means to attain a better match between the output of educational and training programs with the occupational skill requirements of the existing jobs, which would help to ameliorate youth unemployment.

This program was initiated in Brazil in 1942 under the name of National Apprenticeship Service of Industrial Training (SENAI). It was organized by industrial employers in response to the budgetary restraints for the expansion of the educational system in Brazil. It is supported by a payroll tax on industrial forms. It is designed to assist industry in training new skilled workers and master craftsmen, for on-the-job training of skilled and semi-skilled workers and for training supervisors and technicians. In the past two decades it has been adopted in other countries in the region: Colombia (SENA), Venezuela (INCE), Chile (SCT), Peru (SENATI), Argentina (CONET), and Ecuador (SECAP).

In general, training programs are organized in coordination with industrial, commercial and agricultural firms and public corporations which have specific occupational training needs, for either entry-level personnel or for advancing employees to higher positions. Usually, SENAI training programs are set up in response to requests by enterprises and government agencies. But it also develops training programs in accordance with regional manpower surveys.

SENA programs offer the advantage that it will design courses that will provide the specific training needs of an industry which otherwise will have difficulty in finding persons with the required skills. Trainees are usually employees of the firms who are recruited as apprentices, and will combine job experience and on-the-job training in the firms, and formal classroom classes in SENA facilities. Classes will include also general education subjects. This arrangement offers the clear advantage that the trainee is already incorporated into the job for which he is being prepared to undertake, and theoretical and practical training are designed to correspond to the skills required to perform that job. This way, education and work are closely linked and fitted with each other.

The program is clearly oriented to the already employed and as initially organized, its programs were not designed for the unemployed, or even for those seeking employment for the first time. So in Colombia SENA has been pressed to institute programs for out of work youth in both rural and urban areas. The experience in reducing youth unemployment is still to be seen.[24]

From the side of the firms, these SENA type of programs have been successful. It has proven to be an effective way to assure the training needs of all types and levels of occupational skills; skilled workers, specialized technicians, supervisory personnel, and managers. It has been able to provide the array of programs that will supply the skill diversity and level of complexity of the occupational structure of the firms. In this sense it has proven to be a more adequate model for LDCs than vocational education in the formal school system.

However, these programs contribute to solve the educated youth unemployment problem in as much as it fills the employment slots in the economy and matches the qualifications of the aspiring candidates to those positions. But according to some critics it is vitiated with the same defects of formal schooling systems in that they are oriented to the modern sector and arouses in its graduates aspirations for higher position jobs, including managerial, non-manual, and non-technical type of jobs. In fact there is evidence that in Colombia, a large percentage of SENA trainees uses its training courses as a leverage to move out of the blue collar world. They use it as an instrument to finance additional academic education and ultimately reach the coveted status of high school graduate.[25]

Another factor that moves SENA trainees to pursue formal schooling,

Rafael L. Irizarry

which is mostly academic or general education curriculum is the pervasion of 'credentialism' among employers. Survey studies of employers show that they give more value to pre-employment formal schooling diplomas to grant the higher position and better paid jobs which have more opportunity for upward mobility.[26]

The substitution of pre-employment out-of-school educational experiences will not assure the better entry positions nor will they count for promotion in the future. 'It is then unrealistic to encourage individuals to pursue out-of-school education with the goals of reaching the same level of income parity with those who have attended formal schools. In sum, out-of-school education may do little to foster greater access to economic resources.'[27] These companies will value out-of-school education experiences that are acquired after the individual is with the company, and are sponsored by the employer.[28]

Education for Self Employment and the New Vocationalization

In terms of their role as a policy to reduce youth unemployment, particularly of those with high level education, the technical training courses offered by schools and SENA type of programs are of limited consequence. According to the current assessments of international agencies their major handicap resides in the fact that like academic education they are oriented to jobs, values and lifestyles of the modern and urban sector. They are indeed inserted in the institutional and cultural context of the modern sector, and their goals, curricula and orientations are shaped by them.

The fact is that the process of expansion of the modern sector of the economy in LDCs has lost its dynamism in terms of absorbing the growing numbers of the economically active sectors of the population. Even though it is still expanding in some countries in terms of the volume of capital investment and output, this is being attained with modern, capital intensive and labor saving technology designed and manufactured in developed countries. Given the structural relation of economic and technological dependency of LDCs on developed countries, they adopt these technological devices in an indiscriminate way. In countries where their human resources are abundant and idle, they adopt technological forms of production that make little use of them. In addition, the problem is compounded when technologically intensive firms, many of them subsidiaries of transnational corporations, displace small and medium size local firms which use labor intensive forms of production. So, some countries that are in intermediate stages of industrialization register a shrinkage in the relative (and sometimes absolute) numbers of employed in the industrial productive sectors. Worse still, this same process is now taking place at an accelerated pace in the agricultural sector with the adoption of green revolution techniques of cultivation, and technological forms of recollection and processing. It is now also common to see the invasion of agri-business firms in Latin America, which do have significant impact in increasing output, but with relatively small numbers of laborers.[29]

214

So in view of the relative stagnation in the creation of employment opportunities in the modern sectors international agencies of development recognize the futility of the present educational and training programs — both in schools and out of schools; academic or technical, because these are oriented to place graduates in jobs in the modern sector. But given the situation that such opportunities are diminishing in relation to the growing working force, they are now looking for other alternatives.

The new trend to counteract the growing numbers of unemployed youth is to re-direct their sights to the traditional (or informal) sectors of the economy. For the past decade students of the process of development in LDCs are increasingly taking note of the fact that the traditional (or informal) sector of the economy accounts for a significant number of jobs in these economies; in many cases, up to 75 per cent, and in all developing countries, the employment opportunities continue to grow at a faster pace than the number of jobs in the modern sector.[30] This sector comprises all of those economic activities — production, trade and services that are either realized by one person on his own, or by a small unit which employs very few individuals who are often related by family ties to the owner of the enterprise. They use primitive or low productivity forms of organization, production techniques or delivery of services, and usually operate at the margin of all regulations and laws that govern economic activity in a country. It includes the peasant that cultivates his small plot of land with his relatives; the cottage or household industry, small shopkeepers, brick carriers, vendors, street peddlers and providers of personal and household services. There is variation in the earnings of individuals of this sector which, ranges from bare subsistence levels to ones that correspond to those levels of income of skilled workers of the modern sector. Usually those with the highest earnings are small entrepreneurs who run shops or small-scale manufacturing enterprises.

In Africa and Asia, estimates on employment show that as many as 30 to 40 per cent of the working population are on their own (or self-employed) in a small farm or a small shop in the unorganized part of the urban economy.[31] In Latin America, 40 to 60 per cent of the economically active population of the urban centers were in the informal sector, though they accounted for only 20 per cent of added value of production and services activities.[32] From 1950 to 1970 self-employed and non-salary family related workers increased their proportion of the work force at a rate of 9.6 to 11.7 per cent.[33]

This growth of the traditional sector runs counter to what accelerated industrialization and social modernization theories and policies of economic development had precognized; that in time the modern sector of the economy would absorb the majority of all the labor force.[34] But as these strategies were implemented within the structural context of dependency, this has restrained the diversification, expansion and spreading out of modern forms of activity to the whole economic and social sphere of LDCs.

This failure has led to a new paradigm of development on the part of international agencies. Its different versions can be conceptualized as 'development for basic needs,' 'redistribution with growth,' and 'equitable modernization.'[35] Its basic premise is that development policies must focus on this poverty ridden backward sector of the population and its economic activities. More resources should be diverted to uplift its living conditions and to improve its technical capability of production, and thereby increase its earnings and its share in the economic wealth of the country.

In harmony with this approach to the economy, educational strategies have shifted attention from the formal educational institutions, and their specialization and high level professional programs to nonformal (out-of-school) programs which cater to the specific needs of poorer population groups. These strategies attempt to increase access to educational opportunities through a variety of flexible, specific purpose and short duration courses directed to the different population groups; children, youth, women, men, etc. They are guided more by performance criteria than credentials as those of schools. They comprise a variety of courses that include literacy programs, health information, attitudinal change and skill formation.[36]

The present policies to reduce educated youth unemployment arise from the recognition of these processes in the economic and educational spheres: on the one hand, the availability of a greater number of jobs in the traditional than in the modern sector; and on the other hand, the dampening effects that informal education can have on the inflated aspirations of educated youth, and its effectiveness in providing the specific skills required for jobs in the traditional sector.

For the international agencies (more so than national governments) the crux of the matter of education in LDCs is, in the words of King, '. . . how to lower the aspirations of pupils and make them accord better with the work possibilities of the rural (and urban) areas,' and how to switch the attention of pupils away from paid jobs altogether.[37] Specifically, the idea is to instill in the pupils the attitude and orientations and provide them with the relevant skills to undertake entrepreneurship (or self-employment) and by so doing create jobs and employ others.[38]

This policy implies a radical change in the organization and orientation of the school systems. Educational formal institutions and their curricula in LDCs are founded on the theoretical premises of modernization strategies, which prescribed a subservient role of preparing qualified manpower for the modern sector. Also, as will be discussed later on, the expectations and motives of the young (and of their supporting parents) are that schooling constitutes the passage way out of the traditional sector into a job in the modern sector. Now the proposed policies are directed to alter this state of things altogether. They propose that schools prepare pupils to become self-employed, and that they do so in the traditional sector because this is not viable in the modern sector which is increasingly monopolized by large-scale modern corporations. They also envision orienting pupils to be willing and qualified to take on any sort of employment in the traditional sector.

For the schools, this entails establishing close links with work in the unorganized sector, and assimilating the culture, values, and lifestyles of the population of this sector. This means they have to redirect the curriculum to rural, village and urban slum life, its drabness and the peculiar forms of work; thrift and ingenuity for day to day survival. Schools have to be impregnated with the orientations and methodologies of non-formal education programs which have been developed to attend to the social needs and skill requirements of this population group.

Some Examples

National Youth Services

The National Youth Services type of project was a precursor to the present efforts to develop educational programs to attain the objectives of channeling school leavers and graduates towards the traditional sector. This project was carried out in some African and English-speaking Caribbean countries during the 1960s as part of government reconstruction and development efforts after attaining political independence.

They were intended for the growing number of primary school leavers, which was higher than the absorptive capacity of secondary schools and labor markets. According to Paulston, this is one of the few non-formal educational programs that was more or less planned and coordinated at a national level to attract school leavers who were unemployed and provide them with effective vocational training programs, as well as to ensure political socialization.[39]

Many of these programs offered full-time residential training, which was camp style of residence. At the same time that they received training they were given politically oriented courses so as to identify with the goals of national unity and development. Also they engaged in development-oriented work such as road building, erosion control, new agricultural settlements. They were given training in discipline, physical fitness and instilled willingness to do hard work.[40] Academic content of courses was minimized so as not to arouse aspirations for secondary schooling, and practical training was emphasized. In some countries, training was concentrated in agricultural techniques and former trainees were supported in the development of new agricultural areas when they finished their training.[41]

Most of the ex-trainees did not find employment, and the costs were as high or higher than secondary schools.[42] In addition in some cases these programs only recruited about 10 per cent of its potential clientele . Furthermore, young people had unattractive images of this program. King cites youth comparing this experience to life in German prisoner-of-war camps, that it is like jail, and that you have to prove that you can dig well.[43] Paulston points out that African Youth Services are small and becoming smaller, because of their high costs, and to the greater importance and resources assigned by governments to upper levels of formal education.[44]

The New Vocationalization

As pointed out before, vocational technical programs of both schools and of out-of-school programs were directed to provide skills for jobs in modern firms, but the job opportunities in this sector have been dwindling in relation to the growing work force. In the case of Africa, the problem is compounded by the fact that the student body was a highly selected elite, including that of the vocational programs.

Their career aims and probable employment were in the civil service or large companies; and very few went on to be employed in one of the trades they acquired in school.[45]

According to King, the 'new' orientations of vocational education are directed to link the school courses and training at all levels of education with the local community and the production activities of the traditional sector. In the primary level they are practicalizing the curriculum with manual arts and home economics. In Sri Lanka, they have added more than eighty courses of pre-vocational studies that are related to the cottage industries of that country. Ethiopia is developing community-skill training centers. In Kenya, they are planning a nine-year basic school with the best two years offering skills for self employment.

Instead of studying and practicing with the technology of the modern sector, they are dealing more with the 'native' or village technology (which is the typical and generalized form of organization of economic activities in the traditional sector). This is done by incorporating work into schools, and using this village technology. It constitutes an attempt to replicate that world of work of the traditional sector in the school — something that has proven difficult to do according to the experience of Tanzania.[46]

All of these reforms in the primary level are seen by King as corresponding to 'subsistence type of self employment'. He asserts that these programs stress the reintegration of the primary school youth into ordinary village life; they adapt his skills to village needs, and prepare them to work alongside people in the village. They emphasize correct attitudes, hard work and reconciliation with village mores.[47]

As to secondary level education, the trend in some countries like India is to diversify the offerings so as to increase the proportion of terminal vocational streams, but with the difference from past policies of orienting these offerings to occupational courses that correspond to the opportunities for self-employment.[48]

But according to King the major thrust of present policies is to develop out-of-school programs concentrating in higher level skill formation that will enable trainees to go into self-employment. Instead of being oriented to modern sector firms like the Latin American SENA type of model or the British model of the Industrial Training Act, these new models are linked to the community and the economic activities of the informal sector. Some of the projects which are being supported by the World Bank are: Village Polytechnics in Kenya, Integrated Rural Education Centers in Sudan and Malawi, Community Skill Training Centers in Sierra Leone and Tanzania. In Lesotho the Community Skill Centers are being developed in association with rural high schools.[49] These projects give more emphasis in village and peasant economy skills. Such skills are different to the typical ones provided by trade training which are specialized, and require modern type of tools and workshops. In contrast the skills required for the peasant economy are more broad and diversified — a kind of jack-of-all-trades.[50] A peasant requires to know about agriculture, repair of tools and simple machinery, carpentry, and so on.

As to the young in the urban sector, there is a variety of jobs with a wide range of skills whose level of complexity and training requirements range from those that do not require any specific trained skills like vendors to others that are complex and high level technical ones such as artisans, automobile mechanics and small industrial machinery operation and maintenance. Some are in fact acquired in formal vocational training; others through formal arrangements of apprenticeship, and others through on the job, casual or informal means; but the majority acquire their skills through apprenticeship, including the entrepreneurs of petty production firms[51].

Given this myriad of skills and varying levels of complexity, it is difficult to develop a coherent and comprehensive program of training for the traditional sector. On the other hand, the main form of skills acquisition, apprenticeship, is impossible to monitor. Apprenticeship in the traditional sector takes different forms and fulfills different ends. Many artisans or shop owners take on apprentices as cheap and disposable labor and encase them in a very specific task, which does not allow for the craftman's skill acquisition on the part of the apprentice.

Studies made of the relation between different forms of training, including formal education, present conflicting versions of the nature of the relation between education, training and employment and occupational mobility in the traditional sector. In view of this complex reality, national governments and international agencies have been more cautious in promoting specific training programs. Policy recommendations for training youth in the urban area are therefore more general and propose the following lines of action:

— adult literacy programs;
— radio or newspaper information compaigns on existing legislation, methods of organizing cooperatives, possibilities of obtaining technical assistance or credits, and training streams available;
— vocational-training centers with a flexible structure offering part-time education or evening classes to apprentices to supplement their general, theoretical and technical training, or to entrepreneurs who wish to improve their knowledge in specific fields.[52]

Finally to assure a successful entry into entrepreneural activity, mastery of productive skills are not enough. They also require a minimum of capital to start off an enterprise in either the rural or urban unorganized sector of the economy.

Thus, for example in India, the banking system is providing loans to small business and entrepreneurs of the unorganized sector of the economy to acquire the machinery and tools for their enterprise. So educational agencies are advocating use of this policy of the banking sector to provide the initial support for self-employment of graduates of training programs.[53]

In relation to the university level, the same theme of linking education, work and the community is repeated. This linkage has a two-fold purpose. On the one hand, its advocates see this integration of university students into work in the community as a means of learning about the reality of this social, economic and cultural world of the traditional sector, which comprises the major part of the population of LDCs. Work experience of students in the community is increasingly validated as a substantial component of the curriculum. On the other hand, students' involvement in the community is geared towards making a contribution to satisfy specific needs of a technical nature in the community. The student then is able to apply theory learned in the university to problems in villages or urban slums. So, for example, students of the different scientific and technical areas help with the repair of farm implements, deal with the problems of paper pulp, textile yarns, or compost pits, or with the questions of agriculture or animal raising and husbandry. Students of commerce help with the accounting procedures in village co-operatives, medical students work with the health needs of the population; and so on. 'This leads to continuous revision of the curricula to fit in with the data and analysis resulting from these exercises. Higher education gains as much as the local community in this two-way relationship.'[54]

The author cited, who introduced these reforms in the University of Madras, considers that this curricular program of linking education, work and community will contribute to ameliorate the problem of unemployment of university graduates. This curricular orientation to the community should weaken the link between completion of higher education and job entry into the modern sector. In addition, given the reduction of employment opportunities in this sector, students there will search for other alternatives such as self employment enterprises — 'on farms and in animal husbandry areas, as technicians and entrepreneurs of small self-managed industries, in opening new avenues in the repair and maintenance of machines and implements, in the processing, finishing and distributive trades, etc.'[55]

This work-in-the-community based education will also help to ameliorate educated youth unemployment by providing the appropriate skills for the technical needs of the traditional sector's most important economic activities. For example, Adiseshiah argues that there are unmet demands in the area of fluctuating and low productivity primary agricultural industry; the nutrition and health care needs of the mass of the people for which university graduates should be trained.[56]

Finally, other complementary reforms required to contain the spiralling demand for higher education are to change the examination system, and to substitute the sequence of the three levels of the educational system where each of the lower levels is structured in such a way that it is conducive to the subsequent upper level. The main issue at hand is to break the connection between educational credentials of the formal school system and employment. The recruitment for employment should be based on performance criteria rather than educational credentials. Also, everyone should be provided basic education, and thereafter there should be opportunities for everyone to enter into the subsequent educational levels at any time in a person's life. The access to higher levels of education should not be mainly dependent on a person's educational credentials, money or social status, but on a person's work experience, and knowledge and competency acquired through other means such as work and non-formal education. Thereby higher education will be provided according to recognized social needs of higher level expertise and specialization.[57]

The Structural Obstacles to Educational Policies for Employment in the Traditional Sector

For reasons of space we shall only outline what are the main difficulties for the successful implementation of policies that attempt to link education and employment in the traditional sector. Many of the social forces prevailing in neutralizing the other policies discussed before: limitation of enrollments in the higher educational levels and channelling students into technical type of courses are also set into motion to impede their implementation.

In the first place, all social groups in LDCs including the lower income masses of the traditional and marginalized sectors look upon acceding to employment in the modern sector as the only means to attain an adequate standard of living. For them, this constitutes the means to escape from poverty and the inanity and often the misery of slum or rural village life. In general, the earnings of the different occupational groups in the modern sector are two to three times higher than that of their occupational counter-parts in the traditional sector.[58] The passageway from the traditional to the modern sector is through the process of formal education and the attainment of credentials: the higher the levels of schooling attained, the probabilities of entering or securing a position in the modern sector increase correspondingly. A study of PREALC of San Salvador shows that as the number of years of schooling rises in the labor force, the proportion employed in the modern sector increases. While in the group with 0–3 years of schooling, 27 per cent are employed in the modern sector, in the group with 13 years or more 91 per cent is employed in a modern sector job.[59] In addition the income levels of groups according to levels of schooling employed in the modern sector are two to three times that of their counterparts in the traditional sector.[60]

The population groups of the traditional sector are clearly aware of this structure of employment opportunities and their corresponding economic and social rewards. Therefore they aspire for their children the best of formal educational opportunities. This is poignantly illustrated by a survey made by Ewert among a group of rural residents in Zaire. The adults expressed that they prefer that the government channel those resources invested in non-formal education to use them to build schools for the young.[61]

The success of the efforts of inducing the young to take employment in the traditional sector will depend to a great extent on the improvement of the standards of living and of the quality of social welfare services of this sector, and to an increase in its share of national wealth. But the fact is that though the traditional sector increasingly accounts for the number of employment opportunities its share of national income has been decreasing. Given its low productivity its share of total value of output in the urban sector in Latin America is about 20 per cent, when the proportion of employment is 40 to 60 per cent. In Colombia it is reported that the proportion of total added value that corresponds to the traditional sector has gone down from 45 to 34 per cent during the period 1951–1964. From 1950 to 1960, the income of self-employed, wage earners and domestic employees of the traditional sector in Perú went down by 1.9 per cent, in contrast to the 4.9 per cent rate of increase of the income of public employees, office workers and laborers in modern industry[63]. It is then evident that the gap in income and standards of living of the work force of each of these two sectors has been widening, making more unattractive the idea of training for employment in the urban traditional sector.

A similar process of polarization is taking place in the rural traditional sector. The recent entry of agri-business type of production in the rural areas of Latin America is creating a modern sector of agricultural production whose expansion is being carried out at the social cost of the mass of the rural population. This modernization of agriculture is characterized by large accumulation of capital, technological complexity, and large extensions of land of high yield. These business firms employ a small number of professionals and technicians, and semi-skilled permanent laborers, and a relatively larger number of unskilled workers on a temporary basis. These firms are supported by the state with grants of public land, subsidies, easy credit terms and technical assistance. On the other hand small and intermediate farmers are suffering stagnation because they lack support and means to adopt modern techniques of production, as well as the methods for efficient administration, financing and marketing. The present 'styles of development' based on highly technified large scale corporations have resulted in the maintenance of two-thirds of rural households below the poverty levels.[64] Furthermore, in a context where there are very high demographic pressures over land, the opportunities for self employment are certainly very dim.

A final observation is that the proposals for schools or out-of-school programs to provide training in the skills employed in the economic activities of the traditional sector may well turn out to be redundant. For the fact is that the skills required in this sector are ordinarily acquired through work in these activities through apprenticeship, or informal or casual on-the-job learning. This occurs in urban petty production as well as in the peasant economy. A child's socialization in this social world comprises from his early stages the acquisition of the skills needed to work in the urban or rural unorganized economy. It may well occur that schools or other out-of-school programs may pretend to serve as a substitute, for a process that takes place day to day in the lives of the laboring groups of this sector. These are the hypotheses to be tested in relation to this new approach to educational development in the Third World.

In concluding, we would argue the point that educated youth unemployment is a generalized phenomenon in LDCs, and that as these countries' economies become more industrialized and modern, the magnitude of this phenomenon increases. The policies proposed to deal with this problem do not take into account the fact that this phenomenon is rooted in the structural configuration of dependency. By this we refer to a pattern of economic development that is highly dependent on developed countries' financial capital, technology, machinery, equipment and its corresponding parts, industrial processing inputs, and technological know-how. This pattern of dependent industrialization tends to be technological intensive, fragmented, and concentrated. It does not spread out or expand so it does not incorporate labor in a proportionate degree to its capital and volume of output. This process is now also taking place in agriculture with agri-business type of organization and production. This pattern only reinforces the minuscule modern sector where the benefits of development are increasingly concentrated for a minority of the population. This pattern of industrialization and agricultural modernization runs totally counter to the present proposals of improving the productive capacity of the traditional sector where the majority of the population is located. So an educational strategy that depends on the increase and improvement of employment opportunities and their economic rewards in the traditional sector will have a very limited impact in reducing youth unemployment.

This problem must be seen in the context of a comprehensive development strategy. It must alter the present structures of dependency, and pursue a policy of self-reliance, direct efforts to phase out altogether the division of society in two economic, social and cultural spheres: one modern with levels and styles of living that are similar to those of Western developed countries, and the other traditional, backward and poverty ridden; and redistribute the highly skewed distribution of income and assets. Any strategy for development and single-focus policies to solve specific problems in LDCs are destined to fail if they do not tackle these three dimensions of the underdevelopment and dependency syndrome of the Third World.

Notes

1 HARBISON, F. and MYERS, C.A. (1964) *Education, Manpower and Economic Growth: Strategies of Human Resource Development*, New York, McGraw Hill.
2 MEIER, G.M. (1964) *Leading Issues in Development Economics*, New York, Oxford University Press, p. 266.
3 CHENERY, H. et al. (1974) *Redistribution with Growth*, Oxford, Oxford University Press.
4 For a more detailed exploration of this process of dependent industrialization and its sequel of higher rates of unemployment see IRIZARRY, R.L. (1980) 'Overeducation and unemployment in the third world: the paradoxes of dependent industrialization', *Comparative Education Review*, 24 (3), October, pp. 338–52.
5 ADISESHIAH, M. (1982) 'Access, relevance and employment relation and higher education dimensions of the new international order' in BIKAS, C.S. (Ed) *Higher Education and the New International Order*, Paris, UNESCO.
6 BLAUG, M. (1973) *Education and the Employment Problems in Developing Countries*, Geneva, International Labour Office.
7 ADISESHIAH, M. (1982) *op cit.*, p. 32.
8 United Nations, Economic Commission for Latin America (CEPAL) (1982) *El desarrollo de América Latina y sus repercusiones en la educación, alfabetismo y escolaridad basica* (Cuadernos de la CEPAL), Santiago, Chile, United Nations, p. 25.
9 BLAUG, M. (1973) *op cit.*, p. 10
10 United Nations, Economic Commission for Latin America (CEPAL) (1982), *op cit.*, p. 9.
11 UNESCO (1975) *Statistical Yearbook 1975*, table 3.2.
12 United Nations, Economic Commission for Latin America (CEPAL) (1982), *op cit.*, p. 20.
13 BLAUG, M. (1973) *op cit.*, pp. 44–84.
14 *Ibid*, pp. 42–3.
15 LASKA, J.A. (1968) *Planning and Educational Development in India*, New York, Teachers College Press, p. 77.
16 HEIMER, F.-W. (1975) 'Education and politics in Brazil', *Comparative Education Review*, 19 (1), February, pp. 51–67.
17 BLAUG, M. (1973) *op cit.*, p. 43.
18 McGINN, N.F. et al. (1980) *Education and the Modernization of the Republic of Korea (1945–1975)*, Cambridge, Mass, Harvard University Press.
19 BLAUG, M., LAYARD, R. and WOODHALL, M. (1969) *The Causes of Graduate Unemployment in India*, London, Allen Lane, the Penguin Press, p. 100.
20 WORLD BANK, (1974) *Education Sector Working Paper*, Washington, D.C., p. 13.
21 FOSTER, P. (1965) 'The vocational school fallacy in development planning' in

Rafael L. Irizarry

ANDERSON, C.A. and BOWMAN, M.J. (Eds) *Education and Economic Development*, Chicago, Aldine Publishing Co; also KING, K. (1980) 'Education and self-employment' in International Institute for Educational Planning, *Education, Work and Employment*, Volume II, Paris, p. 243.

22 ESTAFEN, B.D. (1970) *The Comparative Management of Firms in Chile*, International Business Research Series, No. 4, Bloomington, Graduate School of Business Division of Research, University of Indiana, p. 6a; University of Puerto Rico, Center for Social Research (1972) *Puerto Rico's Present and Prospective Technical, Skilled and Clerical Manpower and Training Needs*, 1968–1975, Rio Piedras, Puerto Rico, p. 236; and FULLER, W.P. (1976) 'More evidence supporting the demise of pre-employment vocational trade training: a case study of a factory in India', *Comparative Education Review*, 20 (1), February, pp. 30–41.

23 GHANDI, K. (1977) *Issues and Choices in Higher Education, A Sociological Analysis*, New Delhi, BR Publishing Corporation.

24 PAULSTON, R.G. (1973) 'Non-formal educational alternatives' in COLE, S.B. and THOMPSON, T.J., *New Strategies for Educational Development: The Cross-cultural Search for Non-formal Alternatives*, Lexington, Lexington Books; HARBISON, F. and SELTZER, G. (1973) National training schemes' in COLE S.B. and THOMPSON, T.J. (Eds) *op cit.*; EDFELT, R. (1975) 'Occupational education and training: the role of large private industry in Brazil' in LA BELLE, T.J. (Ed) *Educational Alternatives in Latin America*, Los Angeles, University of California, Latin American Center Publications; and LA BELLE, T.J. (1975) 'The impact of non'formal education on income in industry: Ciuda Guyana, Venezuela' in LA BELLE, T.J. (Ed) *op cit.*.

25 PURYEAR, J.M. (1975) 'Recruitment to industrial apprenticeship programs in Colombia: the case of SENA' in LA BELLE, T.J. (Ed) *op cit.*, pp. 431–2; and PAULSTON, R.G. (1973) *op cit.*, p. 188.

26 LA BELLE, T.J. (Ed) (1975) *op cit.*, p. 288; BRUNO, J.E. and VAN ZEYL, C. (1975) 'Educational ideology in Venezuela: a counterforce to innovation' in LA BELLE, T.J. (Ed) *op cit.*, p. 466; and SANYAL, B.C. and YACOUB, EL SAMMANI A. (1975) *Higher Education and Employment in the Sudan*, Paris, UNESCO, International Institute for Educational Planning, p. 170.

27 LA BELLE, T.J. (Ed) (1975) *op cit.*, p. 288.

28 *Ibid.*

29 United Nations, Economic Commission for Latin America (CEPAL) (1982), *op cit.*, p. 41.

30 HALLAK, J. and CAILLODS, F. (1981) *Education, Training and the Traditional Sector* (Fundamentals of Educational Planning Series: 31), Paris, UNESCO, International Institute for Educational Planning.

31 BLAUG, M. (1973) *op cit.*, p. 54.

32 TOKMAN, V.E. (1981) 'Influencia del sector informal urbano sobre la desigualdad económica', *El Trimestre Económico*, Vol. 48, no. 4, October–December, Mexico, pp. 931–64.

33 *Ibid*, p. 956.

34 LEWIS, W.A. (1977) 'Economic development with unlimited supplies of labor' in ARGAWALA, A.N. and SINGH, S.P. (Eds) *The Economics of Underdevelopment*, New Delhi, Oxford University Press.

35 CHENERY, H. (1974) op cit.; and MELLOR, J.W. (1976) *The New Economics of Growth: A Strategy for India and the Developing World*, Ithaca, New York, Cornell University Press.

36 COOMBS, P. and AHMED, M. (1974) *Attacking Rural Poverty: How Non-formal Education Can Help*, Baltimore, Johns Hopkins University Press; LA BELLE, T.J. and VERHINE, R.E. (1975) 'Education, social change and social stratification' in LA BELLE, T.J. (Ed) *op cit.*; and KING, K. (1980) *op cit.*

37 KING, K. (1980) *op cit.*, p. 23.
38 BLAUG, M. (1973) *op cit.*, p. 54.
39 PAULSTON, R.G. (1973) *op cit.*, p. 70
40 *Ibid*, p. 72.
41 *Ibid*, p. 73.
42 *Ibid*, p. 74.
43 KING, K. (1980) *op cit.*, p. 253.
44 PAULSTON, R.G. (1973) *op cit.*, pp. 73–4.
45 KING, K. (1980) *op cit.*, p. 234.
46 *Ibid*, pp. 231–3.
47 *Ibid*, p. 227.
48 National Council of Educational Research and Training (1976) 'Higher secondary education and its vocationalization' New Delhi, p. 1, cited by KING, K. (1980) *op cit.*, p. 235.
49 KING, K. (1980) *op cit.*, p. 236.
50 *Ibid*, p. 238.
51 HALLAK, J. and CAILLODS, F. (1981) *op cit.*, p. 121.
52 *Ibid*, p. 122.
53 *Ibid*, p. 239.
54 ADISESHIAH, M. (1982) *op cit.*, pp. 31–2.
55 *Ibid*, p. 33.
56 *Ibid*, p. 234.
57 *Ibid*, pp. 34–5; BLAUG, M. (1973) *op cit.*, pp. 66–7; and GOMEZ, V.M. (1981) 'Expansion, crisis y prospectiva de la educación en la America Latina', *El Trimestre Económico*, Vol. 48, No. 1, January–March, pp. 121–55.
58 BRODERSOHN, V. (1982) 'La prolematica del empleo en Centroamerica' *El Trimestre Económico*, Vol. 49, No. 2, April–June, pp. 387–421.
59 Cited by BRODERSOHN, V. (1982) *op cit.*, p. 411.
60 SCHIEFELBEIN, E. (1977) 'Relaciones entre educación y empleo en el Paraguay', *Revista paraguaya de sociolgía*, Year 14, No. 39/40, May, pp. 7–30.
61 EWERT, D.M. (1980) 'Formal vs non-formal education: the African experience' paper presented at the National Adult Education Conference, St Louis, Missouri, November, ERIC-ED 197–065.
62 TOKMAN, V.E. (1981) *op cit.*, p. 936.
63 *Ibid*, p. 957
63 United Nations, Economic Commission for Latin America (CEPAL) (1982), *op cit.*, pp. 41–3.

References

DAS, A.K. (1981) 'Unemployment of educated youth in Asia: a comparative analysis of the situation in India, Bangladesh and the Philippines' UNESCO, International Institute of Educational Planning, Occasion Paper — No. 60, mimeographed.

RAMA, G.W. (1979) *Educación, imágenes y estilos de desarrollo*, Cuadernos de la CEPAL, Santiago, Chile, CEPAL/ILPES.

SANYAL, B.C. (1982) 'Alternative structures of higher education', *International Review of Education*, Vol 28, No. 2, pp. 239–57 .

SANYAL, B.C. and KINUNDA, M.J. (1977) Higher Education for Self-Reliance: The Tanzanian Experience, Paris, International Institute for Educational Planning.

SOBEL, I. (1978) 'The human capital revolution in economic development: its current history and status', *Comparative Education Review*, Vol. 22, No. 2, June, pp. 278–308.

Rafael L. Irizarry

Szyliowicz, J. (1973) *Education and Modernization in the Middle East*, Ithaca, Cornell University Press.
Tedesco, J.C. (1977) 'Educación e industrialización en la Argentina', *Revista paraguaya de sociología*, Year 14, No. 39/40, May–December, pp. 125–94.

Contributors

Frank Bacon was President of the Association of Teachers in Technical Institutions, now the National Association of Teachers in Further and Higher Education (NATFHE) in 1965–66, and founding father and Organizing Secretary of the National Association of Staff Development. In October 1983 the *NATFHE Journal* remembered him 'for his dedication and good humour and for being something of an original. Unique for being the only Doctor of Divinity to be President of the Union'.

John Cameron has been a member of faculty in the School of Development Studies at the University of East Anglia, Norwich, since its inception in 1973. He went to the University after studying economics at the University of Essex where he acquired a basic understanding of politics, sociology and Marxism. He has spent eighteen months in Nepal resulting in three major publications (published by the Oxford University Press, Aris and Phillips and the OECD) on Nepal's political economy — particularly the conditions faced by the landless. From 1977–81 he was engaged in researching and writing a book on the basic principles of economics in a comparative, politically-aware framework. This book was published in 1983 by Longman.

Ian Charles is a Lecturer in Communications at Paddington College, London. His interest in Norway dates back to 1968, when he read for an Honours degree in European/Scandinavian Studies, which included a year spent at the University of Oslo. More recently, he has been conducting research into the 16–19 education system of Norway, as the theme of a PhD degree by part-time study at the Centre for Applied Research in Education (CARE), University of East Anglia. In connection with this work he lived in Norway for the academic year 1981–82, carrying out field-work and teaching in Norwegian tertiary institutions. In September 1981 he was commissioned by the DES to write a report on the post-compulsory education provision in Norway.

John Claus is a doctoral student in the Department of Education, Cornell University, Ithaca, New York. His interests include the design and evaluation of educational programmes for disadvantaged youth, the use of anthropological methods and perspectives in educational research, and issues concerning the goal and achievement of equal educational opportunity. His dissertation is an ethnographic analysis of a secondary vocational programme.

Don Dippo is a doctoral student in the Department of Sociology in Education at the Ontario Institute for Studies in Education. He is completing a dissertation entitled 'Politics and Practice in Education for Work'.

Stephen Hamilton is an Associate Professor in the Department of Human Development and Family Studies at Cornell University, Ithaca, New York. He received his doctorate from Harvard University and has written and conducted research in the areas of experimental education, employment and training programmes for disadvantaged youth, and the social context of schooling.

Rafael Irizarry is Assistant Professor in Social Sciences at the University of Puerto Rico, Rio Piedras campus and fellow member of the Centre for the Study of the Puerto Rico Reality (CEREP). He completed his doctoral studies in 1981 in the fields of Educational Planning and Social Policy at the Graduate School of Education of Harvard University. He has served as Technical Consultant to the Planning Board of Puerto Rico in the units of Human Resources and Social Planning. From 1974–77 he taught at the Graduate School of Planning of the University of Puerto Rico in the area of Social Planning and Policy.

Saville Kushner is a Senior Research Associate at the Centre for Applied Research in Education (CARE) at the University of East Anglia. Since completing doctoral studies in the field of access to higher education he was one of a team commissioned by the Ford Foundation of America to produce an evaluative case study of bilingual schooling in the USA. He is co-editor (with Barry MacDonald) of the resulting book *Bread and Dreams* published in 1982 by CARE Occasional Publications. For the past three years he has been evaluating Project No 27 of the European Pilot Programme 'Transition from School to Working Life', and is the author of a range of resulting publications.

Jean-Jaques Paul is Attache de Recherche at the Centre National de la Recherche Scientifique (CNRS) of the Institut de Recherche sur l'Economie de l'Education in Dijon.

Christopher Pilley is Senior Development Officer at the Scottish Community Education Council. He has responsibilities in the areas of policy development and research and is concerned with the promotion of an international dimension to that part of the Council's work. Amongst his particular interests are community education's responses to unemployment. He has been involved in a number of study visits abroad, particularly to France.

Henry R Sredl is Professor in the Department of Vocational and Technical Education at Oregon State University. He was formerly Coordinator of the Human Resources Development Speciality and Chairperson of the Industrial Education Division of the Department of Vocational and Technical Education at the University of Illinois at Urbana-Champaign. He has served in many capacities related to programme and personnel planning, development and evaluation. He is currently interested in factors affecting workforce development and transition in the United States and abroad.

Author Index

Subject Index

Note: Where relevant countries are indicated in brackets after index terms. Abbreviations have been used for German Democratic Republic (GDR), German Federal Republic (GFR), People's Republic of China (PRC) and United States of America (USA).

Printed in the United States
by Baker & Taylor Publisher Services